CHORAL MUSIC

A Norton Historical Anthology

Also available from Norton

Mostly Short Pieces: An Anthology for
Harmonic Analysis
    Edited by Mark DeVoto

Norton Anthology of Western Music
    Second Edition
    Edited by Claude V. Palisca

The Norton Scores: An Anthology for Listening
    Fifth Edition
    Edited by Roger Kamien

The Symphony, 1800–1900
    Edited by Paul Henry Lang

An Anthology of Early Renaissance Music
    Edited by Noah Greenberg and Paul Maynard

Anthology of Medieval Music
    Edited by Richard H. Hoppin

Anthology of Classical Music
    Edited by Philip Downs

Anthology of Romantic Music
    Edited by Leon Plantinga

Anthology of Twentieth-Century Music
    Edited with Analytical Comments
    by Robert P. Morgan

CHORAL MUSIC
A Norton Historical Anthology

EDITED BY

Ray Robinson

PALM BEACH ATLANTIC COLLEGE

W · W · NORTON & COMPANY · INC ·
NEW YORK

PRINTED IN THE UNITED STATES OF AMERICA.
All Rights Reserved
W. W. Norton & Company, Inc. 500 Fifth Avenue, New York, N.Y. 10110

Library of Congress Cataloging in Publication Data
Main entry under title:
Choral music.
    1. Choruses. 2. Choruses, Sacred.
I. Robinson, Ray, 1932–
M1495.C54218   784'.2   78–833
ISBN 0-393-99062-0

1 2 3 4 5 6 7 8 9 0

Contents

Contents

Contents

1800–1900

1900–

Contents

Foreword

This volume is practical in intention. It is an anthology designed to facilitate the study of choral music. With appropriate adjustments, it may be used for classes in conducting, choral literature, music history, and even music theory. It presents, under one cover, a repertorial survey of music for the choral medium from Gregorian chant to the present. The book is not a compendium of choral works we love the best. Rather, it is a guide to the development of the choral idiom in all its evolutionary complexity. Thus, the editor has attempted to realize several closely related objectives in selecting pieces for inclusion: first, to document the evolution of musical style from the Middle Ages to the twentieth century as it may be observed in choral music; second, to illustrate the major categories of choral composition (e.g., Mass, motet) in different periods; and third, to provide a convenient and portable library of works by the most important composers of the genre.

The anthology's organization is essentially chronological. After a survey of the sacred choral literature of the Middle Ages and the Renaissance, we are introduced to the secular music of France, Italy, and England in the sixteenth century. Subsequent sections are devoted to both sacred and secular literature of the seventeenth and eighteenth centuries and include a wide diversity of works ranging from pieces of North American origin to examples of Viennese Classicism. The vast panorama of the Romantic period is outlined in detail and the volume concludes with an assortment of works drawn from the expansive choral literature of the twentieth century.

In the early part of the anthology, the complete Mass of Josquin and the other Mass excerpts provide material ranging from the isorhythm of Machaut to the stately lyricism of Palestrina and Byrd. Although it had been the intention of the editor to include only complete Masses in this volume, practical considerations of length made it necessary to limit ourselves to one complete work only. With the motet, the problem of length did not exist, but the difficulty was selecting appropriate examples from the wealth of music available. The guiding principle continued to be the illustration of different musical styles and compositional techniques through the works of the most important composers. Thus, the selections range from Dunstable to Gabrieli in styles from fauxbourdon to polychoral.

The sixteenth century witnessed the religious upheavals occasioned by the Lutheran Reformation, and these had a profound effect on music for worship. Although a great deal was retained from the Catholic tradition, Protestantism brought with it musical innovation ranging from simple settings of psalm translations to opulent polychoral works on chorale texts and tunes. In fact, nothing exemplifies German Protestantism better than the chorale itself—devotional texts set to melodies either newly composed or contrafacted, but which, in either case, usually exhibited a kind of proletarian wholesomeness ideally suited to the new religious spirit. In England, the musical product of the break with the Latin Church was the large repertory of anthems composed in the sixteenth century and after by Tomkins, Byrd, and Gibbons, along with many others.

The sixteenth century also saw the great flowering of polyphonic secular music. Of course, secular vocal music of the polyphonic variety has been known since the twelfth century. But, with some exceptions, this music (as we know it from the examples which have come down to us) was reserved for the musical intelligentsia—a refined and fragile art suited to rendition by the cultivated solo voice. In both text and melody it exhibited a preciosity which characterized it unmistakably as music for an elite, a delicate plant which thrived on the thin air of the court. But in the sixteenth century, secular vocal polyphony assumes a sprightly spontaneity and contagious effervescence which marks it clearly as belonging in the bourgeois *Wohnstube*. Texts are less contrived, melodies more angular, harmonies more regular, rhythms more propulsive, and voice parts more egalitarian. Like the solo song in nineteenth-century America, secular polyphony in the sixteenth century became the tool of conviviality.

Musically, many things changed after 1600. The Baroque seems to have brought with it an antipathy for the old orderliness and balance. Where possible, color and contrast were carried out on a colossal scale, and were regarded as aesthetic virtues. Something of the classic Renaissance style of Palestrina and Josquin lingered, but it was pallid and bloodless. Everything artists and musicians produced had to be larger than life in order to be considered of value. For this reason, perhaps, independent instrumental idioms were developed, and it became a regular practice to combine instruments and voices in the same work, not, as might have been done earlier, for the purpose of support, but rather for the excitement and pathos of a competition—a concerto in the literal sense of the word. The works by Charpentier, Purcell, Buxtehude, and Telemann amply illustrate this musical phenomenon.

The section of the anthology devoted to the Viennese Classical school illustrates the rich heritage that Haydn and Mozart have bequeathed to modern choral performers. A cappella singing was little valued at this time. Most works for chorus employed instruments—a remnant of the Baroque tradition. The popularity of the Italian opera made bel canto singing fashionable everywhere. For this reason, and because most composers up to the end of the eighteenth century worked for patrons and these patrons often were interested in sacred music, a large repertory of Masses, Vesper settings, motets, oratorios, and similar works has been preserved from this period. The works of Haydn and Mozart represent the best of this repertory. But whether such works were composed for the Esterházy Court, the Salzburg Cathedral, or any of the hundreds of similar establishments in and outside of Austria, their unity of style and general high quality reflects the last great flowering of Catholic liturgical music.

The choral medium was less attractive to most composers of the nineteenth century than were symphonic music and opera. Often, with Berlioz or Mahler, for example, they wrote for chorus in order to expand the resources of the symphony orchestra. There was, nevertheless, a respectable amount of nonsymphonic choral music written during the Romantic and Postromantic periods. In Catholic circles, the influence of Cecilianism encouraged a cappella writing in a neo-Palestrina style (Bruckner); among Protestants, the influence of Handel and particularly Bach may be observed (Mendelssohn, Brahms). Secular choral music of the nineteenth century often reflects the influence of the folk-song movement, particularly in Germany (Schumann).

Next, we come to the music of the twentieth century. The styles represented by these works, which are organized according to the nationality of the composer, include the following: 1) works influenced by the revival of interest in folk song and hence exhibiting a nationalistic character (Holst, Bartók, Vaughan Williams); 2) Neoclassic works (Carter, Pinkham, Persichetti, Hindemith, and Stravinsky); 3) serial compositions (Schoenberg.

Webern); and 4) avant-garde works (Penderecki, Felciano). Some excellent examples could not be included since it was impossible to secure copyright releases for them. This is especially to be regretted in the case of the French repertory, which is unfortunately not sufficiently well represented here.

In keeping with the practical nature of this anthology, the works are presented in reliable performing editions. The editor recognizes the virtues, indeed the superior merit, of scholarly editions, particularly when they are recent. But we consider them generally unsuited to an anthology like this for two reasons: they usually depend on an elaborate accompanying critical apparatus (for which we have no room), and they often presume a degree of sophistication in music reading (e.g., in the use of unfamiliar clefs, special signs, older note forms) which not everyone possesses.

Within the limitations imposed by copyright restrictions, every attempt has been made to present the music in the best available performing edition. Somewhat arbitrarily, perhaps, it was decided to include only works for mixed chorus (or its presumed equivalent in the case of early music). This decision, however, had the beneficial side effect of facilitating the realization of one of the objectives of the volume, the study of musical style. It is easier (and more defensible) to compare and contrast styles when the medium is consistently restricted. Other considerations being equal, preference was accorded less well-known works. For example, Handel's *Israel in Egypt* was included instead of the familiar *Messiah* and Vivaldi's *Magnificat* appears in place of his better-known *Gloria*.

A word is in order concerning the need we hope this book will fill. Anthologies are of three types. First, there is the publication series represented by a collection such as *Das Chorwerk*. The works contained therein, although reliably edited, seem to be chosen at random and are arranged in the volume according to no obvious system. Furthermore, the sheer bulk of such a collection makes it more a reference source than a study tool. The second type is the general historical anthology, which is usually systematic and portable, but suffers from the requirements of catholicity—the obligation to represent all types of music. Such books must contain a great deal of dross when only one type of music is being considered. Finally, there is the generic anthology, a collection similar to the preceding type, but devoted only to works in a given form or for a particular medium.

This volume is designed as an anthology of the third type, one which is long overdue in filling a practical as well as pedagogical need. It is the first generic anthology (comparable in scope and method to those already available for other types of music) to deal exclusively with works for vocal ensemble.

It is also necessary to say something about the term *choral music* as it is used for the purpose of this anthology. Naturally, the designation does not mean the same thing in the twentieth century that it meant in the twelfth. Vocal ensembles were considerably smaller in the medieval and Renaissance periods. In fact, polyphony throughout the Middle Ages was regarded as the exclusive province of a group of soloists. Large choirs existed only in monasteries or great churches, where their function was the performance of chant. Gradually, as it became the practice for more than one singer to execute a part of a polyphonic work, ensembles were developed for the rendition of polyphony.

By the fourteenth century, such ensembles were common in churches and elsewhere, so that most functional liturgical polyphony (hymns, sequences, Mass Ordinary settings) may, in this sense, be safely considered choral music. Although we know of isolated instances of larger groups, the prevailing size of choirs for singing polyphony in the Renaissance remained relatively small—usually between 12 and 24 members—what in modern times is called a *chamber choir*. In the period after 1500, until the end of the eighteenth century, vocal ensembles gradually became larger for a variety of reasons (including the influence of the Lutheran Reformation, which viewed congregational singing more favorably than it had been at any time since the early church; the invention of printing, which eventually made possible identical multiple copies of a single work; and the proclivity of the Baroque aesthetic for great masses of sound). Then, the French Revolution and its artistic counterpart, the Romantic movement, found in choral singing the musical corollary to their cherished beliefs in the brotherhood of man and the universality of the aesthetic experience, starting a vogue for choirs of immense proportions. Therefore, for purposes of this publication, choral music is defined as music in more than one part conceived primarily for an ensemble of voices with more than one singer on a part. Hence the exclusion of much worthy nineteenth-century symphonic music using chorus, which is viewed as essentially instrumental, as well as the vast corpus of motets written in the Middle Ages, works which are putatively for soloists.

The editor has striven to make this volume of practical value from a variety of standpoints. Biographical information concerning each composer is provided in Appendix A, arranged alphabetically. In Appendix B, each piece is discussed briefly. This commentary is intended to point out basic stylistic and historical facts and is to be viewed as supplementary to class discussion. Terms with which the student may be unfamiliar are defined in the Glossary. The information contained in Appendix C—a complete list of publication credits for all works included in the Anthology—is intended to facilitate performances of the music. The performance of the music is, after all, the ultimate objective of all music study.

Ray Robinson

Princeton, New Jersey
July 1, 1977

Acknowledgments

This anthology is the product of the human and library resources of the Westminster Choir College. The motivating force behind its realization was the need for a comprehensive collection of choral works for use in choral literature and conducting classes at the College. And, as in any project of this breadth, its completion was possible only with the assistance of many who gave unstintingly of their time and energies.

I am indebted to Dennis Shrock and Nancy Wicklund for their encouragement and assistance in the planning and selection of the individual choral works included in this volume. Without their dedication and commitment to it, this project would not have become a reality. To William Dalglish I wish to express appreciation for his assistance in proofreading, rewriting, and technical advice in musicological matters. There are also specific staff members who deserve thanks for their advice and translations: these include Father Gerard Farrell, Walter Schoenefeld, and Marianne Torza. Candie Brown rendered special service in typing, translating, proofreading, and securing permissions from the publishers whose works are included in this volume.

I am also deeply grateful to my wife Ruth for her encouragement and patience during the period in which the anthology was in preparation.

Special acknowledgement is due to the staff of W. W. Norton and Company for consideration and enthusiastic assistance during the period of publication.

Ray Robinson

CHORAL MUSIC

A Norton Historical Anthology

1. Anonymous, *Magnificat*
anima mea

Anonymous, *Magnificat anima mea*

bra - chi - o su - o: dis - per - sit su - per - bos men - te cor - dis su - i.

7. De - po - su - it po - ten - tes de se - de,   et ex - al - ta - vit hu - mi - les.

8. E - su - ri - en - tes im - ple-vit bo - nis: et di - vi - tes di - mi-sit in - a -

- nes.   9. Sus - ce - pit Is - ra - el pu - e - rum su - um,   re - cor - da - tus

mi - se - ri - cor - di - e su - ae.   10. Si - cut lo - cu - tus est ad

pa - tres nos - tros,   A - bra - ham et se - mi - ni e-jus in sae - cu - la.

11. Glo-ri - a Pa - tri et Fi - li - o,   et spi - ri - tu - i San - cto.

12. Si - cut e - rat in prin - ci - pi - o et nunc, et sem - per,   et in sae - cu - la

sae - cu - lo - rum. A - men.

Magnificat anima mea Dominum.	My soul magnifies the Lord.
Et exsultavit spiritus meus in Deo salutari meo.	And my spirit rejoices in God my Savior.
Quia respexit humilitatem ancillae suae: ecce enim ex hoc beatam me dicent omnes generationes.	For he has regarded the low estate of his handmaiden: for behold, henceforth all generations will call me blessed.
Quia fecit mihi magna qui potens est: et sanctum nomen ejus.	For he who is mighty has done great things for me: and holy is his name.
Et misericordia ejus a progenie in progenies timentibus eum.	And his mercy is on those who fear him from generation to generation.
Fecit potentiam in brachio suo: dispersit superbos mente cordis sui.	He has shown strength with his arm, he has scattered the proud in the imagination of their hearts.
Deposuit potentes de sede, et exaltavit humiles.	He has put down the mighty from their thrones, and exalted those of low degree.
Esurientes implevit bonis: et divites dimisit inanes.	He has filled the hungry with good things, and the rich he has sent empty away.
Suscepit Israel puerum suum, recordatus misericordiae suae.	He has helped his servant Israel, in remembrance of his mercy.
Sicut locutus est ad patres nostros, Abraham et semini ejus in saecula.	As he spoke to our fathers, to Abraham, and to his posterity forever.
Gloria Patri, et Filio, et Spiritui Sancto.	Glory be to the Father, and to the Son, and to the Holy Spirit.
Sicut erat in principio, et nunc, et semper, et in saecula saeculorum, Amen.	As it was in the beginning, is now, and ever shall be; world without end, Amen.

Luke 1:46–55

2. Anonymous, *Hodie Christus natus est*

Hodie Christus natus est:
hodie Salvator apparuit:
hodie in terra canunt Angeli,
laetantur Archangeli:
hodie exsultant justi, dicentes:
Gloria in excelsis Deo, alleluia.

Today Christ was born:
today the Savior appeared:
today on earth the angels sing,
the Archangels rejoice:
today the just exalt, saying:
Glory to God in the highest, alleluia.

3. Anonymous, *Haec dies, quam fecit Dominus*

Anonymous, *Haec dies, quam fecit Dominus*

Haec dies, quam fecit Dominus:
exsultemus, et laetemur in ea.
Confitemini Domino, quoniam
    bonus:
quoniam in saeculum misericordia
    ejus.

This day, which the Lord has made:
we exult and rejoice in it.
Trust in the Lord, for He is good:

for his mercy endures forever.

4. Guillaume de Machaut, Kyrie from *La Messe de Nostre Dame* (c. 1364)

Machaut, *La Messe de Nostre Dame*: Kyrie

Kyrie eleison.
Christe eleison.
Kyrie eleison.

Lord have mercy upon us.
Christ have mercy upon us.
Lord have mercy upon us.

5. Guillaume Dufay, Gloria from
Missa Se la face ay pale (c. 1460)

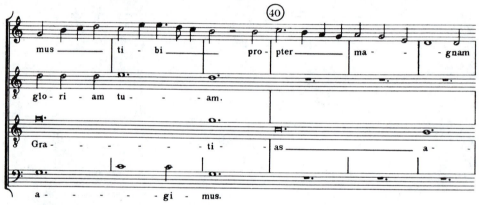

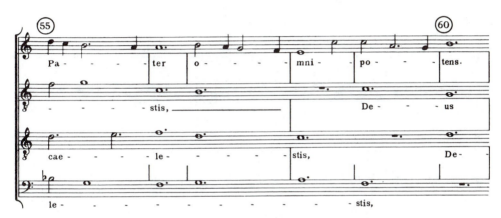

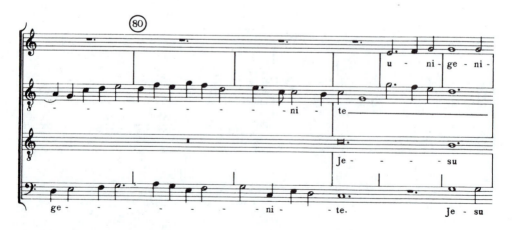

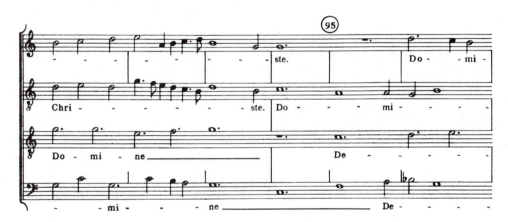

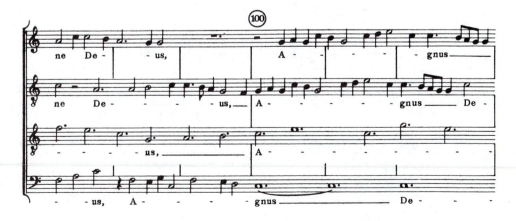

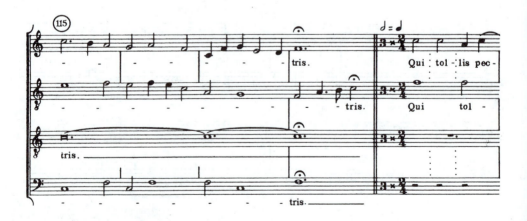

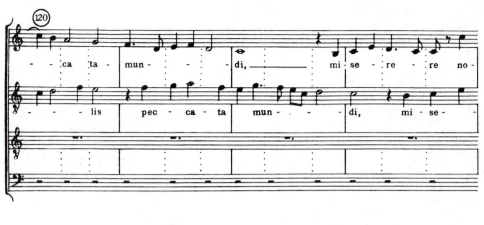

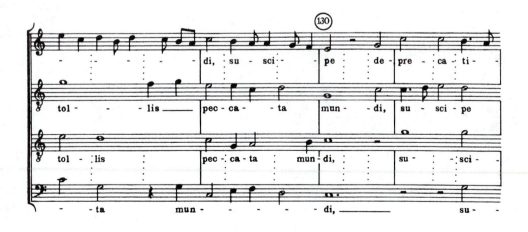

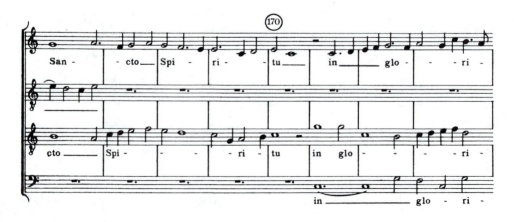

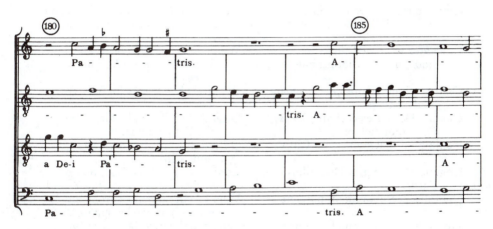

Gloria in excelsis Deo. Et in terra pax hominibus bonae voluntatis.

Laudamus te. Benedicimus te. Adoramus te. Glorificamus te.

Gratias agimus tibi propter magnam gloriam tuam.
Domine Deus, Rex caelestis, Deus Pater omnipotens.
Domine Fili unigenite, Jesu Christe.

Domine Deus, Agnus Dei, Filius Patris.
Qui tollis peccata mundi, miserere nobis.
Qui tollis peccata mundi, suscipe deprecationem nostram.
Qui sedes ad dexteram Patris, miserere nobis.
Quoniam tu solus sanctus. Tu solus Dominus. Tu solus Altissimus, Jesu Christe.
Cum Sancto Spiritu, in gloria Dei Patris. Amen.

Glory be to God in the highest. And on earth peace to men of good will.

We praise Thee. We bless Thee. We adore Thee. We glorify Thee.

We give Thee thanks for Thy great glory.
O Lord God, heavenly King, God the Father almighty.
O Lord, the only-begotten Son, Jesus Christ.

Lord God, Lamb of God, Son of the Father.
Who taketh away the sins of the world, have mercy upon us.
Who taketh away the sins of the world, receive our prayer.
Who sitteth at the right hand of the Father, have mercy upon us.
For Thou alone art holy. Thou alone art Lord. Thou alone, O Jesus Christ, art most high.
Together with the Holy Ghost, in the glory of God the Father. Amen.

6. Johannes Ockeghem, Credo from *Missa Mi-Mi* (c. 1465)

Transposed up a minor third from the original.

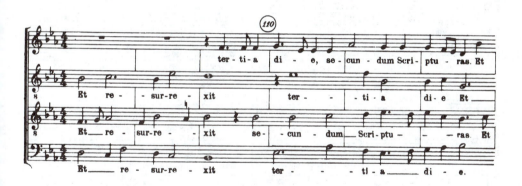

Credo in unum Deum, Patrem
omnipotentem, factorem coeli
et terrae, visibilium omnium,
et invisibilium.
Et in unum Dominum Jesum
Christum, Filium Dei
unigenitum.
Et ex Patre natum ante omnia
saecula.
Deum de Deo, lumen de lumine,
Deum verum de Deo vero.
Genitum, non factum,
consubstantialem Patri: per
quem omnia facta sunt.
Qui propter nos homines, et
propter nostram salutem
descendit de coelis.
Et incarnatus est de Spiritu Sancto
ex Maria Virgine; Et homo
factus est.

I believe in one God, the Father
almighty, maker of heaven and
earth, and of all things visible
and invisible.
And in one Lord Jesus Christ, the
only-begotten Son of God.

Born of the Father before all ages.

God of God, light of light, true God
of true God.
Begotten, not made; of one substance
with the Father: by whom all
things were made.
Who for us men, and for our
salvation, came down from
heaven.
And was made flesh by the Holy
Ghost of the Virgin Mary: And
was made man.

Crucifixus etiam pro nobis; sub Pontio Pilato passus, et sepultus est.

Et resurrexit tertia die, secundum Scripturas.

Et ascendit in coelum: sedet ad dexteram Patris.

Et iterum venturus est cum gloria, judicare vivos et mortuos: cujus regni non erit finis.

Et in Spiritum Sanctum, Dominum, et vivicantem: qui ex Patre Filioque procedit.

Qui cum Patre et Filio simul adoratur, et conglorificatur: qui locutus est per Prophetas.

Et unam sanctam catholicam et apostolicam Ecclesiam.

Confiteor unum baptisma in remissionem peccatorum.

Et exspecto resurrectionem mortuorum.

Et vitam venturi saeculi. Amen.

He was also crucified for us, suffered under Pontius Pilate, and was buried.

And on the third day He rose again, according to the Scriptures.

And ascended into heaven: He sitteth at the right hand of the Father.

And He shall come again with glory to judge the living and the dead; and of His Kingdom there shall be no end.

And in the Holy Ghost, the Lord and Giver of life, who proceedeth from the Father and the Son.

Who together with the Father and the Son is adored and glorified: who spoke by the Prophets.

And in one holy, catholic, and apostolic Church.

I confess one baptism for the remission of sins.

And I expect the resurrection of the dead.

And the life of the world to come. Amen.

7. Josquin Des Prez,
Missa Pange lingua (publ. 1539)

KYRIE

GLORIA

CREDO

SANCTUS

AGNUS DEI
I

See the following pages for texts:
Kyrie, page 15
Gloria, page 28
Credo, pages 36–37
Sanctus, page 70
Agnus Dei, page 74

8. Giovanni Pierluigi da Palestrina, Sanctus and Benedictus from *Missa Papae Marcelli* (publ. 1567)

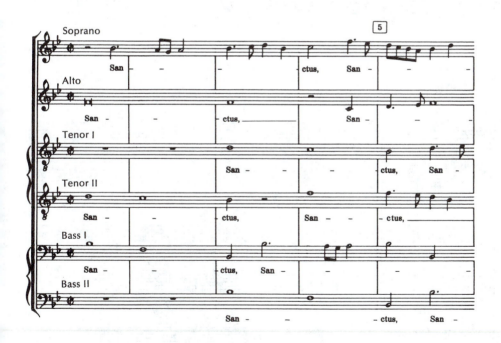

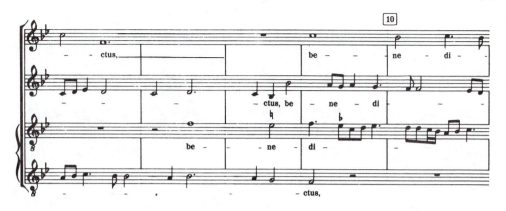

Hosanna is repeated

Sanctus, Sanctus, Sanctus Dominus Deus Sabaoth.	Holy, Holy, Holy Lord God of hosts.
Pleni sunt coeli et terra gloria tua.	Heaven and earth are filled with Thy glory.
Hosanna in excelsis.	Hosanna in the highest.
Benedictus qui venit in nomine Domini.	Blessed is He that cometh in the name of the Lord.
Hosanna in excelsis.	Hosanna in the highest.

9. William Byrd, Agnus Dei from *Mass for Four Voices* (publ. c. 1605)

Byrd, "Agnus Dei" from MASS FOR FOUR VOICES, edited by Frederick Hudson (E 997). Reprint permission granted by the publisher. Transposed down a whole tone from the original.

Agnus Dei, qui tollis peccata mundi, miserere nobis.

Lamb of God, who taketh away the sins of the world, have mercy upon us.

Agnus Dei, qui tollis peccata mundi, miserere nobis.

Lamb of God, who taketh away the sins of the world, have mercy upon us.

Agnus Dei, qui tollis peccata mundi, dona nobis pacem.

Lamb of God, who taketh away the sins of the world, grant us peace.

10. John Dunstable,
Quam pulcra es (c. 1420)

Quam pulcra es et quam decora,
carissima in deliciis.
Statura tua assimilata est palme,
et ubera tua botris.

Caput tuum ut Carmelus,
collum tuum sicut turis eburnea.
Veni, dilecte me,
egrediamur in agrum,
et videamus si flores fructus
    parturierunt,
si floruerunt mala Punica.
Ibi dabo tibi ubera mea. Alleluia.

How beautiful and how decorous,
most dear of sweet things.
Your figure is like a palm tree,
and your breasts like clusters of
    grapes.
Your head is like Carmel,
your neck like a tower of ivory.
Come, my beloved,
let us go into the field,
and see if the blossoms of the fruit
    have appeared,
and the pomogranates flowered.
There will I give you my breasts.
    Alleluia.
        Song of Solomon 7:4–7, 11–12

11. Dufay, *Ave Regina coelorum* (*a* 3) (c. 1420)

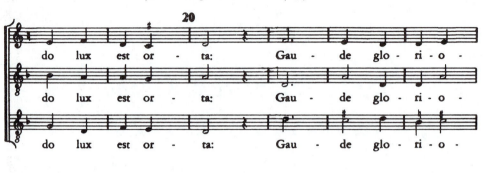

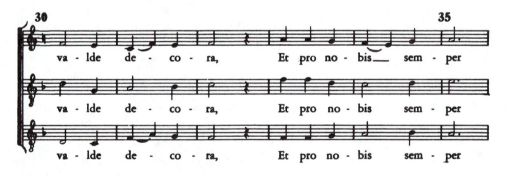

Ave Regina coelorum,
Ave Domina Angelorum:
Salve radix sancta,
Ex qua mundo lux est orta:
Gaude gloriosa,
Super omnes speciosa:
Vale, valde decora,
Et pro nobis semper Christum exora,
Alleluia!

Hail, Queen of the heavens,
Hail, Mistress of the angels:
Holy Root, from which has come
The light of the world, we greet you.
Rejoice! O glorious one,
Hail most fair one,
In beauty far surpassing all.
Pray for us always to Christ, our Lord.
Alleluia.

12. Josquin, *Ave Maria, gratia plena* (publ. 1568)

AVE MARIA GRATIA PLENA, Copyright 1948, Mercury Music Corp. Used by permission.

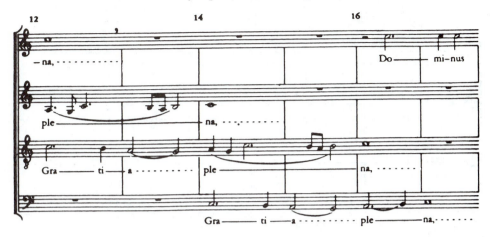

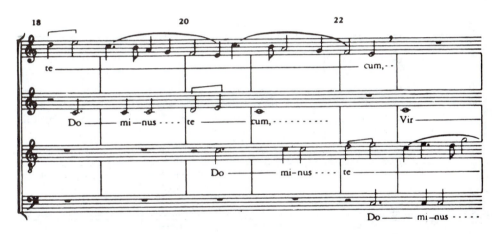

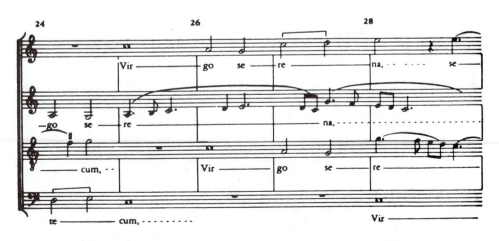

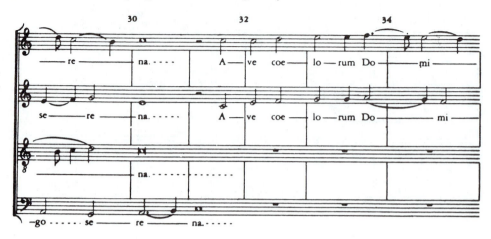

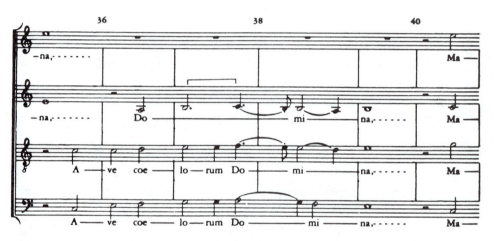

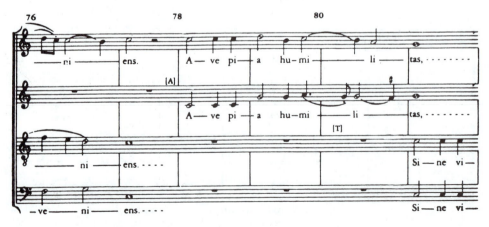

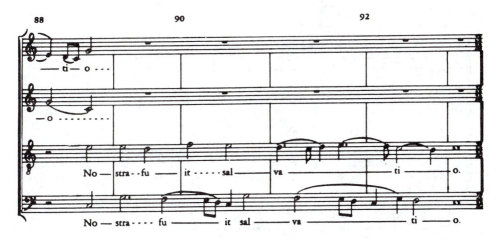

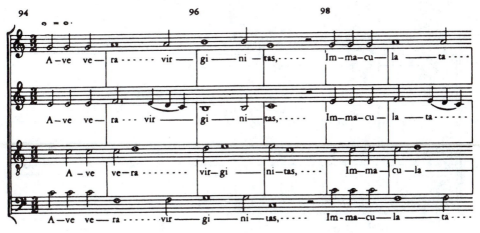

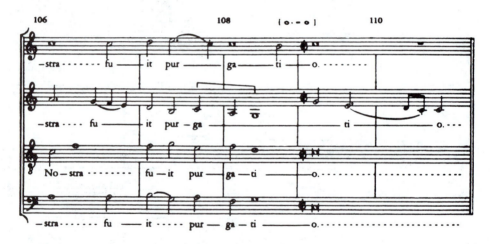

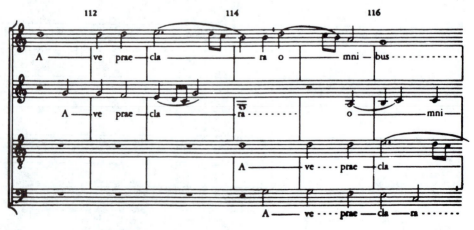

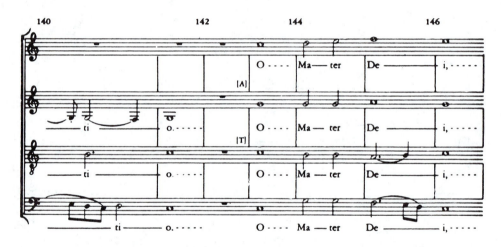

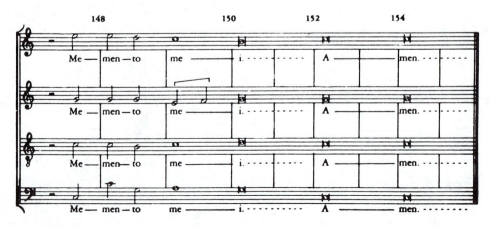

Ave Maria,
Gratia plena,
Dominus tecum,
Virgo serena.

Ave coelorum Domina,
Maria plena gratia,
Coelestia, terrestria,
Mundum replens laetitia.

Ave cujus nativitas
Nostra fuit solemnitas;
Ut lucifer lux oriens,
Verum solem praeveniens.

Ave pia humilitas,
Sine viro foecunditas,
Cujus annunciatio
Nostra fuit salvatio.

Ave vera virginitas,
Immaculata castitas,
Cujus purificatio
Nostra fuit purgatio.

Ave praeclara omnibus
Angelicis virtutibus,
Cujus fuit assumptio
Nostra glorificatio.

O Mater Dei,
Memento mei.
Amen.

Hail Mary,
Full of grace,
The Lord is with Thee,
Virgin fair.

Hail, Mistress of the Heavens,
Mary, full of grace,
With heavenly and earthly joy
Thou fill'st the world.

Hail Thou, whose birth
Became our feast,
As the morningstar, a rising light,
Thou precedest the true sun.

Hail, blessed humility,
Inviolate fecundity,
Whose Annunciation
Became our salvation.

Hail, true virginity,
Unspotted chastity,
Whose purification
Became our expiation.

Hail Thou, who shinest
With all angelic virtues,
Whose Assumption
Became our glorification.

O Mother of God,
Be mindful of me.
Amen.

13. Orlando di Lasso,
In hora ultima (publ. 1604)

Used by permission of Roger Dean Publishing Company, 324 West Jackson, Macomb, Illinois 61455

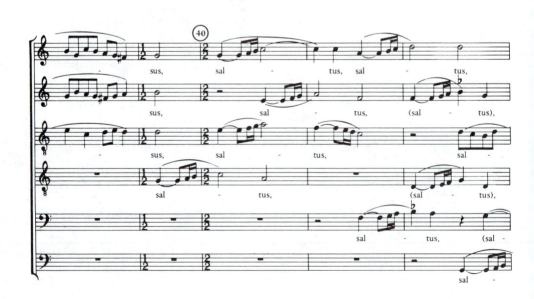

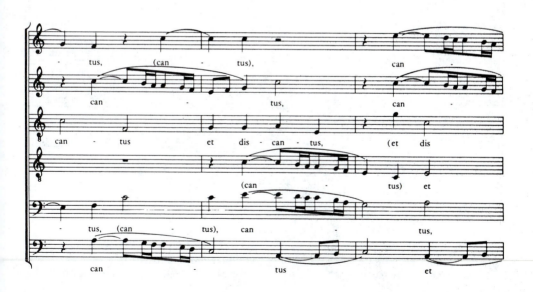

In hora ultima peribunt omnia:
tuba, tibia, et cythara;
jocus, risus, saltus, cantus et discantus.

At the final hour all will pass away:
trumpet, flute, and harp;
jokes, laughter, dancing, singing, and
   harmony.

Translated by Alan Harler

14. Palestrina, *Ave Maria, gratia plena* (publ. 1571)

Palestrina, *Ave Maria, gratia plena*

ti - a ple - na;   Do - mi - nus,   Do - mi - nus

- - - - na;   Do - mi - nus te -

ti - a ple - na;   Do - mi - nus te - cum,   Do -

ti - a ple - na;   Do - mi - nus te - cum, Do - mi - nus te - cum,

te - cum: be - ne - di - cta

cum: be - ne - di - cta tu, be - ne - di

- mi - nus   te - cum: be - ne - di - cta tu,   be - ne -

Do - mi - nus te - - - - - cum: be - ne -

tu   in mu - li - e - ri - bus,   in mu - li - e - - -

- cta tu   in mu - li - e - ri - bus, in mu - li - e -

di - cta tu   in mu - li - e -

di - cta tu in mu - li - e - ri - bus,

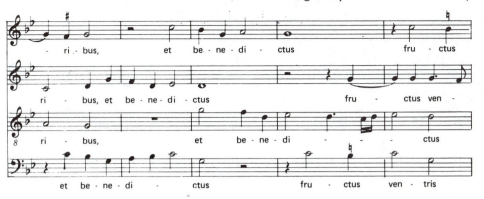

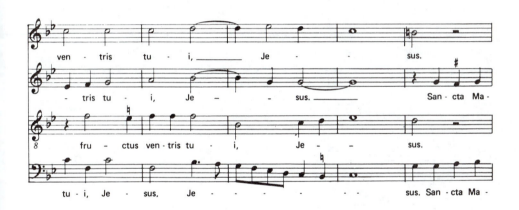

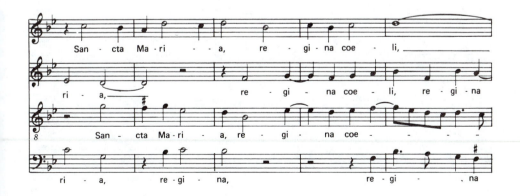

to - ri - bus, ut cum e - le - ctis te _____ vi - de -

ri - bus, ut cum e - le - ctis te _____ vi -

ri - bus, ut cum e - le - ctis te vi -

to - ri - bus, ut cum e - le - ctis te vi -

a - - - - - mus, ut

de - a - - mus, _____ ut

de - a - - - mus, te vi - de - a - mus, ut

de - a - mus, te vi - de - a - mus, ut

cum e - le - ctis te vi - de - a - - -

cum e - le - ctis te vi - de - a -

cum e - le - ctis te vi - de a - -

cum e - le - ctis te vi - de - a - mus, _____

Ave Maria, gratia plena;
Dominus tecum: benedicta tu in
    mulieribus,
et benedictus fructus ventris tui,
    Jesus.
Sancta Maria, regina coeli, dulcis et
    pia;
O mater Dei, ora pro nobis
    peccatoribus, ut cum electis te
    videamus.

Hail Mary, full of grace;
The Lord is with you: blessed are
    you among women,
and blessed is the fruit of your womb,
    Jesus.
Holy Mary, queen of heaven, sweet
    and holy;
O mother of God, pray for us sinners,
so that among the elect we may see
    you.

                                          Luke 1:42

15. Tomás Luis de Victoria,
O quam gloriosum (publ. 1572)

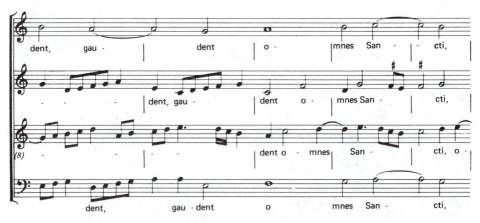

O quam gloriosum est regnum, in quo cum Christo gaudent omnes Sancti! Amicti stolis albis sequuntur Agnum quocumque ierit.

O how glorious is the kingdom in which all holy men rejoice in Christ, men garbed in white who attend the Lamb, with whom Christ goes.

16. Giovanni Gabrieli,
O magnum mysterium (publ. 1615)

O magnum mysterium,
et admirabile sacramentum,
ut animalia viderent Dominum
    natum,
jacentem in praesepio:
Beata Virgo, cujus viscera meruerunt
    portare Dominum Christum:
Alleluja.

O great mystery,
and wonderful sacrament,
of living beings who see the birth of
    the Lord,
sleeping in a manger:
Blessed Virgin, in whose unblemished
    womb was carried the Lord:
Alleluia.

17. Thomas Tallis, *O nata lux de lumine* (publ. 1575)

O nata lux de lumine by Thomas Tallis, revised edition by Anthony Greening. © Oxford University Press, 1969. Reprinted by permission.

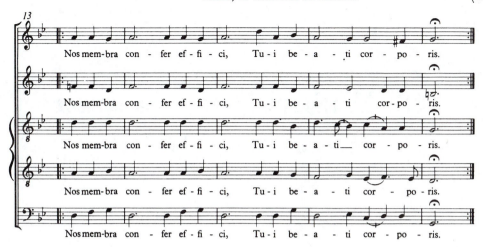

O nata lux de lumine,
Jesu redemptor saeculi,
Dignare clemens supplicum
Laudes preces que sumere.

Qui carne quondam contegi

Dignatus es pro perditis.

Nos membra confer effici,
Tui beati corporis.

O light born of light,
Jesu, the savior of our age,
Graciously be pleased to receive
The prayers and praises of your
    servants.
You, who in time, deigned to be
    clothed in flesh
For love of those who were
    abandoned.
Grant that we may become the
Members of your blessed body.

18. William Byrd, *Ave verum Corpus* (publ. 1605)

Ave verum corpus by William Byrd, revised edition by John Morehen. © Oxford University Press, 1972. Reprinted by permission.

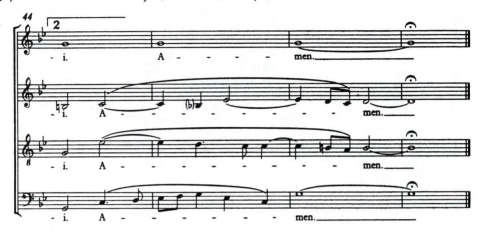

Ave verum Corpus,
natum de Maria Virgine:
Vere passum,
immolatum in cruce pro homine:
Cujus latus perforatum,
unda fluxit sanguine:
Esto nobis praegustatum in mortis
   examine.
O dulcis, O pie, O Jesu Fili Mariae,
   miserere mei. Amen.

Hail, true body,
born of Virgin Mary:
Thou who truly suffered,
sacrificed upon the cross for mankind:
Thou whose side was riven,
whence the stream of blood did flow:
O may thou, dear Lord, be given at
   death's hour to be my food.
O tender, O pure, O Jesus Son of
   Mary, have mercy upon me.
   Amen.

19. Johann Walther, *Ein feste Burg ist unser Gott* (1537)

Ein feste Burg ist unser Gott,
ein gute Wehr und Waffen.
Er hilft uns frei aus aller Not,
die uns jetzt hat betroffen.
Der alt böse Fiend
mit Ernst ers jetzt meint;
gross Macht und viel List
sein grausam Rüstung ist;
auf Erd ist nicht seins Gleichen.

Martin Luther

A strong fortress is our God,
a good defense and weapon.
He sets us free from all peril,
that has now befallen us.
The old evil foe
is now in earnest;
great power and much cunning
are his cruel armor;
on earth there is not his equal.

Translated by Marianne Torza

20. Johannes Eccard, *Christ lag in Todesbanden* (publ. 1644)

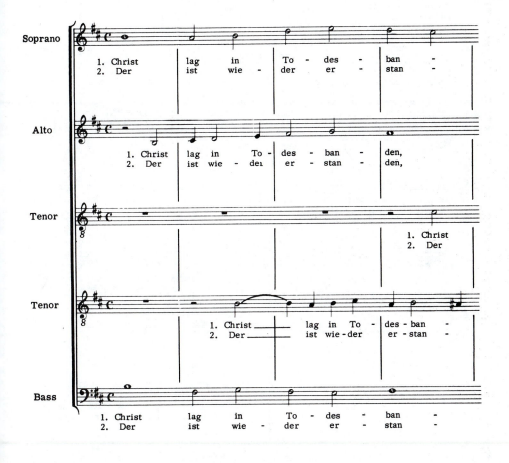

Christ lag in Todesbanden,
für unsre Sünd gegeben.
Des wir sollen fröhlich sein.
Gott loben und ihm dankbar sein,
und singen Alleluia.

Martin Luther

Christ lay in death's dark bondage,
who for our sin was given;
Wherefore we should joyful be,
give praise to God thankfully,
And sing we Alleluia.

Translated by Ron Haizlip

21. Hans Leo Hassler, *Komm, Heiliger Geist* (1608)

Komm, Heiliger Geist, Herre Gott
erfüll mit deiner Genaden Gut
deiner Geläubigen Herz, Mut and
    Sinn,
dein inbrünstige Lieb entzünd in
    ihn.
O Herr, durch deines Lichtes Gelanz

zu einem Glauben versammlet
    hast das Volk aus
aller Welt ein Zungen,

das sei dir, Herr, zu Lob und Ihr
    gezungen. Alleluja!

Come Holy Spirit, Lord God,
and fill with thine all-merciful grace
the hearts, minds, souls of those who
    follow Thee,
and kindle them with thine
    impassioned love.
O Lord, through the brightness of
    Thy Light
hast Thou gathered in one faith all
    peoples
from all tongues throughout the
    world,
that they might sing, Lord, Thy
    praise and honor. Alleluja!

Translated by Ron Haizlip

22. Leonhard Lechner, Part I
from *Historia der Passion und Leidens unsers einigen Erlösers und Seligmachers Jesu Christi* (1594)

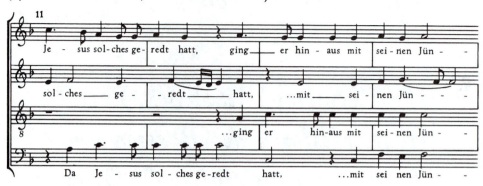

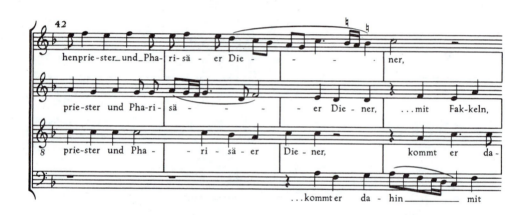

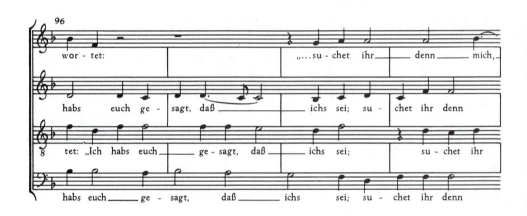

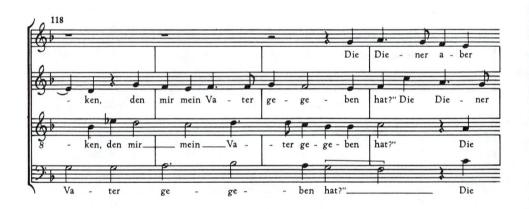

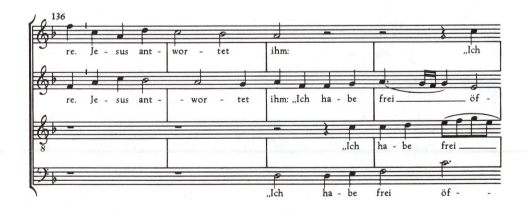

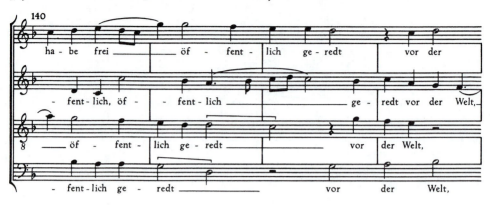

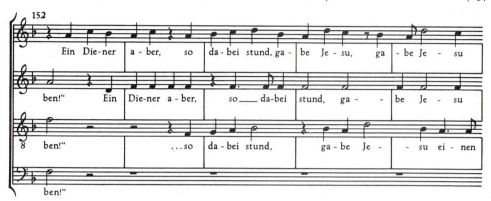

Das Leiden unsers Herren Jesu Christi aus dem Evangelisten Johanne. Da Jesus solches geredt hatt, ging er hinaus mit seinen Jüngern über den Bach Kidron; da war ein Garten, in den ging Jesus mit seinen Jüngern. Judas aber, der ihn varriet, wusste den Ort auch, denn Jesus versammelt sich oft daselbst mit seinen Jüngern. Judas aber, der ihn verriet, genommen die Schar und der Hohenpriester und Pharisäer Diener, kommt er dahin mit Fakkeln, Lampen und mit Waffen. Als nun Jesus wusste alles, was ihm begegnen sollte, ging er hinaus und sprach zu ihnen: "Wen suchet ihr?" Sie antwortten ihm: "Jesum von Nazareth." Jesus spricht zu ihnen: "Ich bins." Judas aber, der ihn verriet, stund auch bei ihnen. Als nun Jesus zu ihnen sprach: "Ich bins," wichen sie zurück und fielen zu Boden. Da fraget er sie abermals: "Wen suchet ihr?" Sie aber sprachen: "Jesum von Nazareth." Jesus antwortet: "Ich habs euch gesagt, dass ichs sei; suchet ihr denn mich, so lasset diese gehn." Da hatte Simon Petrus ein Schwert und zog es aus und schlug nach des Hohenpriesters Knechte und hieb ihm sein recht

The passion of our Lord Jesus Christ according to the Gospel of John. After these words, Jesus went out with his disciples over the brook Kidron; there was a garden there, and he and his disciples went into it. The place was known to Judas, his betrayer, because Jesus had often met there with his disciples. So Judas took a detachment of soldiers, and police provided by the High Priest and the Pharisees, equipped with lanterns, torches and weapons, and made his way to the garden. Jesus, knowing all that was coming upon him, went out to them and asked: "Who is it you want?" "Jesus of Nazareth," they answered. Jesus said to them: "I am he." And there stood Judas the traitor with them. When Jesus said to them, "I am he," they drew back and fell to the ground. Again Jesus asked, "Who is it you want?" Again they answered, "Jesus of Nazareth." Then Jesus said, "I have told you that I am he. If I am the man you want, let these others go." Thereupon Simon Peter drew the sword he was wearing and struck at the High Priest's servant, cutting off his right ear. Jesus then said to Peter: "Sheathe your sword: This is the cup

Ohr ab. Da sprach Jesus zu Petro: "Steck dein Schwert in die Scheide! Soll ich den Kelch nicht trinken, den mir mein Vater gegeben hat?" Die Diener aber bunden ihn und führeten ihn aufs erste zu Hannas. Der fraget Jesum um seine Jünger und um sein Lehre. Jesus antwortet ihm: "Ich habe frei öffentlich geredt vor der Welt, ich hab allzeit gelehrt in der Schul und im Tempel; frag die, so es gehöret haben!" Ein Diener aber, so dabei stund, gabe Jesu einen Bakkenstreich und sprach: "Sollst du dem Hohenpriester also antworten?" Jesus antwortet: "Hab ich übel geredt, so beweise es, dass bös sei; hab ich aber recht geredt, warum schlägst du mich?" Und Hannas sandte ihn gebunden zu dem Hohenpriester Kaiphas.

my Father has given me; shall I not drink it?" The troops now arrested Jesus and secured him. They took him first to Annas. He questioned Jesus about his disciples and about what he taught. Jesus replied: "I have spoken openly to all the world, I have always taught in synagogue and in the temple; Why question me?" When he said this, one of the police who was standing next to him struck him on the face, exclaiming: "Is that the way to answer the High Priest?" Jesus replied, "If I spoke amiss, state it in evidence; if I spoke well, why strike me?" So Annas sent him bound to Caiaphas the High Priest.

John 18: 1–12, 19–20, 22–24

23. Claude Goudimel, *Ainsi qu'on oit le cerf bruire* (publ. 1565)

Ainsi qu'on oit le cerf bruire,	As a hart longs for the brooklet
Pourchassant le frais des eaux:	Flowing in a quiet place,
Ainsi mon coeur qui souspire,	So my thristing soul does long, Lord,
Seigneur, apres tes ruisseaux,	For thine all-refreshing grace;
Va tous-jours criant, suivant,	My soul cries out for thine aid,
Le grand, le grand Dieu vivant:	For sight of the living God.
Helas! donques quand sera-ce,	O when shall mine eyes behold thee?
Que verrai de Dieu la face?	When shall I see God face to face?
Jours et nuits pour ma viande	Oft my tears, in long night watches,
De pleurs me vay soustenant,	Have been bitter food for me;
Quand je voy qu'on me demande,	Mocking men, to try my patience,
Où est ton Dieu maintenant?	Cried, "Why has thy God left thee?"
Je fond en me souvenant,	Why art thou cast down, my soul?
Qu'en troupe j'alloy menant,	Why art thou disquieted?
Priant, chantant, grosse bande	Hope in God, and I shall praise him.
Faire au temple son offrande.	I will trust him eternally.

Psalm 42

24. Jan Pieterszoon Sweelinck, *Chantez à Dieu chanson nouvelle* (publ. 1613)

PSALM 96, Copyright 1941, Mercury Music Corp. Used by permission.

Chantez à Dieu chanson nouvelle,
Chantez, ô terr' universelle,
Chantez, et son Nom bénissez,
Et de jour en jour annoncez
Sa delivrance solemnelle.

Sing new songs to God,
Sing, O world,
Sing, and bless his holy Name,
And from day to day tell
Of his solemn deliverance.

Psalm 96

25. William Byrd, *Sing Joyfully*
(publ. 1589)

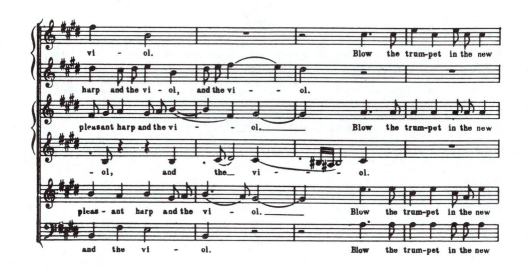

Psalm 81:1–4

26. Orlando Gibbons, *This Is the Record of John* (publ. 1641)

VERSE

Then said they un-to him:___What art thou? That we may give,__that we may give an an-swer un-to them___ that sent us.

What say'st thou of thy-self?

And he said,___ I am___ the voice of him that cri - eth in the wil - der - ness: Make

27. Claudin de Sermisy, *J'ay fait pour vous cent mille pas* (publ. 1528)

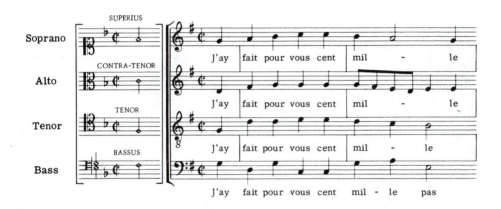

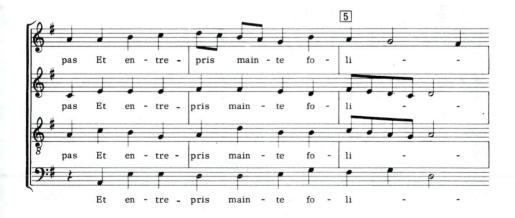

e. Ves - cu sans rei - gle ni com - pas, Dont je suys

e. Ves - cu sans rei - gle ni _____ com - pas, Dont je suys

e. Ves - cu sans rei - gle ni com - pas, _____ Dont je suys

e. Ves - cu sans rei - gle ni com - pas, Dont je suys

en ___ me - lan - co li - - e. Las, que se -

en me - lan - co li - - e. Las, que se -

en me - lan - co li - - e. Las, que se -

en me - lan - co li - - e. Las, que se -

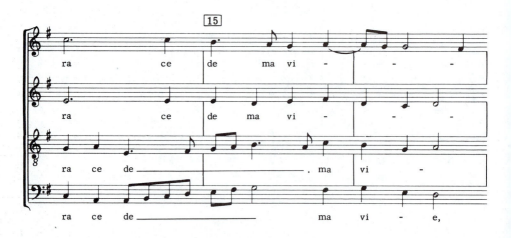

ra ce de ma vi - - -

ra ce de ma vi - - -

ra ce de _____ . ma vi -

ra ce de _____ ma vi - e,

J'ay fait pour vous cent mille pas

Et entrepris mainte folie.
Vescu sans reigle ni compas,
Dont je suys en melancolie.
Las, que sera ce de ma vie,
Il ne me survient que malheurs,

Pour ung plaisir mille douleurs.

I have made for you one hundred
    thousand steps
And many foolish undertakings.
I've lived without rule or compass,
For which I am melancoly.
Alas, what will my life become?
It befalls me nothing but
    unhappiness.
For one pleasure, a thousand pains.

28. Clément Janequin,
Le Chant des oyseaux
(publ. 1529)

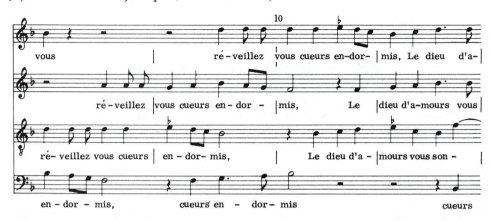

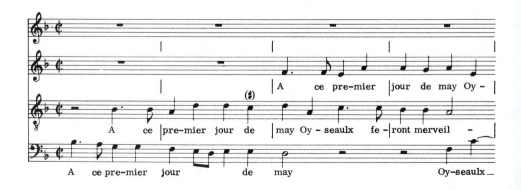

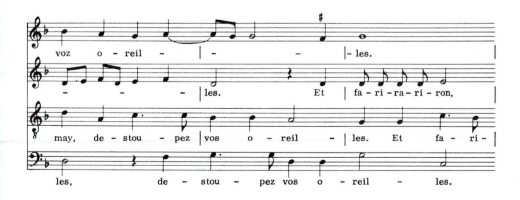

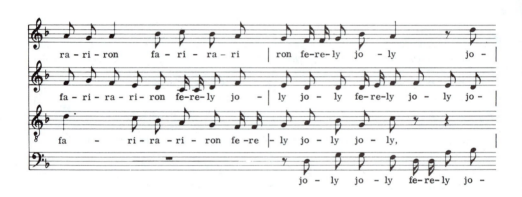

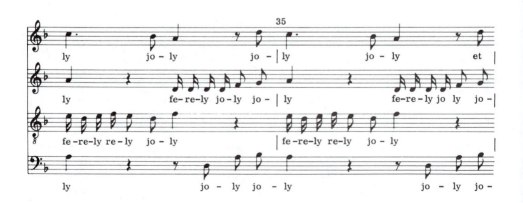

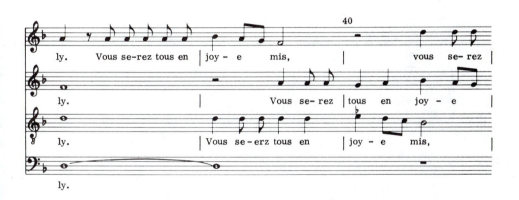

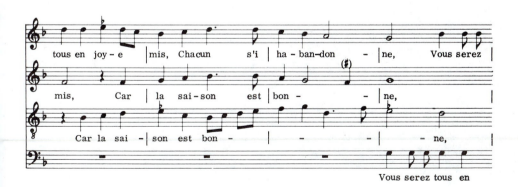

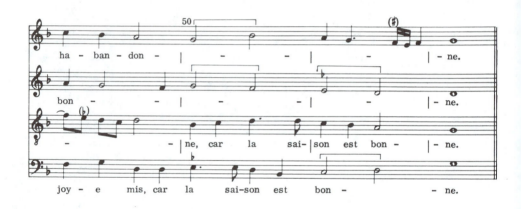

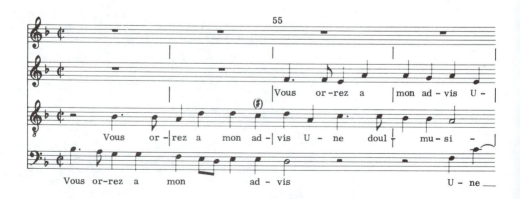

Vous orrez a mon ad - vis, Que fe-ra le

ne doulce mu - si - que, Que fe - ra le roy mau - vis

que, Que fe - ra le roy mau - vis, Le merle aus -

— doulce musi - que, Que fe - ra le roy mau - vis D'u -

roy mau-vis D'u - ne voix au - ten - ti - - -

D'u - ne voix au - ten - ti - - - que. Ti

si L'e- stour-nel se-ra par - my D'u - ne voix au - ten - ti -

ne voix au-ten - ti - - que, d'u - ne voix au-ten-

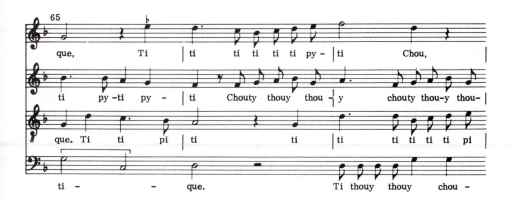

que, Ti ti ti ti ti ti py - ti Chou,

ti py -ti py - ti Chouty thouy thou - y chouty thou-y thou-

que. Ti ti pi ti ti ti ti ti ti ti pi

ti - - que. Ti thouy thouy chou -

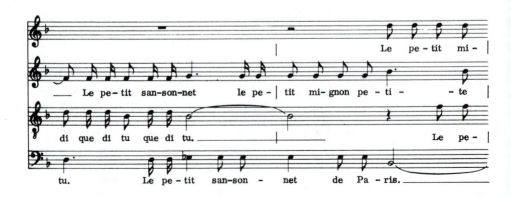

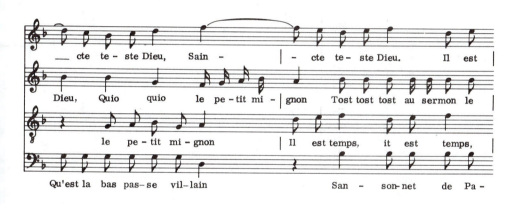

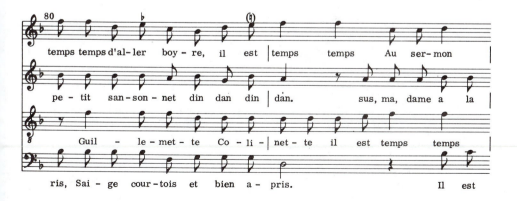

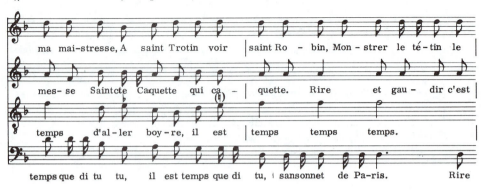

ma mai-stresse, A saint Trotin voir | saint Ro - bin, Mon - strer le té - tin le

mes- se Sainctcte Caquette qui ca- | quette. Rire et gau - dir c'est

temps d'al-ler boy-re, il est | temps temps temps.

temps que di tu tu, il est temps que di tu, ᵢ sansonnet de Pa-ris.   Rire

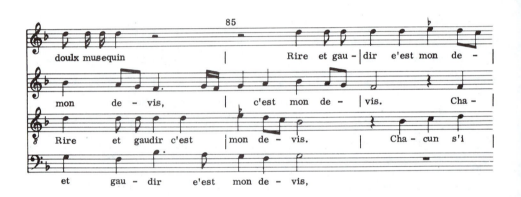

doulx musequin | Rire et gau-|dir e'est mon de -

mon de - vis, | c'est mon de -|vis.   Cha -

Rire et gaudir c'est |mon de - vis. | Cha - cun s'i |

et gau - dir e'est mon de - vis,

vis Cha - cun s'i | ha - ban-don - |ne, rire et gau -

cun s'y ha - ban-|don - - |ne |

ha - ban-don - |- - | - ne, |

rire et gaudir c'est

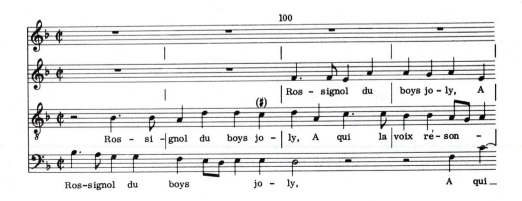

Ros - signol du boys jo - ly,   Pour vous mettre

qui la voix ré - son - ne, Pour vous met - tre hors d'en - nuy

ne, Pour vous met - tre hors d'en - nuy Vos - tre gor -

__ la voix réson - ne, Pour vous met - tre hors d'en - nuy Vos-

hors d'en-nuy   Vos - tre gor - ge jar - gon - - -

Vos - tre gor - ge jar - gon - - - ne.

-ge, Pour vous met - tre hors d'en nuy vos - tre gor - ge jar - gon -

tre gor - ge jar - gon - - ne, vos - tre gor - ge jar -

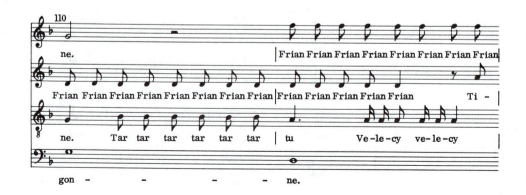

ne.   Frian Frian Frian Frian Frian Frian Frian Frian

Frian Frian Frian Frian Frian Frian Frian Frian Frian Frian Frian Frian   Ti -

ne. Tar tar tar tar tar tar tu Ve - le - cy ve - le - cy

gon - - - - ne.

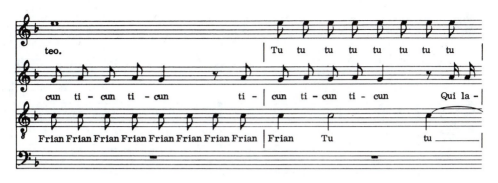

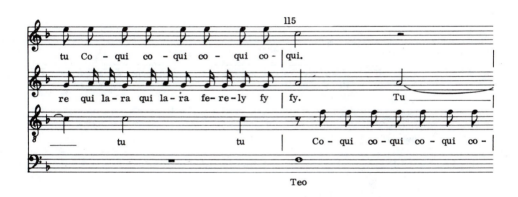

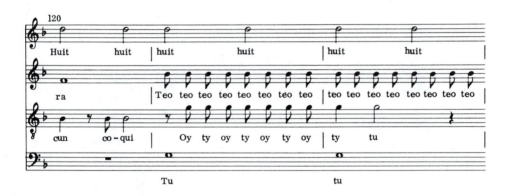

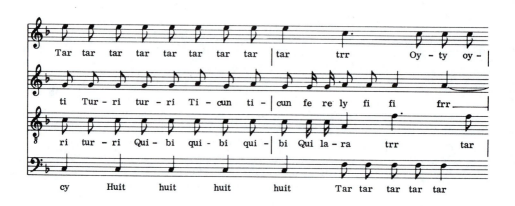

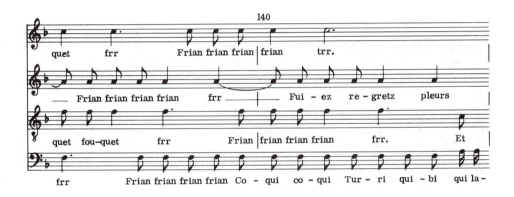

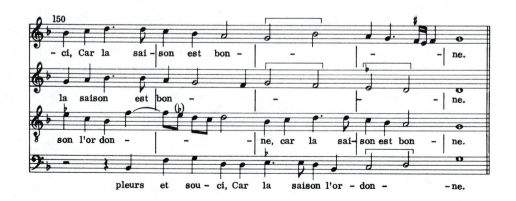

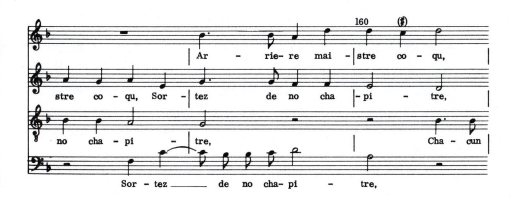

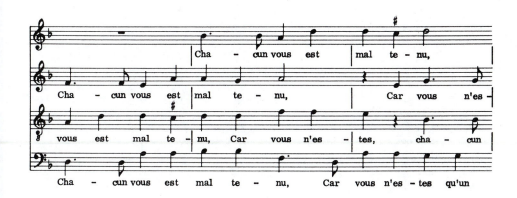

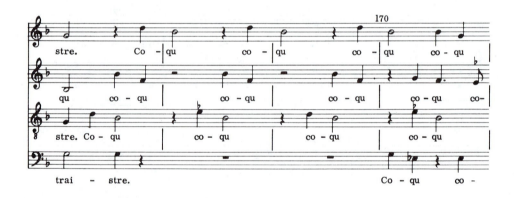

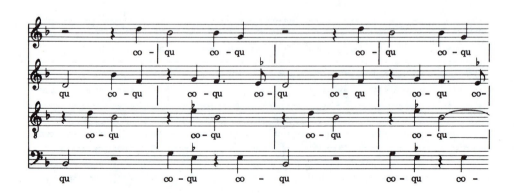

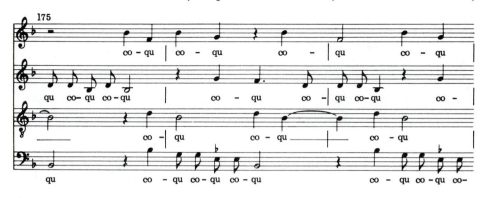

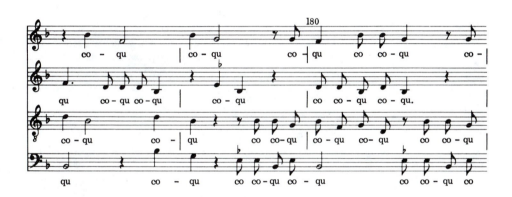

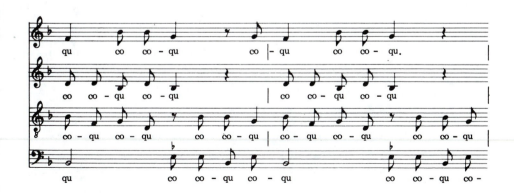

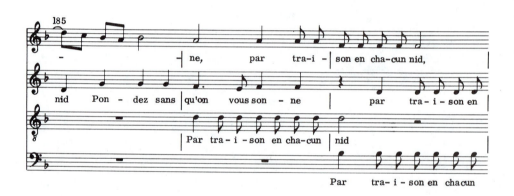

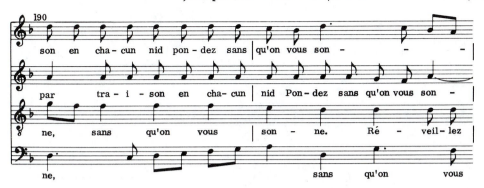

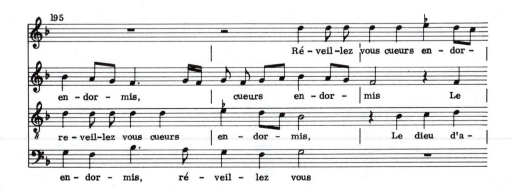

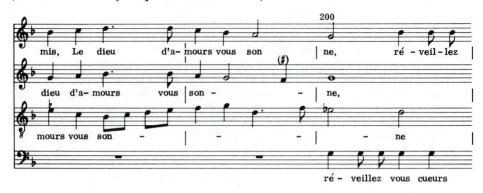

Réveillez vous, cueurs endormis,
Le dieu d'amours vous sonne.
A ce premier jour de may,
Oyseaulx feront merveilles,
Pour vous mettre hors d'esmay.
Destoupez voz oreilles.
Et fa-ri-ra-ri-ron, fe-re-ly joly.
Vous serez tous en joye mis,
Chacun s'i habandonne,
Vous serez tous en joye mis,
Car la saison est bonne.
Vous orrez, à mon advis,
Une doulce musique
Que fera le roy mauvis
D'une voix autentique:
Ti, ti, chouthy, thouy . . .
Le petit sansonnet de Paris,
Le petit mignon,
Qu'est la bas passe, villain.
Il est temps d'aller boyre,
Sansonnet de Paris,
Au sermon ma maistresse,
A saint Trotin
Voir saint Robin,
Rire et gaudir c'est mon devis,
Chacun s'i habandonne.
Rossignol du boys joly,
A qui la voix résonne,
Pour vois mettre hors d'ennuy
Vostre gorge jargonne.
Fuyez, regretz, pleurs et souci,
Car la saison l'ordonne.
Arriere, maistre coucou,
Chacun vous donne au hibou,
Sortez de no chapitre,
Chacun vous donne au hibou,
Car vous n'estes q'un traistre.
Cou, cou.
Par traison, en chacun nid,
Pondez sans qu'on vous sonne,
Reveillez vous, cueurs endormis,
Le dieu d'amours vous sonne.

Awaken, sleeping hearts,
The god of love is calling you.
On this first day of May
Birds will do marvelous things
To take you away from dismay.
Open your ears
And make laughter and merriment.
You will be completely joyful,
Each one indulging,
You will be completely joyful
Because the season is good.
You will hear, at my advice,
sweet music
which the thrush will make
in a resounding voice:
Ti, thouy, chouti, ti, ti.
The little starling of Paris,
This dear little one,
Who passes there, naughty thing,
It is time to go to drink,
Starling of Paris,
To the speeches of my mistress,
To St. Trotin, to St. Robin.
To laugh and make merry is my
     device,
Each one indulging himself.
Nightingale of the lovely wood,
Whose voice resounds
to pass the hours of boredom,
Your throat utters only nonsense,
frian, tu, tu, coqui.
Fly away, regret and care,
Because the season decrees it.
Master cou-cou, leave our place,
Each one gives you to the owl,
Because you are nothing but a traitor,
cou, cou, cou.
By treachery, in each nest,
You produce without anyone's asking
     you to.
Awaken, sleeping hearts,
The god of love calls you.

29. Claude Le Jeune, *Revecy venir du printans* (publ. 1603)

nal d'é - té s'é - clair - cît et la mer cal - me de

nal d'é - té s'é - clair - cît et la mer cal - me de

ses flots A - mo - lit le tris - te cou - rous. Le ca -

ses flots A - mo - lit le tris - te cou - rous. Le ca -

nard s'é - gay' se plon - jant Et se la - ve coint de -

nard s'é - gay' se plon - jant Et se la - ve coint de -

dans l'eau. Et la grû' qui four - che son vol Re - tra -

dans l'eau. Et la grû' qui four - che son vol Re - tra -

ver - se l'air et s'en va. *Repeat RECHANT*

ver - se l'air et s'en va.

CHANT á 3

Soprano
Le so- leil é-clai- re lui – zant D'u-ne plus sé-rai – ne

Alto
Le so- leil é-clai- re lui – zant D'u-ne plus sé-rai – ne

Tenor
Le so- leil é-clai- re lui – zant D'u-ne plus sé-rai – ne

clair - té. Du nu- a- ge l'om-bre s'en fuit __ Qui se ioû' et court et

clair - té. Du nu- a- ge l'om-bre s'en fuit __ Qui se ioû' et court et

clair - té. Du nu- a- ge l'om-bre s'en fuit __ Qui se ioû' et court et

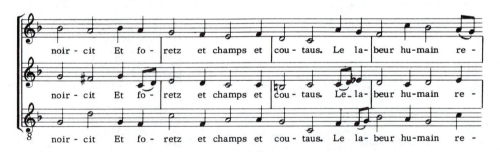

noir - cit Et fo - retz et champs et cou- taus. Le la- beur hu-main re -

noir - cit Et fo - retz et champs et cou- taus. Le la- beur hu-main re -

noir - cit Et fo - retz et champs et cou- taus. Le la- beur hu-main re -

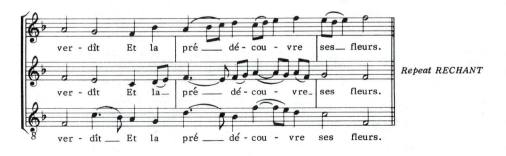

ver - dît Et la pré __ dé- cou- vre ses __ fleurs.

Repeat RECHANT

ver - dît Et la __ pré __ dé- cou- vre __ ses fleurs.

ver - dît __ Et la pré __ dé- cou- vre ses fleurs.

CHANT á 4

Soprano / Alto / Tenor / Bass: De Ve - nus le filz Cu - pi - don L'u - ni -

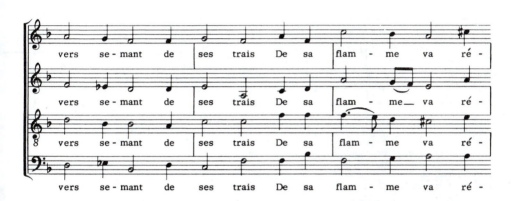

vers se - mant de ses trais De sa flam - me va ré -

chau - fer a - ni - maus qui vo - let en l'air, A - ni -

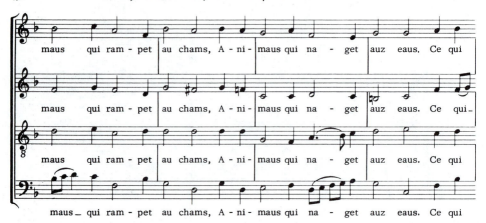

maus qui ram - pet au chams, A - ni - maus qui na - get auz eaus. Ce qui

maus qui ram - pet au chams, A - ni - maus qui na - get auz eaus. Ce qui

maus qui ram - pet au chams, A - ni - maus qui na - get auz eaus. Ce qui

maus qui ram - pet au chams, A - ni - maus qui na - get auz eaus. Ce qui

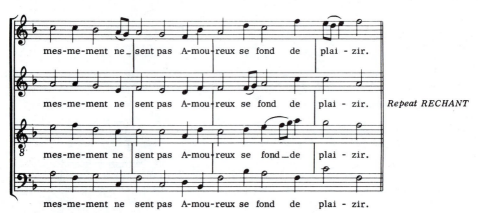

mes-me-ment ne sent pas A-mou-reux se fond de plai - zir.

mes-me-ment ne sent pas A-mou-reux se fond de plai - zir. *Repeat RECHANT*

mes-me-ment ne sent pas A-mou-reux se fond de plai - zir.

mes-me-ment ne sent pas A-mou-reux se fond de plai - zir.

CHANT á 5

Soprano   Ri - ons aus - si nous, et cher - chons Les é -

Soprano   Ri - ons aus - si nous, et cher - chons Les é -

Alto   Ri - ons aus - si nous, et cher - chons Les é -

Tenor   Ri - ons aus - si nous, et cher - chons Les é -

Bass   Ri - ons aus - si nous, et cher - chons Les é -

Repeat RECHANT

Revecy venir du printans,	Once again has come springtime,
L'amoureuz et belle saison.	The season of love and beauty.
Le courant des eaus recherchant	The current of waters which seek again
Le canal d'été s'éclaircit	The summer channel is now clear
Et la mer calme de ses flots	And the calm sea with its waves
Amolit le triste courrous.	Softens cheerless anger.
Le canard s'égay' se plonjant	The duck delights in his diving
Et se lave coint dedans l'eau.	and washes himself coyly in the water.
Et la grû' qui fourche son vol	And the crane, with forked flight,
Retraverse l'air et s'en va.	Criss-crosses the sky and disappears.
Revecy venir . . . (*refrain*)	Once again . . . (*refrain*)

Le soleil éclaire luizant,
D'une plus sereine clairté.
Du nuage l'ombre s'en fuit,
Qui se ioû' et court et noircit
Et foretz et champs et coutaus.

Le labeur humain reverdît
Et la pré découvre ses fleurs.
Revecy venir . . . (*refrain*)

De Venus le filz Cupidon
L'univers semant de ses trais
De sa flamme va réchaufer
Animaus qui volet en l'air,
Animaus qui rampet au chams,

Animaus qui naget auz eaus.
Ce qui mesmement ne sent pas
Amoureux se fond de plaizir.
Revecy venir . . . (*refrain*)

Rions aussi nous, et cherchons
Les ébas et jeus du printans.
Toute chose rit de plaizir,
Sélébron la gaye saizon.
Revecy venir . . . (*refrain*)

The sun brightly shining,
With a light most serene.
The shadow of the clouds flee,
Playing and running and blackening
The forests and meadows and
    hillocks.

Human labour blossoms
And the meadow uncovers its flowers.
Once again . . . (*refrain*)

Cupid, the son of Venus,
Scatters his arrows upon the universe,
And with his flame rekindles
The animals who fly in the sky,
The animals who crawl upon the
    fields,
The animals who swim in the waters.
Even those who have no feeling
Fall in love and melt with pleasure.
Once again . . . (*refrain*)

Let us therefore laugh, and let us seek
The revels and games of springtime.
All things laugh with pleasure,
Let us praise the gay season.
Once again . . . (*refrain*)

30. Jacob Arcadelt, *Il bianco e dolce cigno* (publ. 1539)

o, et io pian-gen - do giung' al fin del___ vi - ver mi -

o, et io pian-gen - do giung' al fin del vi - ver mi

o, et io pian-gen - do giung' al fin del vi - ver mi -

o. et io pian-gen do giung' al fin del vi - ver mi -

o, stran' e di - ver - sa sor - te, ch'ei mo - re scon-so - la -to, et

o, stran' e di-ver-sa sor - te, ch'ei___ mo - re scon-so - la -to,

o, stran' e di-ver-sa _____ sor - te, ch'ei mo re scon-so - la -to,

o, stran' e di - ver - sa sor - te

io mo - ro be - a - - - to, mor -

et io mo - ro be - a - - - to, mor -

et io mo ro, et io mo - ro be - - - to, mor -

et io mo - ro be - a - - to, mor -

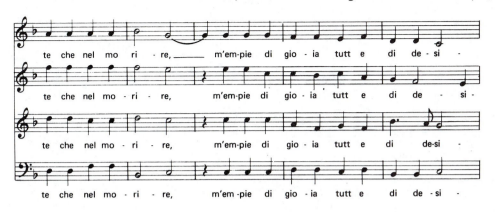

Il bianco e dolce cigno cantando more,
et io piangendo giung'al fin del
    viver mio.
Stran'e diversa sorte, ch'ei more
    sconsolato,
et io moro beato.

Morte che nel morire,
m'empie de gioia tutt'e di desire.
Se nel morir'altro dolor non sento,
di mille mort'il di sarei contento.

               Alfonso d'Avolos

The sweet white swan dies singing,
While I weep as I reach my life's end.

How strange that he dies disconsolate

And I die happy.

Weary to the point of death,
Drained of all joy and desire,
I meet death without sorrow,
Content to die a thousand deaths a
    day.
        Translated by Dennis Shrock

31. Giovanni Gastoldi, *Il bell' umore* (publ. 1591)

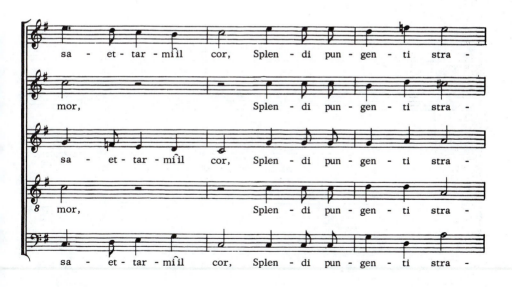

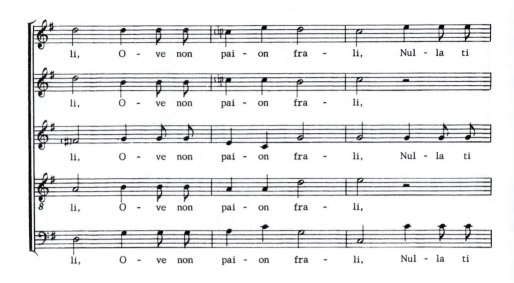

Viver lieto voglio,
senza gran cordoglio, la, la, la.
In poi restar Amor,
Di saettarmi il cor,
Splendi pungenti strali,
Ove non paion frali,
Nulla ti stimo o poco,
E di te prendo gioco, la, la, la.

I will have a gay life.
Free from grief and sorrow, la, la, la.
But Love will still remain,
To pierce my heart with pain,
He shoots a stinging arrow,
Trying my life to narrow,
He cannot thus involve me,
Freedom will ere resolve me, la, la, la.

Translated by Maynard Klein

32. Claudio Monteverdi, *Ecco mormorar l'onde* (publ. 1590)

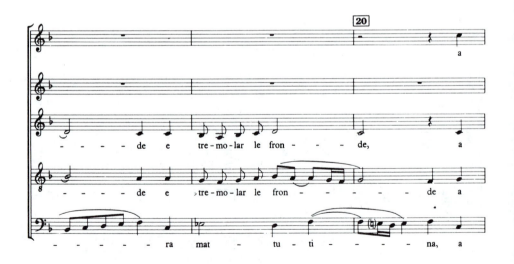

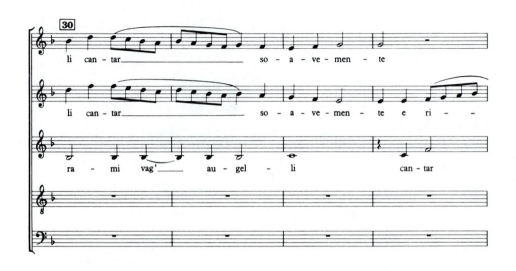

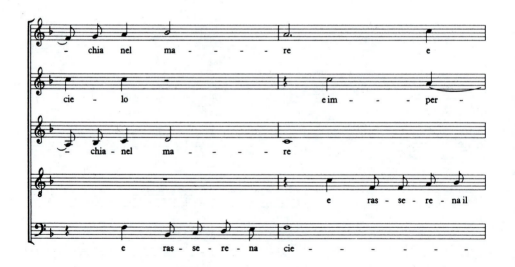

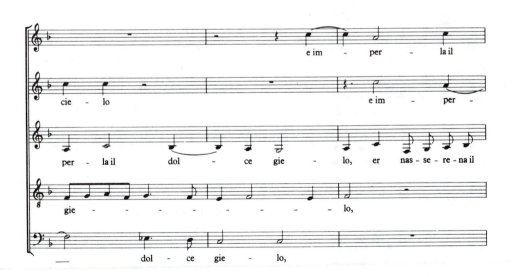

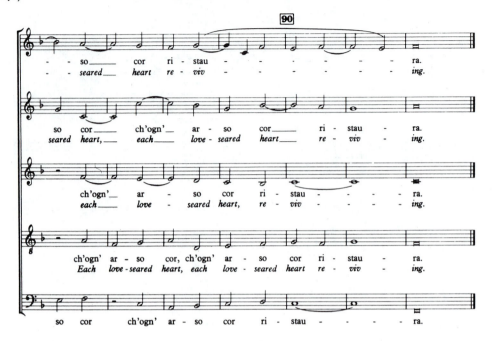

Ecco mormorar l'onde,
e tremolar le fronde,
a l'aura mattutina e gl'arboscelli,

e, sovrai i verdi rami vag'

augelli cantar soavemente
e rider l'oriente:
ecco già l'alb' appare
e si specchia nel mare
e rasserena il cielo
e imperla il dolce gielo
e gl'alti monti indora.
O bella e vag' aurora.
L'aura è tua messaggiera e tu de
     l'aura,
ch'ogn' arso cor ristaura.
          Torquato Tasso

Hark! low murmurs the water,
The bushes are aflutter,
In morning's breeze the groves are
     gently stirring
O'er leafy branches am'rous birds
     are winging
And singing, sweetly singing;
The east is bright with laughter,
And lo, the dawn is waking,
The sea her mirror making
And calming all the heavens,
Light frost the meadows pearling
And lofty mountains gilding.
Lovely and gay Aurora!
Soft wind do herald thee, and thou
     my Laura
Each seared heart reviving.
      Translated by Millicent Rose

33. Luca Marenzio, *Crudele acerba* (publ. 1599)

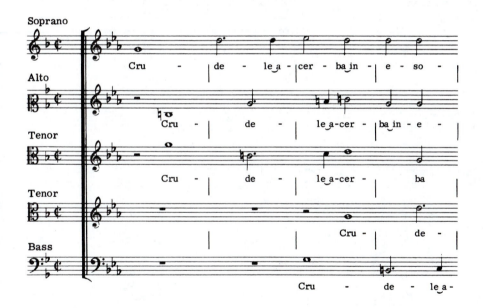

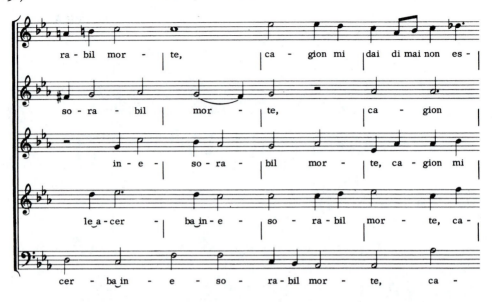

ra - bil mor - te, ca - gion mi dai di mai non es -

so - ra - bil mor - te, ca - gion

in - e - so - ra - bil mor - te, ca - gion mi

le a - cer - ba in - e - so - ra - bil mor - te, ca -

cer - ba in - e - so - ra - bil mor - te, ca -

ser lie - to di mai non es - ser lie -

mi dai di mai non es - ser lie - to,

dai di mai non es - ser lie -

gion mi dai di mai non es - ser lie -

gion mi dai di mai non es - ser lie -

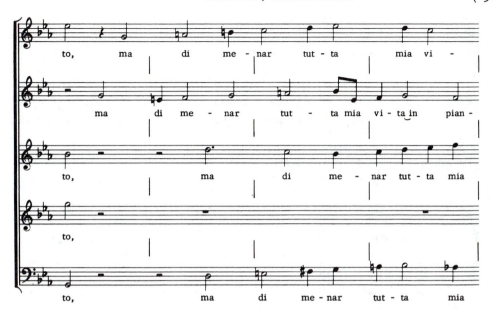

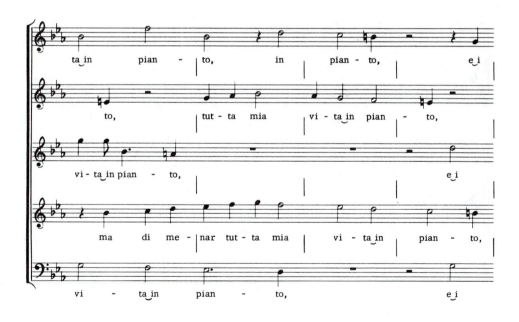

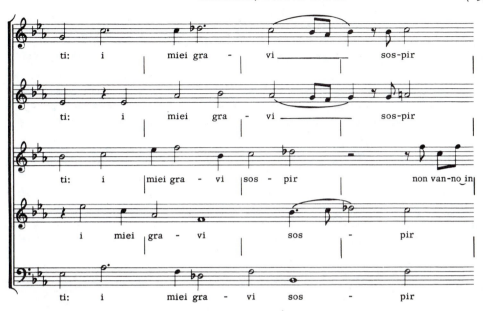

Crudele acerba inesorabil morte,

cagion mi dai di mai non esser lieto
ma di menar tutta mia vita in pianto,

e i giorni oscuri e le dogliose notti:

i miei gravi sospir non vanno in rime,

e'l mio duro martir vince ogni stile.

Petrarch

O cruel, sharp and uncompromising death,

how you have taken away all my joy and left me to spend my life in weeping,

in days of darkness and nights of anguish;

all my sorrows and my sighs yield no more verses,

and my bitter complaints will inspire no songs.

34. Carlo Gesualdo, *Moro lasso* (publ. 1611)

Moro lasso al mio duolo,
e chi mi può dar vita,
ahi, che m'ancide e non vuol darmi
    vita.

O dolorosa forte,
chi dar vita mi può,
ahi, mi da morte.

I die, alas! from my pain,
And who can give me life,
Alas, kills me and will not give me
    life.

Oh painful lot,
Who can give me life,
Alas, gives me death.

35. Thomas Morley, *Fire, Fire*
(publ. 1595)

la   la   la!   O   la   la   la!

la la la la!   la la la la la la la   la la la   la!

la   la   la!   la la   la   la la   la   la!

la   la   la!   la   la   la ____ la la   la!

la   la   la!   la   la   la!

36. Thomas Weelkes, *When David Heard* (c. 1608)

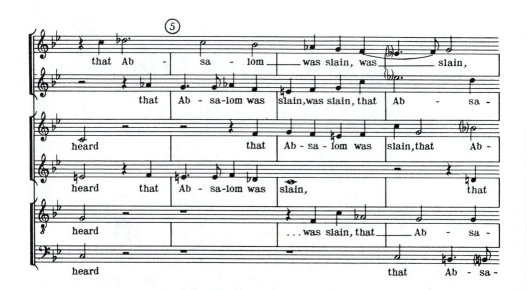

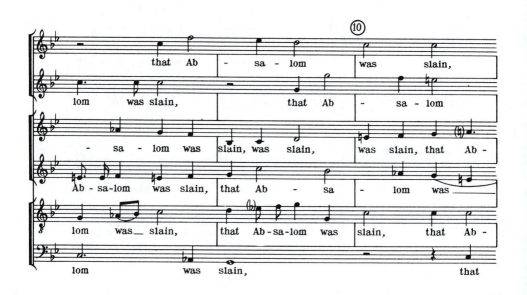

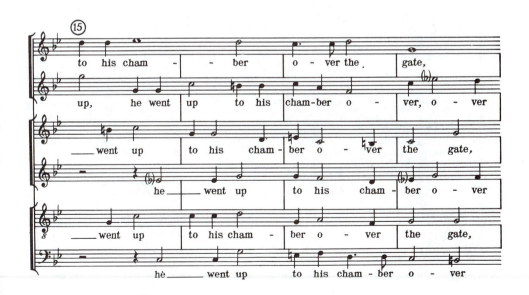

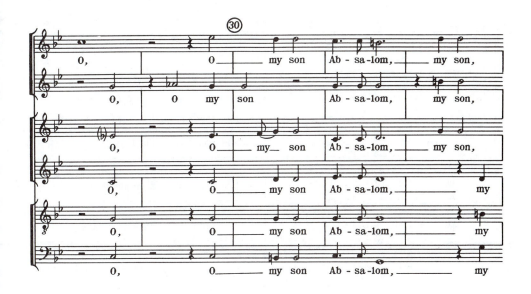

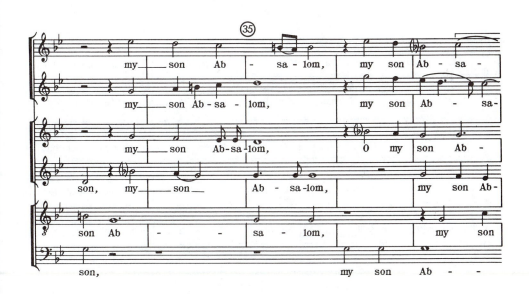

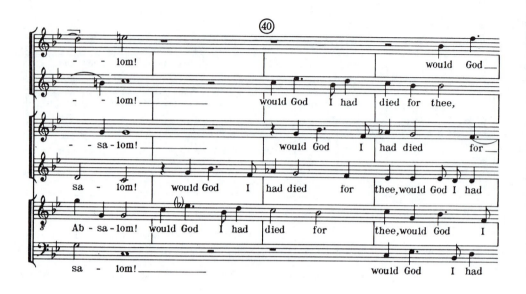

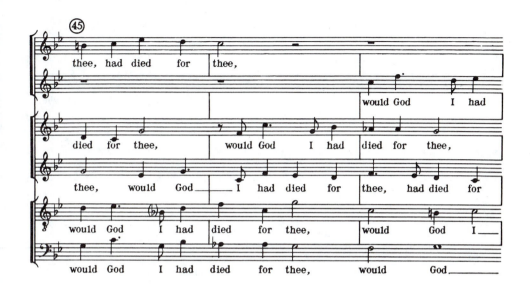

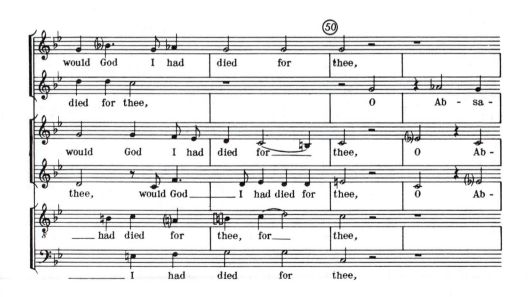

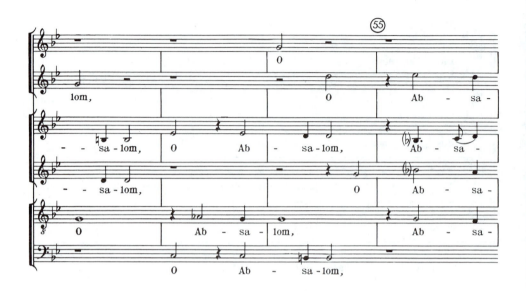

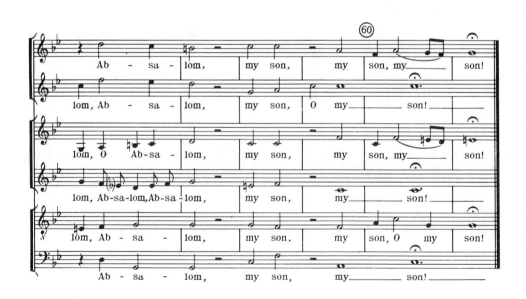

II Samuel 18:23

37. John Wilbye, *Adieu Sweet Amarillis* (publ. 1598)

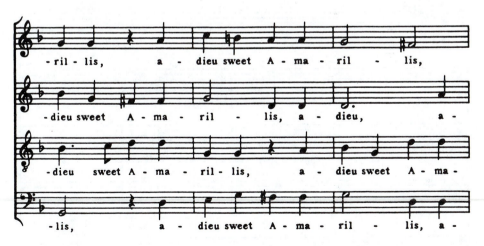

38. Monteverdi, *Laetatus sum* (publ. 1610)

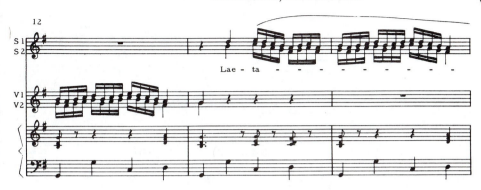

in his quae dic - ta sunt mi - hi: In do - mum Do - mi -

ni _____ i - bi - mus.

Stan - tes, stan - tes e - rant, e - rant pe - des, e - rant pe - des no - stri,

Laetatus sum in his quae dicta sunt
    mihi: In domum Domini
    ibimus.
Stantes erant pedes nostri in atriis
    tuis, Jerusalem.
Jerusalem, quae aedificatur ut
    civitas: cujus participatio ejus
    in idipsum.
Illuc enim ascenderunt tribus, tribus
    Domini: testimonium Israel ad
    confitendum nomine Domini.

Quia illic sederunt sedes in judicio,
    sedes super domum David.

Rogate quae ad pacem sunt
    Jerusalem: et abundantia
    diligentibus te.
Fiat pax in virtute tua: et abundantia
    in turribus tuis.
Propter fratres meos et proximos
    meos, loquebar pacem de te:
Propter domum Domimi Dei nostri
    quaesivi bona tibi.
Gloria Patri, et Filio, et Spiritui
    Sancto.
Sicut erat in principio, et nunc, et
    semper, et in saecula saeculorum.
    Amen.

I rejoiced at the words of those who
    said unto me: "Let us go into
    the house of the Lord."
Now our feet are standing inside
    your gates, O Jerusalem.
Jerusalem, built as a firmly compact
    city.

For there the tribes go up, the tribes
    of the Lord: For it is Israel's
    convenant to acknowledge the
    name of the Lord.
The thrones of judgment were erected
    there, the ruling thrones of the
    house of David.
Ask peace for Jerusalem, and
    abundance for those who love
    you.
Let peace be within you, and
    abundance within your walls.
For my brothers and my neighbors,
    I have spoken peace unto you.
For the house of the Lord our God,
    I have sought good for you.
Glory be to the Father, and to the
    Son, and to the Holy Ghost,
As it was in the beginning, is now,
    and ever shall be. Amen.

Psalm 122

39. Giacomo Carissimi, *Plorate filii Israel* from *Jepthe* (1669)

From: Carissimi "Historia die Jepthe" (edited by Gottfried Wolters) Loses Blatt Nr.
730. Möseler Verlag, Wolfenbüttel.

Plorate filii Israel, plorate omnes virgines et filiam Jepthe unigenitam in carmine doloris lamentamini.

Weep, ye children of Israel, weep all ye virgins, and bewail Jephtah's only daughter with a song of mourning.

Translated by Eckart Weber

40. Antonio Vivaldi, *Magnificat, Et exsultavit,* and *Et misericordia* from *Magnificat* (c. 1730)

24
om- nes,
om- nes,
ec- - - ce e- - nim, ex hoc be- a- - tam, be- a- - tam me di- cent om- - - nes, om- nes
om- nes,
om- nes,
[♯] [♯6]

28
ge-ne-ra-ti-o- nes,
♯ 7 6 6 6 5 5 6 6 5

ius   et san - - ctum, san - ctum no - - men, san-ctum no - - men e - - - ius.

See page 3 for text.

41. Marc-Antoine Charpentier, Kyrie from *Messe de minuit pour Noël* (c. 1680)

See page 15 for text.

42. Jean-Philippe Rameau,
Laboravi clamans (before 1722)

Laboravi clamans, raucae factae sunt
    fauces meae,
defecerunt oculi mei, dum spero in
    Deum meum.

I am wearied with crying out, my
    throat is sore,
my eyes grow dim as I wait for God
    to help me.

Psalm 69, verse 3

43. Henry Purcell, *Come, Ye Sons of Art* from *Come, Ye Sons of Art* (1694)

Chorus
Soprano

Come, come, ye   Sons__ of Art,   come, come   a - way,   come, come, ye

Alto

Come, come, ye   Sons__ of Art,   come, come   a - way,   come, come, ye

Tenor

Come, come, ye   Sons   of Art,   come, come, a - way,   come, come, ye

Bass

Come, come, ye   Sons   of Art,   come, come, a - way,   come, come, ye

Sons— of Art, come, come a - way,   tune all— your voi - ces and

Sons— of Art, come, come, a - way,   tune all— your voi - ces and

Sons   of Art, come, come, a - way,   tune all —— your voi - ces and

Sons   of Art, come, come a - way,   tune all   your voi - ces and

in – struments play, to celebrate, to celebrate this tri – umphant day.

in – stru – ments play, to celebrate, to celebrate this tri – umphant day.

in – struments play, to celebrate, to celebrate this tri – umphant day.

in – struments play, to celebrate, to celebrate this tri – umphant day.

Tune all your voi-ces, and in-struments play, to celebrate, to celebrate this

Tune all your voi-ces, and in-struments play, to celebrate, to celebrate this

Tune all your voi-ces, and in-struments play, to celebrate, to celebrate this

Tune all your voi-ces, and in-struments play, to celebrate, to celebrate this

tri – um-phant day, to celebrate, to celebrate this tri – um-phant day.

tri – um-phant day, to celebrate, to celebrate this tri – um-phant day.

tri – um-phant day, to celebrate, to celebrate this tri – um – phant day.

tri – um-phant day, to celebrate, to celebrate this tri – um-phant day.

44. George Frideric Handel, *And There Came All Manner of Flies* from *Israel in Egypt* (1739)

Tutti.　Org.　Tutti.

45. Michael Praetorius,
Psallite (1612)

Psallite unigenito Christo Dei filio!
Psallite Redemptori Domino,
    puerulo,

iacenti in praesaepio!
Ein feines Kindelein liegt in dem
    Krippelein;
Alle lieben Engelein dienen dem
    Kindelein,
singen ihm gar fein.

Singt und klingt!
Jesu, Gottes Kind und Marien
    Söhnelein!
Unserm lieben Jesulein im
    Krippelein
beim Öchslein und beim Eselein!

Praise Christ, the only-begotten son
    of God!
Praise God the Redeemer, little
    Child
Lying in the manger!
In the cradle lies a fine tiny little
    Child!
All the lovely angels serve the little
    Child,
Singing grandly.

Ring and sing!
Sing about the Child of God little
    Son of Mary!
He's our little Jesus in his little cradle

With ox and ass and with sheep.

46. Heinrich Schütz, Opening Section from *Musikalische Exequien* (1636)

6

sie - he, das_ ist Got-tes Lamm, das der Welt Sün - de trägt._

Nacket werde ich wiederum dahin fahren,
der Herr hats gegeben der Herr hats genommen,
der Name des Herren sei gelobet.

Herr Gott Vater im Himmel erbarm dich, erbarm dich über uns.
Christus is mein Leben,
Sterben ist mein Gewinn.
Siehe, das ist Gottes Lamm,
das der Welt Sünde trägt.
Jesu Christe, Gottes Sohn,
erbarm dich über uns.
Leben wir, so leben wir dem Herren,
Sterben wir, so sterben wir dem Herren,
darum wir leben, oder sterben,
so sind wir des Herren,
Herr Gott heiliger Geist,
erbarm dich über uns.

Naked shall I also return one day thither,
The Lord God hath given, the Lord God has taken,
the Name of the Lord be blessed forever.

Lord God, Father in Heaven, have mercy, have mercy on us all.
Life to me is Jesus,
death to me is but gain.
See ye here the Lamb of God,
that taketh all our sin.
Lord, Christ Jesus, Son of God,
have mercy on us all.
Living, we live unto the Lord God;
Dying, we but die unto the Lord God;
whether in living, or in dying,
we are of the Lord God.
Lord God, Holy Spirit,
have mercy on us all.

English translation by
Henry S. Drinker and
Arthur Mendel

47. Dietrich Buxtehude, *In dulci jubilo* (1685)

wärn wir da,_____ ei - a, wärn wir da!

wärn wir da,_____ ei - a, wärn wir da!

wärn wir da,_____ ei - a, wärn wir da!

In dulci jubilo
nun singet und seid froh!
Unsers Herzens Wonne liegt
in praesepio
und leuchtet als die Sonne
matris in gremio. Alpha es et O.

O Jesu parvule,
nach dir ist mir so weh:
Tröst mir mein Gemüte,
o puer optime
durch alle deine Güte,
o princeps gloriae! Trahe me post te.

O patris caritas,
O nati lenitas!
Wir wären all verdorben
per nostra crimina,
so hat er unser erworben
coelorum gaudia.
Eia, wärn wir da!

Ubi sunt gaudia?
Nirgend mehr denn da,
da die Engel singen
nova cantica
und die Schellen klingen
in regis curia.
Eia, wärn wir da.

In sweet joy
Let us sing and be joyful!
Our heart's joy lies
in the manger
And shines like a bright star
in the mother's lap. You are the
    beginning and the end.

O little Jesus,
My heart is sore for Thee:
Comfort my soul,
O best child,
Through all your good,
O glorious prince! Draw me in with
    you.

O dear father,
O gentle son!
We all were deeply stained
for our sins,
But He has gained for us
the joy of heavens.
O that we were there!

Where are the joyful?
Nowhere more there, then,
Where the angels sing
a new song
There the bells are ringing
in the court of the king.
O, that we were there.

48. Johann Sebastian Bach, *Jesu, meine Freude,* BWV 227 (1723)

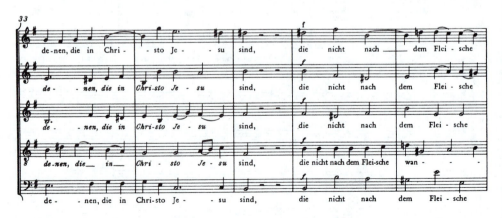

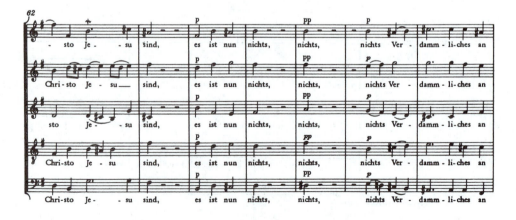

Choral

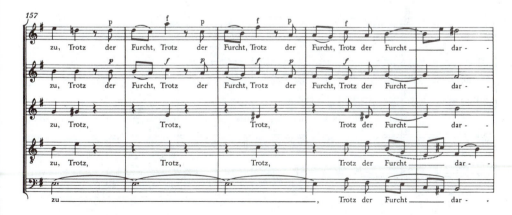

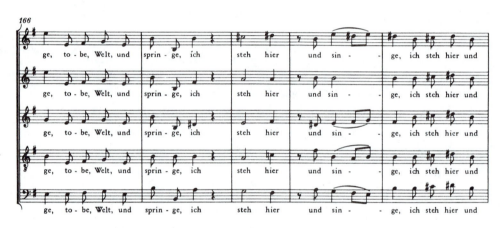

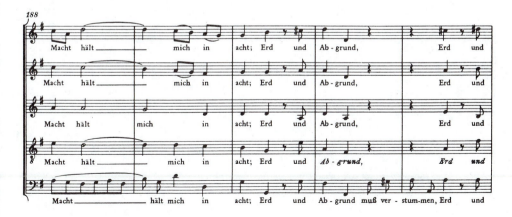

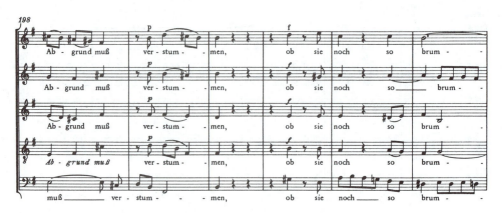

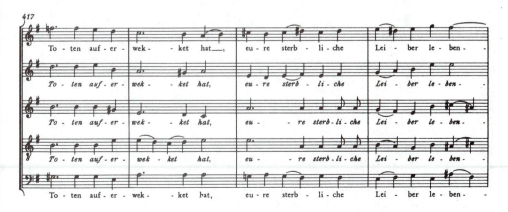

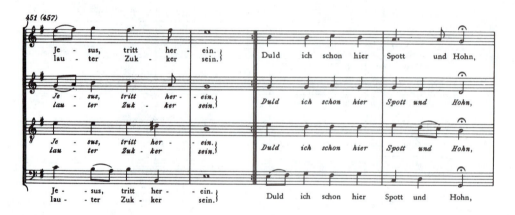

Jesu, meine Freude,
Meines Herzens Weide,
Jesu, meine Zier,
Ach, wie lang', ach lange
Ist dem Herzen bange
Und verlangt nach dir!
Gottes Lamm, mein Bräutigam,
Ausser dir soll mir auf Erden
Nichts sonst Liebers werden.

Jesu, priceless treasure,
Source of purest pleasure,
Truest friend to me,
Ah, how long I've panted,
And my heart hath fainted,
Thirsting, Lord, for Thee!
Thine I am, O spotless Lamb!
I will suffer naught to hide Thee,
Naught I ask beside Thee.

Es ist nun nichts Verdammliches
an denen, die in Christo Jesu
sind, die nicht nach dem
Fleische wandeln, sondern nach
dem Geist.

So there is now no condemnation unto
them which are in Jesus Christ,
them who walk not by the flesh
corruptly,
but as the Spirit leads.

Unter deinen Schirmen
Bin ich vor den Stürmen
Aller Feinde frei.
Lass den Satan wittern,
Lass den Feind erbittern,
Mir steht Jesus bei!
Ob es itzt gleich kracht und blitzt,
Ob gleich Sünd' und Hölle schrecken:
Jesus will mich decken.

In Thine arm I rest me,
Foes who would molest me
Cannot reach me here,
Though the earth be shaking,
Ev'ry heart be quaking,
Fires may flash, and thunders crash,
Yea, and sin and hell assail me,
Jesus will not fail me.

Denn das Gesetz des Geistes, der da
lebendig machet in Christo
Jesu, hat mich frei gemacht
von dem Gesetz der Sünde und
des Todes.

Thus, then the law of the Spirit
of life in Christ abiding,
now hath made me free from the law
of sin and death.

Trotz dem alten Drachen,
Trotz des Todes Rachen,
Trotz der Furcht darzu!
Tobe, Welt, und springe,
Ich steh' hier und singe,
In gar sich'rer Ruh'.
Gottes Macht hält mich in Acht;
Erd' und Abgrund muss verstummen,
Ob sie noch so brummen.

Death, I do not fear thee,
Thou, thou standest near me;
Grave, I calmly spurn thee,
Though to dust thou turn me!
Strong in hope and faith,
Rising up, and singing,
I shall, heavenward singing,
Soar, and vanquish Death,
Soar, and with the blest shall forever
rest!
He that reigns will rend my chains,
Earth may vanish, Heav'n may sever,
God is God for ever.

Ihr aber seid nicht fleischlich,
sondern geistlich, so anders
Gottes Geist in euch wohnet.
Wer aber Christi Geist nicht
hat, der ist nicht sein.

Ye are not of the flesh,
but of the Spirit,
if in your hearts the Spirit abideth,
ye are not of the flesh,
If Jesu's Spirit be not yours;
ye are not His.

Weg mit allen Schätzen!
Du bist mein Ergötzen,
Jesu, meine Lust!
Weg, ihr eitlen Ehren,
Ich mag euch nicht hören,
Bleibt mir unbewusst!
Elend, Not, Kreuz, Schmach und
    Tod
Soll mich, ob ich viel muss leiden,
Nicht von Jesu scheiden.

So aber Christus in euch ist; so ist
    der Leib zwar tot um der
    Sünde willen, der Geist aber ist
    das Leben um der Gerechtigkeit
    willen.

Gutte Nacht, o Wesen,
Das die Welt erlesen,
Mir gefällst du nicht.
Gute Nacht, ihr Sünden,
Bleibet weit dahinten,
Kommt nicht mehr ans Licht!
Gute Nacht, du Stolz und Pracht!
Dir sei ganz, du Lasterleben,
Gute Nacht gegeben!

So nun der Geist des, der Jesum von
    den Toten auferwekket hat, in
    euch wohnet, so wird auch
    derselbige, der Christum von
    den Toten auferwekket hat,
    eure sterblichen Leiber lebendig
    machen, um des willen, dass
    sein Geist in euch wohnet.

Weicht, ihr Trauergeister,
Denn mein Freudenmeister,
Jesus, tritt herein.
Denen, die Gott lieben,
Muss auch ihr Betrüben
Lauter Zukker sein.
Duld' ich schon hier Spott und
    Hohn:
Dennoch bleibst du auch im Leide,
Jesu, meine Freude.

Hence with earthly treasure,
Thou art all my pleasure,
Jesu, all my choice.
Hence, thou empty glory,
Naught to me thy story,
Told with tempting voice;
Pain, or loss, or shame, or cross,
Shall not from my Saviour move me,
Since He deigns to love me.

If, therefore, Christ abide in you,
then is the body dead because of
    transgression
But the Spirit liveth,
because of righteousness liveth.

Fare thee well,
fare thee well that errest,
Thou that earth preferest,
Thou wilt tempt in vain;
Fare thee well,
fare thee well, transgression,
Hence abhorr'd possession,
Come not forth, not forth again.
Past your hour, O pride and pow'r,
Worldly life, thy bonds I sever,
Fare thee well forever.

If by His Spirit, God,
God, that unpraised Jesus from the
    dead,
dwell in you.
He that raised Christ up from the
    dead,
shall also quicken your mortal bodies,
by His Spirit that dwelleth within
    you.

Hence, all fear and sadness,
For the Lord of gladness,
Jesus, enters in;
They who love the Father,
Though the storms may gather,
Still have peace within;
Yea, whate'er I here must bear,
Still in Thee lies purest pleasure,
Jesu, priceless treasure.

49. Bach, *Nach dir, Herr, verlanget mich*, BWV 150 (1710)

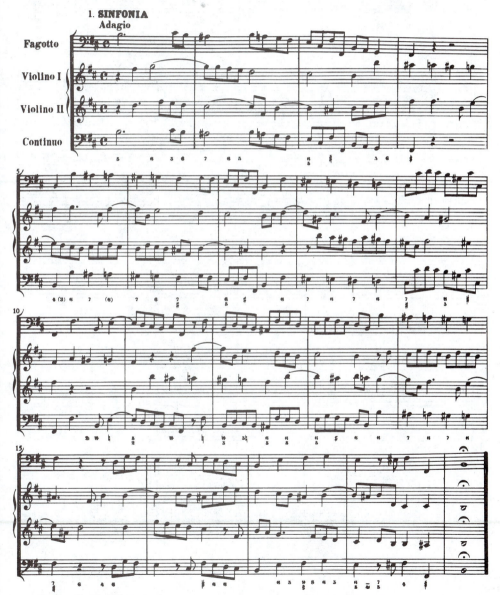

5. ARIE

7. CHOR
Ciaccona

Nach dir, Herr, verlanget mich.
Mein Gott, ich hoffe auf dich.
Lass' mich nicht zu Schanden werden,
dass sich meine Feinde nicht freuen
    über mich.

Doch bin und bleibe ich vergnügt,
obgleich nier zeitlich toben,
Kreuz, Sturm und andre Proben,
Tod, Höll' und was sich fügt.
Ob Unfall schlägt den treuen Knecht
Recht ist und bleibet ewig recht.

Leite mich in deiner Wahrheit und
    lehre mich;
denn du bist der Gott, der mir hilft,
täglich harre ich dein.

Zedern müssen von den Winden
oft viel Ungemach empfinden,
oftmals werden sie verkehrt.
Rat und Tat auf Gott gestellet,
achtet nicht, was widerbellet,
denn sein Wort ganz anders lehrt.

Meine Augen sehen stets zu dem
    Herrn,
denn er wird meinen Fuss
aus dem Netze ziehen.

Meine Tage in den Leiden
endet Gott dennoch zu Freuden;
Christen auf den Dornenwegen
führen Himmels Kraft und Segen;
bleibet Gott mein treuer Schatz,
achte ich nicht Menschenkreuz.

Christus, der uns steht zur Seiten,
hilft mir täglich sieghaft streiten.

Unto thee, Lord, do I lift up my soul.
O my God, I trust in thee;
let me not be ashamed;
let not mine enemies triumph over
    me.

And so my soul may rest content
tho earthly cares beset me,
what-e'er the ills that threat me,
Death and Hell are impotent.
Despite the troubles which assail,
at last will righteousness prevail.

Lead me in thy truth, and teach me;
for thou art the God of my salvation;
on thee do I wait all the day.

Mighty cedars oft are battered.
Often times are bruised and shattered
by the tempest's stormy blast.
Give ye heed to God's direction,
count for naught all other counsel,
to His word, hold ever fast.

Mine eyes are ever toward the Lord;
for he shall pluck my feet
out of the net.

Days that there are filled with sadness,
God at last will turn to gladness:
By the thorny path He takes us,
to the joy in Heav'n that waits us;
ever firm with God I stand,
fearing never, fearing naught from
    mortal man.

We who have the Lord beside us,
steadfast face what-e'er betide us.

Psalm 25:1, 2, 5, 15

50. Bach, *O Haupt voll Blut und Wunden* from *St. Matthew Passion* (1729)

O Haupt voll Blut und Wunden,
voll Schmerz und voller Hohn,
o Haupt, zu Spott gebunden
mit einer Dornenkron,
o Haupt, sonst schön gezieret
mit höchster Ehr und Zier,
jetzt aber hoch schimpfieret,
gegrüsset seist du mir!

Du edles Angesichte,
dafür sonst schrickt und scheut
das grosse Weltgewichte,
wie bist du so bespeit,
wie bist du so erbleichet!
Wer hat dein Augenlicht,
dem sonst kein Licht nicht gleichet,
so schändlich zugericht'?

Oh Head, all scarr'd and bleeding,
and heap'd with cruel scorn!
Oh Head, so fill'd with sorrow,
and bound with crown of thorn!
Oh Head, that was so honor'd,
so lovely fair to see,
and now so low degraded;
my heart goes out to Thee!

Thou countenance so noble
yet now so pale and wan
which all the world should honor,
yet foully spat upon;
O Lord, we will not jeer Thee,
as they who mocked Thee there,
but comfort, love and cheer Thee,
in anguish and despair.

51. Georg Philipp Telemann,
Laudate Jehovam, omnes gentes (1758)

Telemann, *Laudate Jehovam, omnes gentes*

Al - le - lu - ia, al - le -

Al - le - lu - ia, al - le - lu -

Telemann, *Laudate Jehovam, omnes gentes*

Laudate Jehovam, omnes gentes!
Laudibus efferte, omnes populi!
Quia valida facta est super nos
    misericordia ejus,
et veritas Domini in aeternum.
    Alleluia.

O praise ye the Lord God, all ye
    nations!
O praise Him, all ye people!
For his compassion is great to us,
And the truth of the Lord endures
    forever. Alleluia.

Psalm 117

52. William Billings, *I Am Come into My Garden* (1794)

call'd him, I call'd him, I call'd him, I call'd him, but he gave me no an - swer.

[Soprano Solo]

Stay me with fla - gons, com - fort me with ap - ples, for

I am sick of love.

Vigoroso [Tutti]

Make haste, my be - lov - ed, make haste, my be - lov - ed, and be like a

Vigoroso

Song of Solomon 5:1–2, 6; 2:5, 17

53. Josiah Flagg,
Hallelujah (1764)

54. Jeremiah Ingalls, *Northfield* (c. 1800)

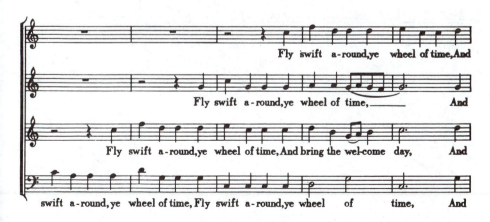

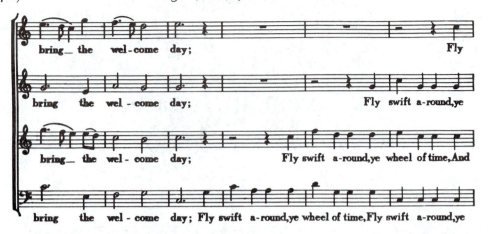

Text by Isaac Watts

55. John Antes, *Christ the Lord, the Lord Most Glorious* (c. 1800)

1. Christ the__ Lord, the Lord most glo - rious, Now is__ born, O__ shout a - loud; Man by__ Him is made vic - to - rious; Praise your Sav - iour, hail your God!
2. Praise the__ Lord, for on us shin - eth Christ the__ Sun__ of__ right - eous - ness; He to__ us in love in - clin - eth, Cheers our souls with pard' - ning grace.

Text by John Miller

56. Wolfgang Amadeus Mozart, *Dixit* from *Vesperae solennes de confessore*, K. 339 (1780)

Dixit Dominus Domino meo: sede a
   dextris meis, donec ponam
   inimicos tuos scabellum pedum
   tuorum.
Virgam virtutis tuae emittet Dominus
   ex Sion, dominare in medio
   inimicorum tuorum.
Tecum principium in die virtutis tuae
   in splendoribus sanctorum, ex
   utero ante luciferum genuite.

Juravit Dominus et non poenitebit
   eum: tu es sacerdos in aeternum
   secundum ordinem Melchisedech.
Dominus a dextris tuis confregit in
   die irae suae reges.

The Lord said unto my Lord, Sit
   thou at my right hand, until I
   make thine enemies thy footstool.

The Lord shall send the rod of thy
   strength out of Zion: rule thou
   in the midst of thine enemies.
Thy people shall be willing in the
   day of thy power, in the beauties
   of holiness from the womb of the
   morning: thou hast the dew of
   thy youth.
The Lord hath sworn, and will not
   repent, Thou art a priest forever
   after the order of Melchizedek.
The Lord at thy right hand shall strike
   through kings in the day of his
   wrath.

Judicabit in nationibus, implebit ruinas, conquassabit capita in terra multorum.

De torrente in via bibet, propterea exaltabit caput.

Gloria patri et filio et spiritui sancto, sicut erat in principio et nunc et semper et in saecula saeculorum. Amen.

He shall judge among the heathen, he shall fill the places with the dead bodies; he shall wound the heads over many countries.

He shall drink of the brook in the way: therefore shall he lift up the head.

Glory be to the Father and to the Son and to the Holy Ghost, as it was in the beginning, is now and ever shall be, world without end. Amen.

Psalm 110

57. Mozart, *Ave verum Corpus,* K. 618 (1791)

See page 132 for text.

58. Mozart, Introit and Kyrie from *Requiem*, K. 626 (1791)

Requiem aeternam dona eis, Domine:	Eternal rest give unto them, O Lord:
et lux perpetua luceat eis.	and let perpetual light shine upon them.
Te decet hymnus Deus in Sion,	A hymn, O God, becometh Thee in Sion;
et tibi reddetur votum in Jerusalem:	and a vow shall be paid to Thee in Jerusalem.
exaudi orationem meam:	O hear my prayer:
ad te omnis caro veniet.	all flesh shall come to Thee.
Kyrie eleison.	Lord, have mercy upon us.
Christe eleison.	Christ, have mercy upon us.
Kyrie eleison.	Lord, have mercy upon us.

59. Franz Joseph Haydn, Gloria from *Missa brevis St. Joannis de Deo* (*Kleine Orgelmesse*) (1775)

See page 28 for text.

60. Haydn, Agnus Dei from
Mass in C (Paukenmesse) (1796)

See page 74 for text.

61. Haydn, *Vollendet ist das grosse Werk* from *Die Schöpfung* (1798)

Haydn "Achieved is the glorious work #2" from The Creation (995). Reprint permission granted by the publisher.

Vollendet ist das grosse Werk,
des Herren Lob sei unser Lied!
Alles lobe seinen Namen,
denn er allein ist hoch erhaben.
Alleluja!

The mighty work is done at last,
to sing the praise of our Lord.
High exalted, great and glorious,
for God alone will be victorious.
Alleluia!

62. Ludwig van Beethoven, Gloria from *Mass in C,* Op. 86 (1807)

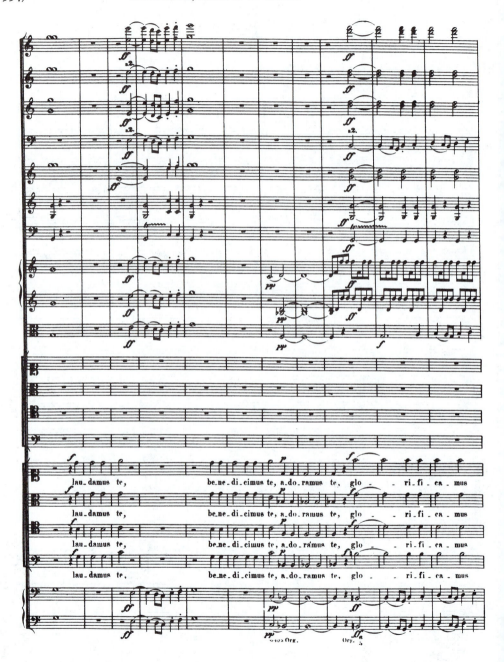

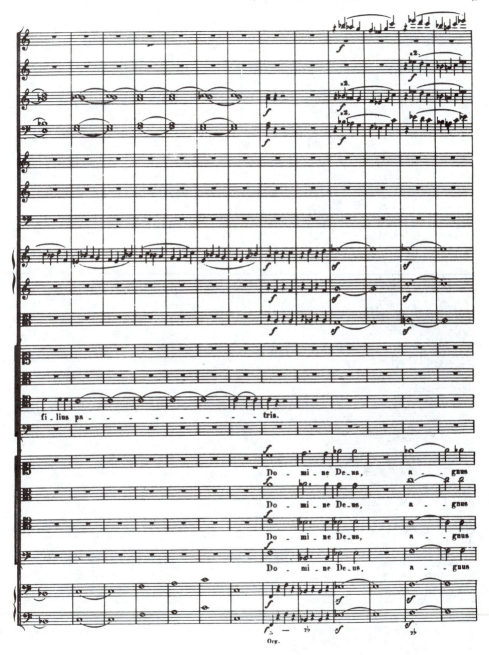

Org. all' ottava.

See page 28 for text.

63. Franz Schubert,
Der Tanz (1825)

Es redet und träumet die Jugend so
    viel,
Von Tanzen, Galloppen, Gelagen,
Auf einmal erreicht sie ein trügliches
    Ziel,
Da hört man sie seufzen und klagen.

Bald schmerzet der Hals,
und bald schmerzet die Brust,
Verschwunden ist alle die
    himmlische Lust.
"Nur diesmal noch kehr' mir
    Gesundheit zurück!"
So flehet vom Himmel der hoffende
    Blick!

K. A. F. Schnitzer

Youth talk and dream so much

Of dancing, carousing, and feasting,
Suddenly they seem to reach an end,
Then one hears them sighing and
    complaining.

At one moment the throat aches,
then it's the chest,
Gone is all the heavenly desire for
    pleasure.
"If only this once good health would
    come back,"
They beseech heaven with a hopeful
    look.

Translated by Marianne Torza

64. Schubert, *Des Tages Weihe*
(1822)

Schicksalslenker, blicke nieder,
Aug ein dankerfülltes Herz,
Uns belebt die Freude wieder,
Fern entfloh'n ist jeder Schmerz.

Und das Leid, es ist vergessen,
Durch die Nebel strahlt der Glanz
Deiner Grösse unermessen,
Wie aus hellem Sternenkranz.

Liebevoll, nahmst du der Leiden

Herben Kelch von Vaters Mund,
Darum ward in Fern und Weiten
Deine höchste Milde kund.

Fortune's pilot, look down
On a thankfilled heart;
We are revived by joy again,
Far fled is every pain.

And suffering, it is forgotten;
Through mists shine the light
Of Your greatness beyond measure
As from a bright wreath of stars.

Lovingly, You took away the bitter
cup
Of suffering from a father's mouth;
Therefore, both far and wide,
Your great mercy has become known.

Translated by Marianne Torza

65. Anton Bruckner,
Christus factus est (c. 1886)

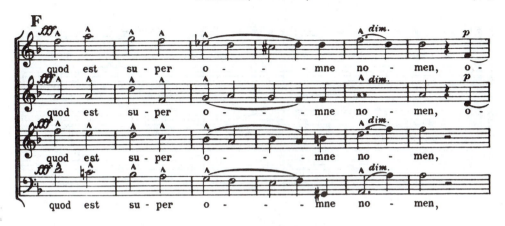

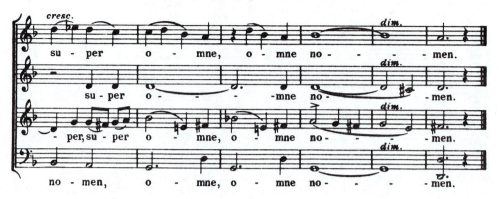

Christus factus est pro nobis obediens usque ad mortem, mortem autem crucis. Propter quod et Deus exaltavit illum, et dedit illi nomen, quod est super omne nomen.

Christ became obedient for us unto death, even the death of the cross. Wherefore God also hath exalted Him, and hath given Him a name which is above every name.

Philippians 2:8–9

66. Hector Berlioz,
Le Ballet des ombres (1829)

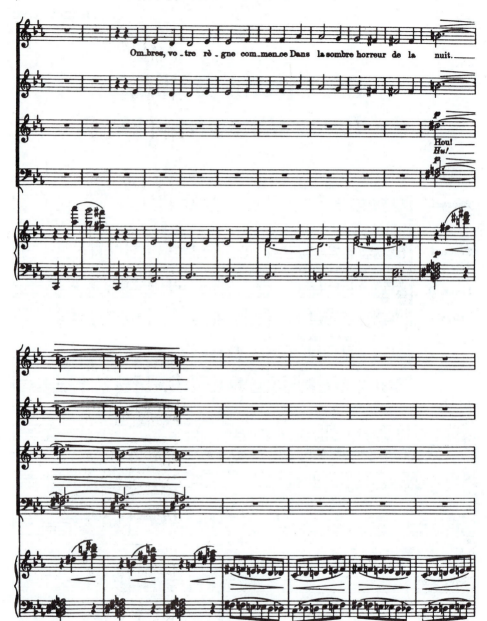

Om_bres, vo _ tre rè _ gne com_men_ce Dans la sombre horreur de la nuit.

Hou!
Hu!

Lors ___ que le souf _ fle des

Lors ___ que le souf _ fle des

(p)

o ___ ra ___ ges A ___ gi ___ te les

o ___ ra ___ ges A ___ gi ___ te les

Pour les rangs point de ja _ lou _ si _ e, Om _ bres de ber _ gers et de

rois! Ou _ bli _ ez

sotto voce
Hou!

sotto voce

vé _ _ _ _ cut. Tous ont pris des rou _ tes di _ ver _ ses Pour ve _ _ nir

Tous ont pris des rou _ tes di _ ver _ ses Pour ve _ _ nir

vé _ _ _ cut. Tous ont pris des rou _ tes di _ ver _ ses Pour ve _ _ nir

tous au mê _ me but. _____ Om _ bres, ou _

tous au mê _ me but.

tous au mê _ me but.

Formez vos rangs, entrez en danse!
L'ombre descend, le jour s'enfuit.
Ombres, votre règne commence
Dans la sombre horreur de la nuit.
Lorsque le souffle des orages
Agite les vertes forêts,
Il vient aussi dans nos bocages

Faire frémir les noirs cyprès.

Formez vos rangs, entrez en danse,
Ombres, prenez-vous par la main,
Troublez cet auguste silence
Qui règne sur le genre humain! Ah!

Pour les rangs point de jalousie,
Ombres de bergers et de rois!
Oubliez que l'orgueil, l'envie

Vous divisèrent autrefois!
L'un n'éprouva que des traverses;

Dans le bonheur l'autre vécut.
Tous ont pris des routes diverses
Pour venir tous au même but.
Ombres, oubliez de la terre
Et les plaisirs et les travaux!
Formez une danse légère
Qui courbe à peine les pavots! Ah!
Formez vos rangs, entrez en danse!
Mais la lune se lève et luit. Hu!

Gagnons l'Elysée en silence,
Et rendons le calm à la nuit!
Mortels, lorsque dans les nuits
   sombres
Notre voix vous réveillera,
Songez bien qu'à la voix des ombres,
Un jour, la vôtre s'unira!
Pourquoi nous craindre, enfants des
   hommes?
Ce que vous êtes nous l'étions,
Et vous serez ce que nous sommes.
Au revoir! nous nous reverrons! Ah!
Oui, vous serez ce que nous sommes.
Au revoir! nous nous reverrons!
               Albert Duboys

Begin the dance, for day is dying,
And slowly wanes the sunset light.
Begin the dance, ye phantoms flying,
Beneath the mantle of the night.
When loud the stormy wind is roaring
Amid the gloomy forest trees,
Around the grave, our home, 'tis
   moaning
Where bends the cypress in the
   breeze.
Begin the dance, ye phantoms, slowly,
Each take the other by the hand
And break the silence of the midnight
That covers all the dreaming land!
   Ah!
Let none dispute for rank or honour,
For clown is equal now with king!
The pride of place, that once we
   sought for,
Is now for us a futile thing!
While one on earth knows nought
   but sorrow,
Another's life in joy is pass'd.
And yet, by various paths conducted,
They reach the self-same goal at last.
Ye ghosts, forget the grief or gladness
Yet knew when in this earthly vale;
Now dance a dance so light, so airy,
It hardly stirs the poppies pale! Ah!
Begin the dance, ye phantoms flying,
While now the moon is shining
   bright; Hu!
Then back to vast Elysium hasten
And calm restore unto the night.
O Men our voices may arouse ye,

Oh! mortals, in the midnight drear!
Remember that one day your voices
Shall blend with these now you hear!
Why fear ye us, benighted mortals?

What ye, that we, too, have been;
And ye shall be, as we are, phantoms.
And join us in the world unseen! Ah!
And ye shall be as we are, phantoms,
We shall meet one day i'th' Unseen!

67. Gabriel Fauré,
Cantique de Jean Racine (1873)

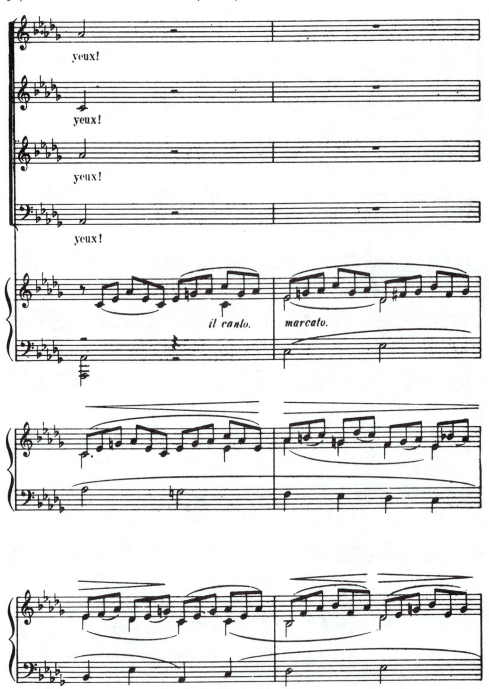

Verbe égal au Très-Haut
Notre unique espérance,
Jour éternel de la terre et des cieux,
Nous rompons le silence.
Divin Sauveur jette sur nous les
    yeux!

Répands sur nous le feu de ta
grâce puissante,
que tout l'enfer fuie au son de ta voix,
Dissipe le sommeil d'une âme
languissante,
qui la conduit à l'oubli de tes lois!

Ô Christ sois favorable à ce
peuple fidèle pour te bénir
maintenant rassemblé,
Reçois les chants qu'il offre
à ta gloire immortelle et de
tes dons qu'il retourne comblé!

O Redeemer divine,
our sole hope of salvation,
Eternal Light of the earth and the sky,
We kneel in adoration.
O Savior, turn on us Thy loving eye!

Send down on us the fire of
Thy grace all-consuming,
whose wondrous might dispersed the
powers of hell, And rouse our
slumb'ring souls with Thy radiance,
that they may waken Thy mercy to
    tell!

O Christ, bestow Thy blessing on us,
we implore Thee, who here are
gathered on penitent knee,
Accept the hymns we chant to Thine
everlasting glory and these Thy gifts
we return unto Thee!
        Translation by Harold Heiberg

68. Felix Mendelssohn,
Heilig (1844)

Heilig, heilig, heilig
ist Gott der Herr Zabaoth!
Alle Lande sind seiner Ehre voll.

Hosianna in der Höh'!
Gelobt sei der da kommt im Namen
des Herrn!

Holy, holy, holy
Lord God of hosts!
All the nations are filled with thy
renown.

Hoseanna on High.
Praise be he who comes in name of
the Lord!

69. Mendelssohn, *He That Shall Endure to the End* from *Elijah* (1846)

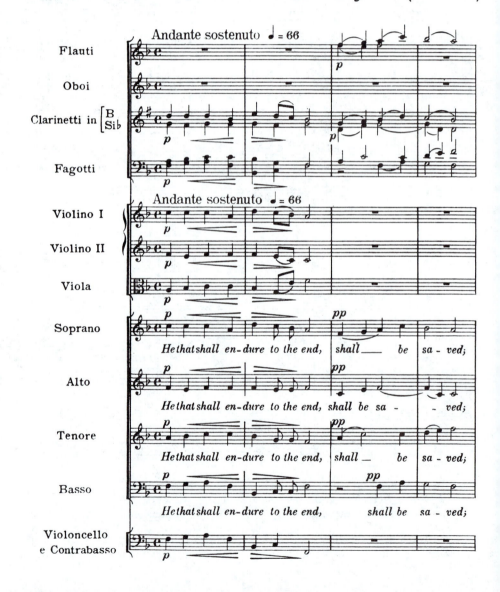

He that shall endure to the end shall be saved.
Matthew 24:13

70. Johannes Brahms, *Schaffe in mir, Gott, ein reines Herz, Op. 29, No. 2 (1860)*

Schaffe in mir, Gott, ein reines Herz
  und gib mir einen neuen
  gewissen Geist.
Verwirf mich nicht von deinem
  Angesicht und nimm deinen
  heiligen Geist nicht von mir.
Tröste mich wieder mit deiner Hilfe
  und der freudige Geist erhalte
  mich.

Create in me a pure heart, O God,
  And give me a new and steadfast
  spirit.
Do not drive me from thy presence
  or take thy holy spirit from me;
Restore in me the joy of thy salvation
  and give me a willing spirit to
  uphold me.

Psalm 51:10–12

71. Johannes Brahms, *Im Herbst,* Op. 104, No. 5 (1888)

Schluss. Feucht wird das Aug, doch in der Trä - ne

Schluss. Feucht wird das Aug, doch in der Trä - ne

Schluss. Feucht wird das Aug, doch in der Trä - ne

Schluss. Feucht wird das Aug, doch in der Trä - ne

Blin - ken, doch in der Trä - ne Blin - ken ent -

Blin - ken, doch in der Trä - ne Blin - ken ent -

Blin - ken, doch in der Trä - ne Blin - ken ent -

Blin - ken, doch in der Trä - ne Blin - ken ent -

strömt des Her - zens se - lig - ster Er -

strömt, ent - strömt des Her - zens se - lig - ster Er -

strömt, ent - strömt des Her - zens se - lig - ster Er -

strömt, ent - strömt des Her - zens se - lig - ster Er -

Ernst ist der Herbst.
Und wenn die Blätter fallen,
sinkt auch das Herz zu trübem Weh
    herein.
Still ist die Flur,
und nach dem Süden wallen die
    Sänger stumm,
wie nach dem Grab.

Bleich ist der Tag,
und blasse Nebel schleiern die Sonne
    wie die Herzen ein.
Früh kommt die Nacht:
denn all Kräfte feiern,
und tief verschlossen ruht das Sein.

Sanft wird der Mensch.
Er sieht die Sonne sinken,
er ahnt des Lebens wie des Jahres
    Schluss.
Feucht wird das Aug',
doch in der Träne Blinken entströmt
des Herzens seligster Erguss.

Autumn is sad.
And when the leaves are falling,
sinks too the heart in troubled grief
    to lave.
Still is the field,
and flown to southwinds calling, are
    songsters still,
as to the grave.

Dreary is the day,
and pallid clouds are veiling the
    sunlight as the spirit free.
Soon comes the night:
then rest all powers empaling;
oblivion falls on all that be.

Tender grows man.
He sees the sun declining,
divines, that life too, as the year,
    must close.
Moist are the eyes,
but thro' the teardrops shining,
outflows the heart and holiest solace
    knows.

Klaus Groth

72. Robert Schumann, *Zigeunerleben,* Op. 29, No. 3 (1840)

Schumann, "Zigeunerleben", op. 29, no. 3, (P 4694). Reprinted by permission of the publisher.

Im Shatten des Waldes, im
    Buchengezweig,
da regt's sich und raschelt und
    flüstert zugleich.
Es flackern die Flammen, es gaukelt
    der Schein
um bunte Gestalten, um Laub und
    Gestein.
Das ist der Zigeuner bewegliche
    Schaar
mit blitzendem Aug' und mit
    wallendem Haar,
gesäugt an des Niles geheiligter
    Fluth,
gebräunt von Hispaniens südlicher
    Gluth.

Um's lodernde Feuer in
    schwellendem Grün,
da lagern die Männer verwildert und
    kühn
da Kauern die Weiber und rüsten
    das Mahl,
und füllen geschäftig den alten Pokal.

Und Sagen und Lieder ertönen im
    Rund,
wie Spaniens Gärten so blühend und
    bunt,
und magische Sprüche für Noth und
    Gefahr
verkündet die Alte der horchenden
    Schaar.

Schwarzäugige Mädchen beginnen
    den Tanz.
Da sprühen die Fackeln in röthlichen
    Glanz.
Es lockt die Guitarre, die Cymbel
    klingt.
Wie wild und wilder der Reigen
    sich schlingt.
Dann ruh'n sie ermüdet vom
    nachlichen Reih'n.
Es rauschen die Buchen im
    Schlummer sei ein.

A woods filled with shadows of beach
    trees and pine,
with whispering branches and leaves
    on the vine.
Where magical flames always flicker
    and shine,
while dancing with rainbows of every
    design.
Here gather the gypsies who roam
    everywhere,
the dashing young gypsies with long
    silky hair,
whose bodies are warmed by the
    Nile's blessed flow,
and tanned by the brilliance of
    Spain's sunny glow.

The warm blazing campfire is lighting
    the trees;
the men strong and handsome are
    taking their ease;
the women assemble preparing the
    food,
and all fill their goblets to brighten
    the mood.
Now stories and songs from an
    unending chain,
as bright as the colorful gardens of
    Spain;
the queen of the gypsies now
    chants loud and clear,
her magical words fight off danger
    and fear.

Now dark-eyed young ladies begin
    with their dance
while flaming red torches bring
    sparkling romance;
with pulsating cymbal and luring
    guitars
the dance grows wilder beneath
    gypsy stars.
The dancers are weary, the campfire
    dies;
they sleep while the beachtrees hum
    sweet lullabies.

Und die aus der glücklichen
　　Heimath verbannt,
sie schauen in Traume das glückliche
　　Land.

Doch wie nun im Osten der Morgen
　　erwacht,
verläsehen die schönen Gebilde der
　　Nacht;
es scharret das Maulties bei
　　Tabesbeginn,
fort zieh'n die Gestallen, wer sagt
　　dir wohin?

　　　　　　　Emanuel Geibel

To visit his homeland a gypsy may
　　yearn,
and now in his dreams he can swiftly
　　return.

But now as in the east the morn draws
　　near,
night's lovely images disappear;

the mules paw the earth as day
　　comes hither,
the folk set out—who can tell you
　　whither?

73. Edward Elgar, *Go, Song of Mine*, Op. 57 (1909)

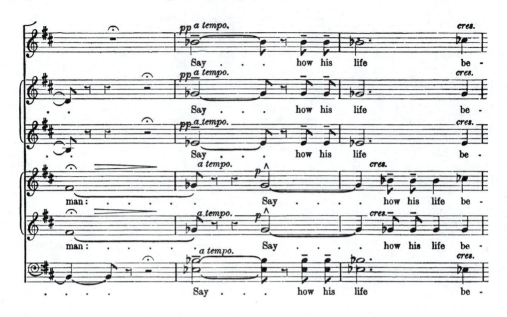

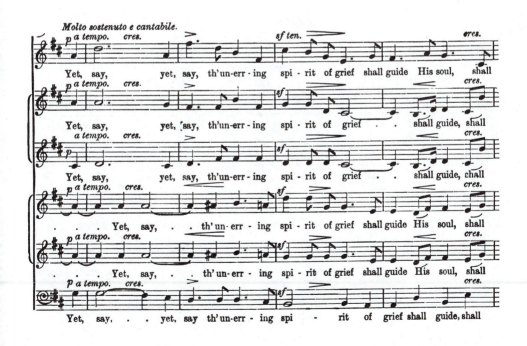

Text by Guido Calvacanti
Translation by D. G. Rossetti

74. Samuel Sebastian Wesley, *Wash Me Throughly from My Wickedness* (after 1855)

Psalm 51:2–3

75. Gioacchino Rossini, Kyrie
from *Petite Messe solennelle* (1864)

See page 15 for text.

76. Giuseppe Verdi, *Ave Maria* from *Quattro pezzi sacri* (1898)

Ave Maria, gratia plena, Dominus
   tecum,
benedicta tu in mulieribus,
et benedictus fructus ventris tui,
   Jesus.
Sancta Maria, Mater Dei,
ora pro nobis peccatoribus nunc
et in hora mortis nostrae. Amen.

Hail, Mary, full of grace, the Lord is
   with you;
Blessed are you among women,
And blessed is the fruit of your
   womb, Jesus.
Holy Mary, Mother of God,
Pray for us sinners now and in the
   hour of our death. Amen.

77. Pavel Chesnokov, *Praise the Name of the Lord,* Op. 11, No. 5 (c. 1900)

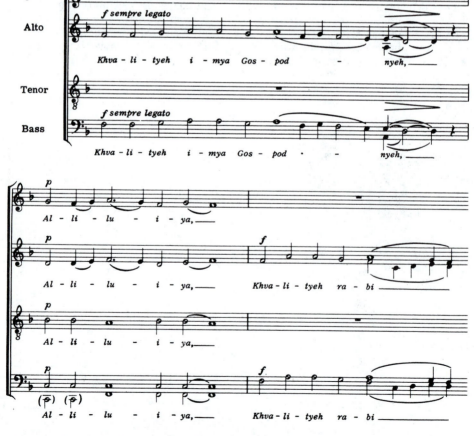

Khvalityeh imya Gospodnye, Alliluiya.

Khvalitye rabi Gospoda, Alliluiya.

Blagoslovyehn Gospod' ot Siona, zhivyi vo Iyehrusalimyeh, Alliluiya.

Ispovyehdaityehsya Gospodyehvi, yako blag, Alliluiya.
Yako v'vyehk milost' Yehvo, Alliluiya.
Ispovyehdaityehsya Bogu Nyehbyehsnomu, Alliluiya.
Yako v'vyehk milost' Yehvo, Alliluiya.

Praise ye the name of the Lord God, Alleluia.

Praise ye Him, ye servants of God, Alleluia.

Blessed be the Lord God who came from Zion, alive and dwelling in Jerusalem, Alleluia.

O sing praises, confess the Name of the Lord, give thanks, Alleluia.
His mercy is forever, Alleluia.
O sing praises, and give thanks to the Lord of Heaven, Alleluia.
His mercy is forever, Alleluia.

Translated by Charles C. Hirt

78. Dimitri Bortnianski,
Cherubic Hymn

Bortnianski, *Cherubic Hymn*

Let us who mystically represent the Cherubim, and who sing the thrice-holy hymn to the life-creating Trinity, now lay aside all earthly cares, Amen. That we may receive the King of All, Who comes invisibly upborne by the angelic hosts, Alleluia.

Translated by Ray Robinson

79. Stephen Foster, *Come Where My Love Lies Dreaming* (publ. 1855)

Text by Stephen Foster

80. Edward MacDowell,
The Brook, Op. 43, No.1 (1891)

Text by Edward MacDowell

81. Arnold Schoenberg,
De profundis, Op. 50b (1950)

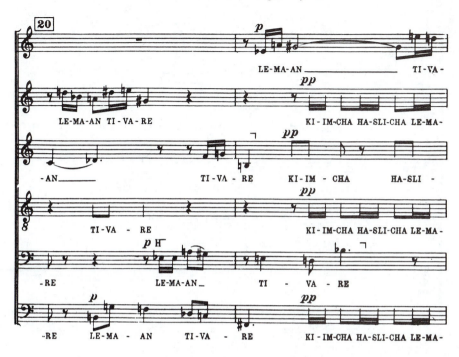

Shir hamaalot
Mima'amakim
keraticha Adonai.
Adonai shimah vekoli
tiyena oznecha kashuvot
Lekol tachanunai.
Im avonot tishmor ya Adonai

Mi yaamod.
Ki imcha haslicha
Lemaan tivare.
Kiviti Adonai
Kivta nafshi
Velidvaro hochalti.
Nafshi l'Adonai mishomrim
Laboker shomrim laboker.
Yachel Yisrael
El Adonai ki im Adonai
Hachesed veharbeh imo fedut

Vehu yifdeh et Yisrael
Mikol avonotav.

From out of the depths
to Thee I cry
with lamenting, O my God.
O my God, give ear to my voice,
and be Thou attentive to my voice
in supplication raised.
If Thou, O Lord, shouldst mark
     iniquities
Lord, who shall stand?
But with Thee there is grace,
Thou art God whom we fear.
My soul waits for the Lord,
I wait for Him,
and in His word is my hope.
I wait for the Lord from the dawn
of one day unto the other.
Let Israel hope
in God, the Lord: for plenteous is
His redemption and with Him is
     mercy found.
He shall redeem His Israel
from all iniquities.

Psalm 130

82. Anton Webern, First Movement from *Cantata No. 1,* Op. 29 (1940)

Zündender Lichtblitz des Lebens
schlug ein aus der Wolke des Wortes.
Donner der Herzschlag folgt nach, bis
er in Frieden verebbt.

Hildegard Jone

Lightning, the kindler of Being struck,
flashed from the word in the storm
cloud. The thunder, the heartbeat follows at last dissolving in peace.

Translated by Eric Smith

83. Max Reger, *O Tod, wie bitter bist du,* Op. 110, No. 3 (1909)

O Tod, wie bitter bist du,
wenn an dich gedenket ein Mensch,
der gute Tage und genug hat,
und ohne Sorgen lebet;
und dem es wohl geht in allen
Dingen und wohl noch essen mag!

O Tod, wie wohl tust du
dem Dürftigen,
der da schwach und alt ist,
der in allen Sorgen steckt
und nichts Bessers zu hoffen
noch zu erwarten hat.

O death, how bitter it is
to remember you for a man
at peace among his goods,
who prospers in everything
and still has the strength
to feed himself.

O death, your sentence is welcome
to a man in want,
whose strength is failing,
to a man worn out with age,
worried about everything,
disaffected and beyond endurance.

84. Paul Hindemith, *En Hiver* from *Six Chansons* (1939)

En hiver, la mort meurtrière
entre dans les maisons;
elle cherche la soeur, le père,
et leur joue du violon.
Mais quand la terre remue,
sous la bêche du printemps,

la mort court dans les rues
et salue les passants.

Rainer Maria Rilke

With the winter, Death, grisly guest
Through the doorway steals in
Both the young and old to guest,
And he plays them his violin.
But when the Spring's spades are
Beating frozen earth beneath blue
    sky,
Then Death his way goes fleeting,
Lightly greeting passersby.

Translated by Elaine de Sincay

85. Hugo Distler, *Es ist ein Ros entsprungen* from *Weihnachtsgeschichte*, Op. 10 (1933)

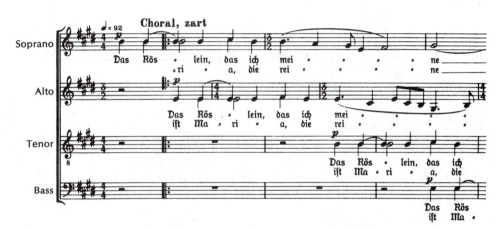

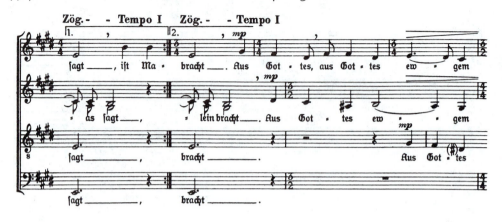

Es ist ein Ros entsprungen
auf einer Wurzel zart,
als uns die Alten sungen:
von Jesse kam die Art
und hat ein Blümlein bracht
mitten im kalten Winter
wohl zu der halben Nacht.
Das Röslein, das ich meine,
davon Jesaias sagt,
ist Maria, die reine
die uns das Blümlein bracht.
Aus Gottes, ewgem Rat
hat sie ein kind geboren
und blieb ein reine Magd.

Lo, how a Rose e'er blooming
from tender stem hath sprung,
of Jesse's lineage coming
as men of old have sung.
It came, a flow'ret bright,
amid the cold of winter,
when half-spent was the night.
Isaiah 'twas foretold it,
the rose I have in mind.
With Mary we behold it,
the Virgin Mother kind.
To show God's love aright,
she bore to men a Saviour,
when half-spent was the night.

86. Arthur Honegger,
Je t'aimerai, Seigneur from
Le Roi David (1921)

Je t'aimerai, Seigneur, d'un amour
    tendre,
Toi dont le bras me sut si bein
    défendre.
Dieu fut toujours mon fort, mon
    protecteur,
ma tour, ma roche et mon libérateur.
Je trouve en lui tout ce que je
    souhaite.
C'est mon bouclier, mon salut, ma
    retraite.
Dès qu'au besoin je l'invoque avec
    foi,
des ennemis délivré je me vois.
Tels qu'un torrent ils pensaient me
    surprendre,
cent fois la mort ses filets me vint
    tendre
et tous les jours quelque péril nouveau
me conduisait sur le bord du
    tombeau.

Thee will I love, O Lord, who art my
    fortress.
Thou art my shield, the horn of my
    salvation.
God is my refuge safe, my protector,
My rock, my strength, my tower and
    deliverer.
In him I find the solace that I long
    for.
He guideth my steps that I may walk
    in comfort.
I call on him and invoke his aid,
And I am saved from my strong
    enemy.
When waves of death encompassed
    me,
and snares of men made me afraid,
Then did he send, and take me from
    above,
And drew me forth out of many
    waters.

Psalm 18:1–4, 16

87. Darius Milhaud, *Babylone* from *Les Deux Cités* (1937)

Un 'grand ca - li - ce plein de vin,   de

vin,   et le feu n'en est pas é - va - po - ré.

Sor -

vin.   Elle est tom - bée.

Tutti

Elle est ton - bée.

tez du mi - lieu d'el - le, mon peu - ple.

Tous, Tous se te - nant à dis - tan - ce di - ront, fré - mis - sant

Elle est tombée Babylone la grande.	Fallen is she, proud Babylon the mighty!
Si Dieu n'édifie pas la maison,	Except the Lord our God build the house,
Si Dieu ne garde pas la cité,	except the Lord the city doth guard,
C'est en vain que se sont travaillés,	the great city is builded in vain,
c'est en vain que travaillent et que se sont travaillés,	'tis in vain that men labor, vainly the watchman doth wake,
et que se travaillent à travailler	vainly do they toil to raise up the walls,
Ceux qui travaillent à le faire.	who build the ramparts of the city.

Elle est tombée Babylone la grande.

Moi, Jean j'entendis la voix d'un aigle
par le milieu de l'aire qui criait:
Ouaï! Ouaï! Voe! Voe! malheur!
    malheur!
Parce que Dieu tout à coup s'est
    repensé d'elle
et il va lui donner à boire
Un grand calice plein de vin.

Elle est tombée.
Tous, Tous se tennant à distance
    diront,
frémissant de terreur: Malheur! Voe!

Ouaï! Ouaï! Babylone la grande
il a péri, le port! Il a péri l'entrepôt;

elle a péri la fabrique,
elle a péri la boutique et personne,
il n'ya plus personne
pour lui acheter ce qu'elle vend.

Marchandises d'argent et d'or
et de pierres précieuses,
et de pourpre et de bois odoriférant

et d'ivoire et toutes sortes de métaux
et de fabrications et de cinnamonne

et de parfums et de gemmes et
    d'encens,
de vin et d'huile et de fleur de farine

et de bêtes de somme et de brebis
et d'âmes d'hommes.
Et toi ô ciel réjouis toi sur elle!

Martyrs poussez des cris de joie sur
    elle
parce que Dieu sur elle a revanché
    votre cause.
Babylone, Elle a péri,
Elle est tombée
Babylone la grande.
                              Paul Claudel

Fallen is she, proud Babylon the
    mighty!
I, John, I did hear an eagle calling
high in the midst of heaven, and he
    cried:
Oh! Oh! Woe! Woe! ah me! ah me!
Know ye that God, of her sins once
    more has grown mindful,
He shall hold to her lips a goblet,
a goblet filled unto the brim
    with wine.

Fallen is she!
All, all who stand without the city
    shall say,
all trembling in their fear: Ah me!
    Woe!

Oh! Oh! Proud Babylon the mighty!
The busy port is gone, now are the
    storehouses gone!
Now is the workshop in ruins,
now is the market in ruins,
the city is deserted;
none will come to buy what she would
    sell.

Merchandise of silver, of gold,
and of precious stones,
and of purple rich and fine, of sweet
    smelling sandalwood,
of ivory and all manner of rare metals
wrought in strange designs, yea, of
    cinnamon
and fragrant perfumes and gems and
    incense rare,
of wine and olives, of sacks of whitest
    wheat flour,
of ewe-lambs and beasts that carry
    the yoke,
and souls of mortals.
Heaven, rejoice that now she is in
    ruins!
Martyrs, lift up your cries of joy to
    heaven,
because the Lord hath now at last
    avenged you upon her!
Proud Babylon, proud Babylon is
    fallen!
Fallen is she, Babylon the mighty!
        Translated by Helen H. Torrey

88. Gustav Holst, *I Love My Love,* Op. 36, No. 5 (1916)

89. Ralph Vaughan Williams,
O vos omnes (1922)

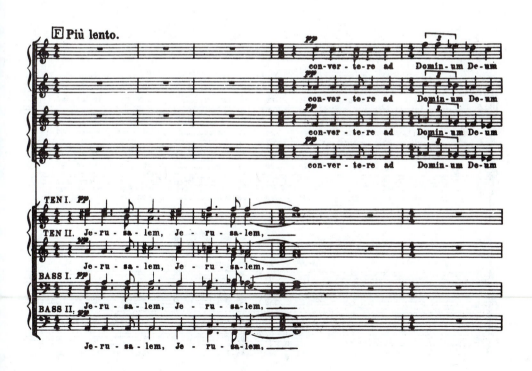

O vos omnes, qui transitis per viam,
  attendite,
et videte si est dolor sicut dolor meus:

quoniam vindemiavit me, ut locutus
est Dominus in die irae furoris sui.

De excelso misit ignem in ossibus
  meis,
et erudivit me: expandit rete
  pedibus meis,
convertit me retrorsum; posuit me
  desolatam,
tota die moerore confectam.

Vigilavit jugum iniquitatum mearum:

in manu ejus convolutae sunt et
  impositae collo meo:
infirmata est virtus mea: dedit me
  Dominus in manu, de qua non
  potero surgere.

Jerusalem, Jerusalem, convertere ad
  Dominum Deum tuum.

O all ye that pass by the way, attend,

and see if there be any sorrow like to
    my sorrow:
for he hath made a vintage of me
as the Lord spoke in the day of his
    fierce anger.

From above he hath sent fire into my
    bones,
and hath chastized me: he hath
    spread a net for my feet,
he hath turned me back: he hath
    made me desolate,
wasted with sorrow all the day long.

The yoke of my iniquities hath
    watched:
they are folded together in his hand,
    and put upon my neck:
my strength is weakened: the Lord
    hath delivered me into a hand
    out of which I am not able to
    rise.

Jerusalem, Jerusalem, return to the
    Lord, your God!
                    Lamentations of Jeremiah
                        1:12, 13, 14

90. Benjamin Britten,
Jubilate Deo (1961)

91. Peter Maxwell Davies, *Alleluia, pro Virgine Maria* from *O magnum mysterium* (1960)

BURDEN

Allegro moderato

f 1st time, *p* second, *f* third time, *pp* < *ff* last time with allarg. to finish

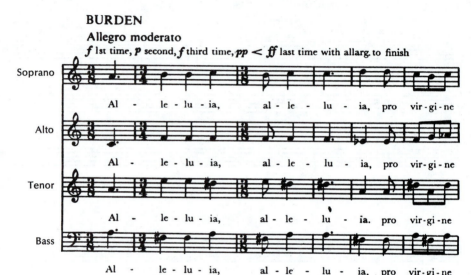

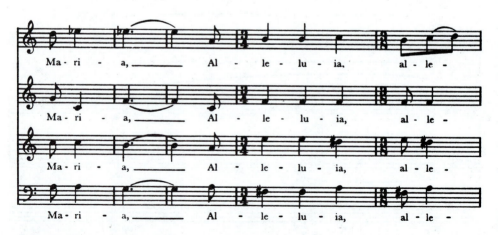

lu - ia, _____ pro vir - gi - ne Ma - ri - a. _____

lu - ia, pro vir - gi - ne Ma - ri - a. _____

lu - ia, _____ pro vir - gi - ne Ma - ri - a. _____

lu - ia, pro vir - gi - ne Ma - ri - a. _____

VERSE

Moderato

p Solo Treble

1. Di - va na - ta - li - ci - a Nos - tra pur-gat vi - ci -
2. Na - to sac - ri - fi - ci - a Re - ges dant tri - pli - ci -
3. Mor - tis vin - cla tru - ci - a Sol - vit di - e ter - ci -

1. Di - va na - ta - li - ci - a Nos - tra pur-gat vi - ci
2. Na - to sac - ri - fi - ci - a Re - ges dant tri - pli - ci
3. Mor - tis vin - cla tru - ci - a Sol - vit di - e ter - ci

1. Di - va na - ta - li - ci - a Nos - tra pur-gat vi - ci
2. Na - to sac - ri - fi - ci - a Re - ges dant tri - pli - ci
3. Mor - tis vin - cla tru - ci - a Sol - vit di - e ter - ci

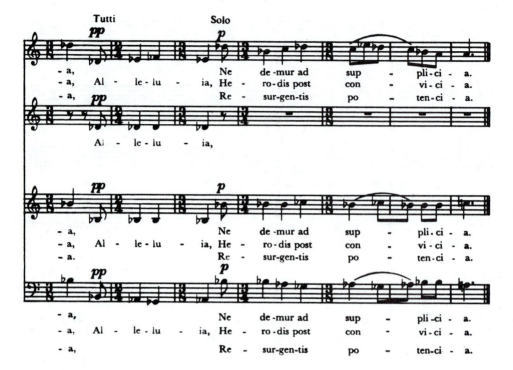

Alleluia, alleluia, pro Virgine Maria
Diva natalicia
Nostra purgat vicia,
Ne demur ad supplicia.

Nato sacrificia
Reges dant triplicia,
Herodis post convicia.

Mortis vincla trucia
Solvit die tercia,
Resurgentis potencia.

Alleluia, alleluia for the Virgin Mary.
The holy birth
purges our sins
Lest we be given to torment.

The kings give
triple offerings to the babe,
After the reproaches of Herod.

On the third day
the power of the risen Christ,
Loosed the grim bonds of death.

92. Michael Tippett,
Nunc dimittis (1961)

- ry of thy peo-ple Is – ra-el.

Lord, to be a light.

Lord, to be a light.

Lord, to be a light

Glor-y be to the Fa-ther, and to the Son,— and to the Ho – ly Ghost:

Glor-y be to the Fa-ther, and to the Son,— and to the Ho – ly Ghost:

Glor-y be to the Fa-ther, and to the Son,— and to the Ho – ly Ghost:

Luke 2:29–32

93. Thea Musgrave,
Rorate coeli (1974)

NOTES ON PERFORMANCE

Accidentals in *unmeasured* bars apply only to the note they precede, except where one note or a pair of notes is immediately repeated.

↓ downbeat to an unmeasured bar

↓ left-hand sign during an unmeasured bar

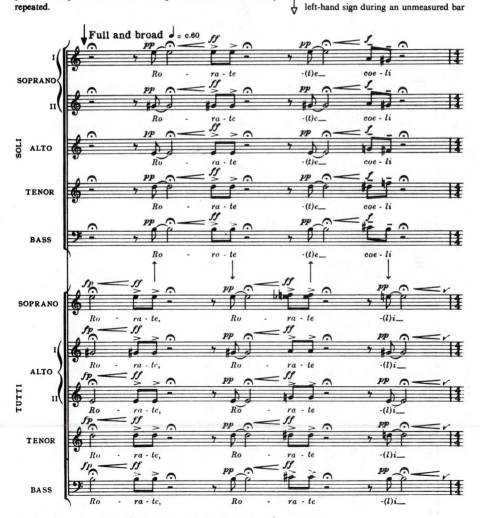

*Ad lib. *not* together. Sing *slowly*, like a tolling bell.

et simile (*not together*) *Repeat as necessary*

et simile (*not together*) *Repeat as necessary*

† Thrones, dominations, were the third and fourth of the nine orders of angels.

*sere = various, pronounce so as to rhyme with clear.

* Pronounce so as to rhyme with clear.

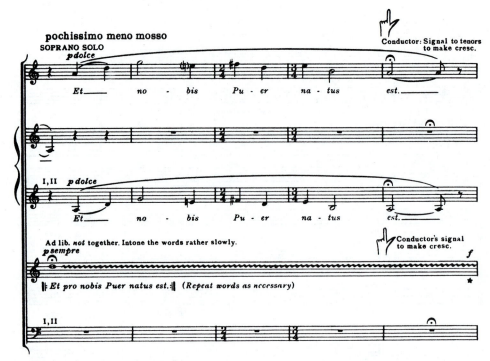

* Break off words immediately on down beat to next bar and continue.

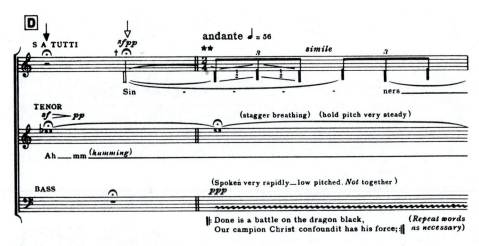

† Sing any pitch within the range indicated
(result should be a closely-spaced cluster)

** Move up and down a semitone from chosen pitch.

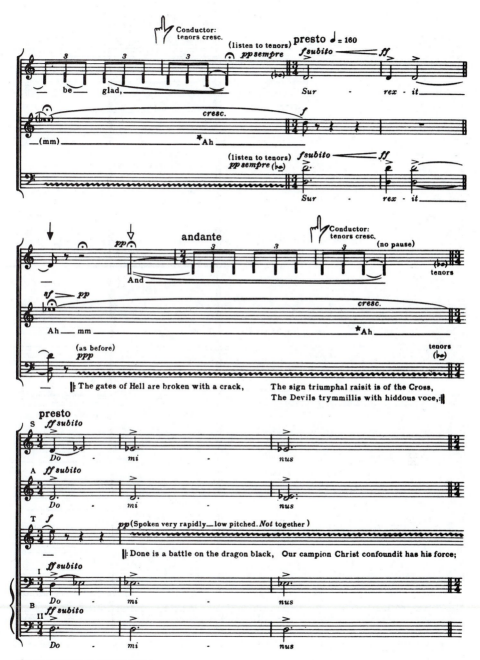

*Open mouth slowly to make cresc.

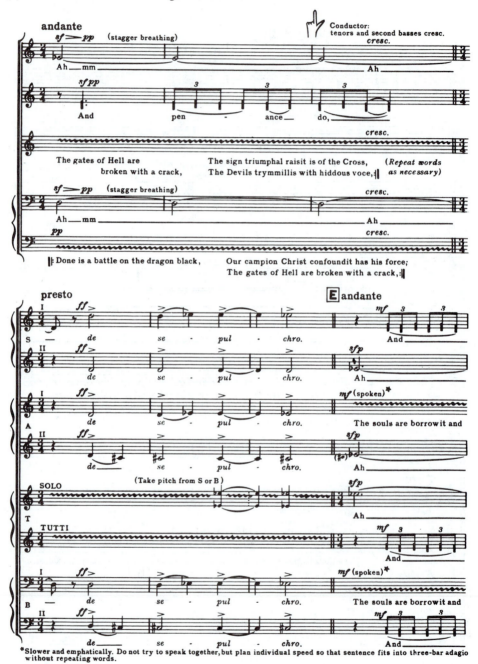

*Slower and emphatically. Do not try to speak together, but plan individual speed so that sentence fits into three-bar adagio without repeating words.

*Move chromatically upwards from chosen pitch.

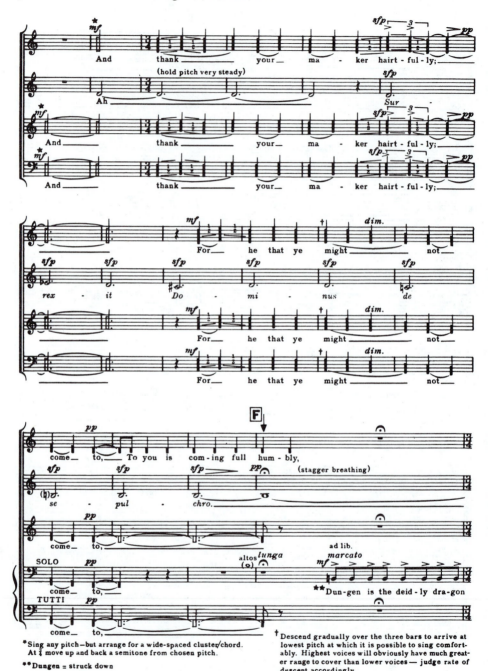

*Sing any pitch—but arrange for a wide-spaced cluster/chord.
At ⅜ move up and back a semitone from chosen pitch.

**Dungen = struck down

†Descend gradually over the three bars to arrive at
lowest pitch at which it is possible to sing comfortably. Highest voices will obviously have much greater range to cover than lower voices — judge rate of
descent accordingly.

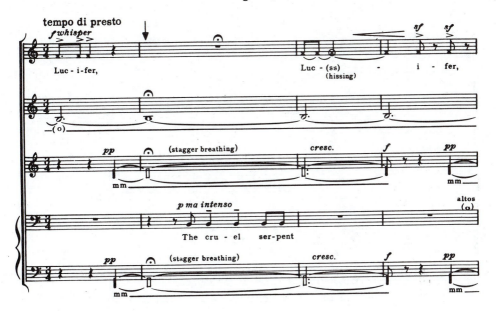

* Do *not* pronounce 'sti' of sting.

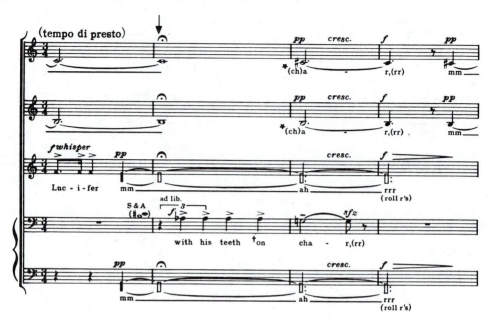

*Do **not** pronounce 'ch' of char.

† on char = ajar

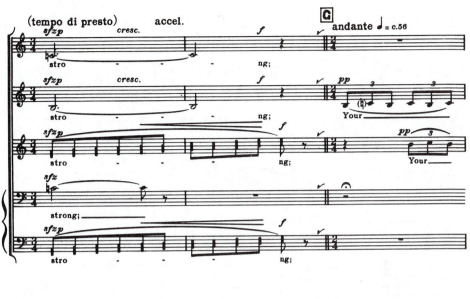

*Sing freely— a little slower than conductor's tempo.
 But do not begin before the given cue.

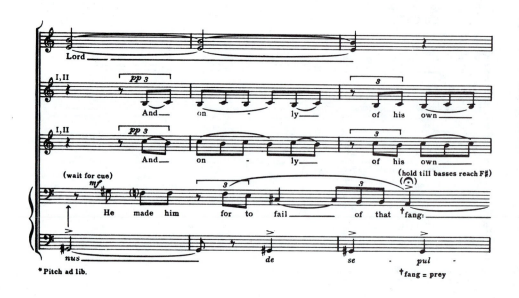

* Pitch ad lib.

† fang = prey

*Pitches ad lib. descend to lowest pitch possible to sing comfortably.

†(soft, but clear: as though coming from a distance)

cline,   And   bow   un - to____ this

cline,   And   bow   un - to____ this

et simile

____ Sol - vet____ sae - clum____ de fa - vil - la,____

TUTTI

p

He for our sake that

bairn   be - nign,____   And   do   your

bairn   be - nign,____   And   do   your

(wait for cue)

Tes - te____ Da - vid____ cum Si - bil - la,____

cresc.

suf - fered to be slain,   And like a   lamb   in   sac - ri - fice was

cresc. poco a poco

ob - ser - vance   di - vine   To

cresc. poco a poco

ob - ser - vance   di - vine   To

(SOLO)

mf

ri - sén up a - gain,   And as gi - ant

TUTTI   p   cresc.   mf

Is like a   li - on   ri - sen up a - gain,   And as gi - ant

*dight,   Is like a   li - on   ri - sen up a - gain,   And as gi - ant

*dight = prepared

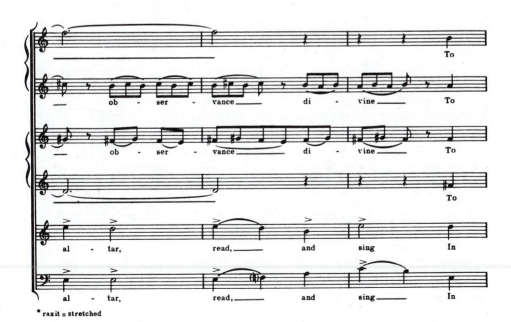

* raxit = stretched

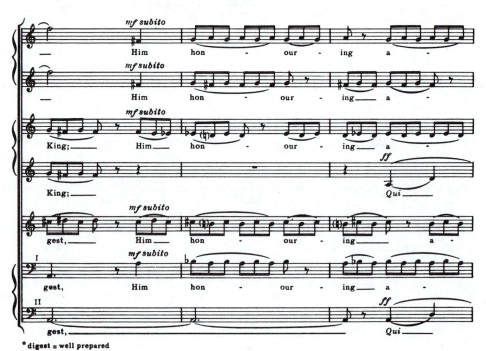

* digest = well prepared

*Pitches ad lib. wide-spaced chords, follow contours.

†Check A with tuning fork and repitch if necessary.

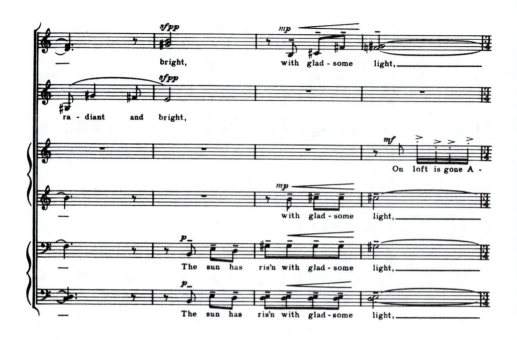

*ad lib. pitches within range indicated: change pitch on each syllable.

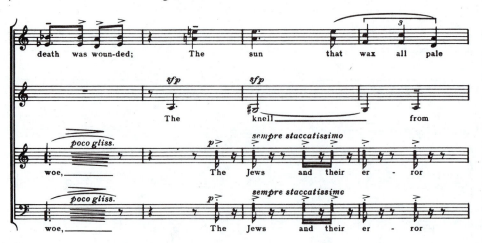

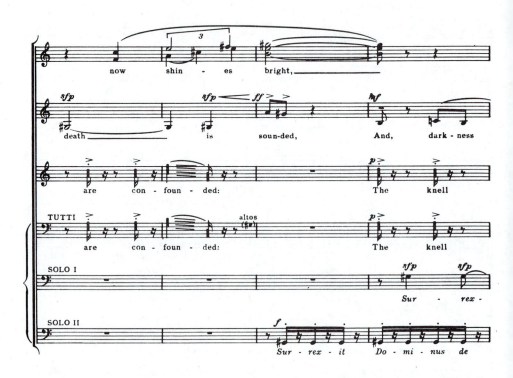

*ad lib. pitches within range indicated: change pitch on each syllable.

* = jailors fled and banished

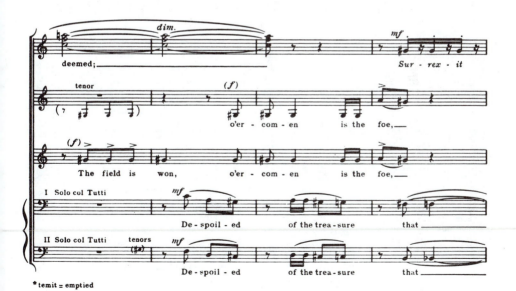

*temit = emptied

*yemit = kept

Text by William Dunbar

94. Béla Bartók, *Wedding Song from Poniky* from *Four Slovak Folk Songs* (1917)

hess, hess, te ri - gó - ma - dár Én ró - zsa - bok - rom -

hess, hess,... te ri - gó - ma - dár...... Én ró - zsa - bok - rom -

ról. .... Rossz férj - hez

ról. .... Rossz férj - hez

Lányát az anya férjhez úgy adta

Idegen országba,
Megmondta neki, meghagyta neki:

Töbé ne is lássa.
Átváltozom én rigómadárá,

Anyámhoz úgy szállok,
Kertjébe ülök egy rózsatöre,

Reája úgy várok.
Az anyja kinéz:
Furcsa egy madár,
Be nagyon búsan szól;
Szállj le csak hess, hess, te rigómadár

Én rózsabokromról.
Rossz férjhez adtál, jó anyám, engem

Idegen országba;
Nehéz a sora hej, bizony annak,
Kinek rossz a párja!

Thus sent the mother her little
    daughter
Into a distant land.
Sternly she bid her: "Follow thy
    husband!
Never return to me!"
"Lo! I shall change me into a
    blackbird,
Shall fly to mother's home;
There I'll be waiting perched in her
    garden
On a white lily's stem."
Out came the mother:
"Who is this blackbird?
Strange is her song and sad,
Forth and begone now, thou little
    birdling,
From my white lily's stem!"
"To a bad husband, mother, has thou
    sent me
Forth to a distant land.
Hard 'tis to suffer such bitter pining
In an illmated bond.

95. Igor Stravinsky, Sanctus from *Mass* (1948)

See page 70 for text.

96. Stravinsky, *Anthem* (1962)

ANTHEM (*The Dove Descending Breaks the Air*). Copyright 1962 by Boosey & Hawkes, Inc. Reprinted by permission of Boosey & Hawkes, Inc.

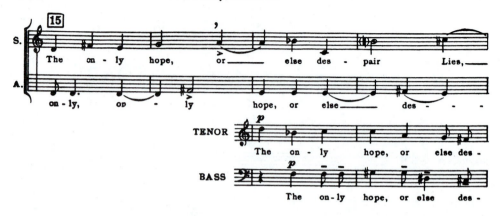

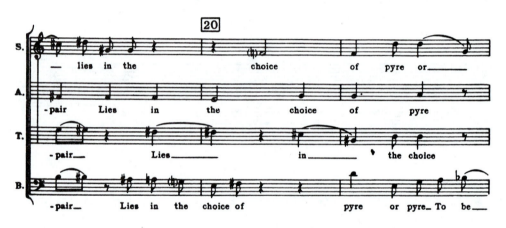

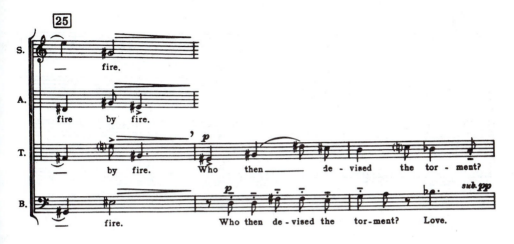

Text by T. S. Eliot

97. Krzysztof Penderecki, *Stabat Mater* (1962)

Duration: 8' 30"

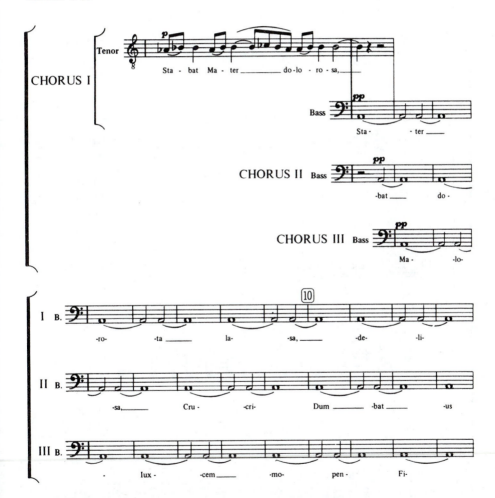

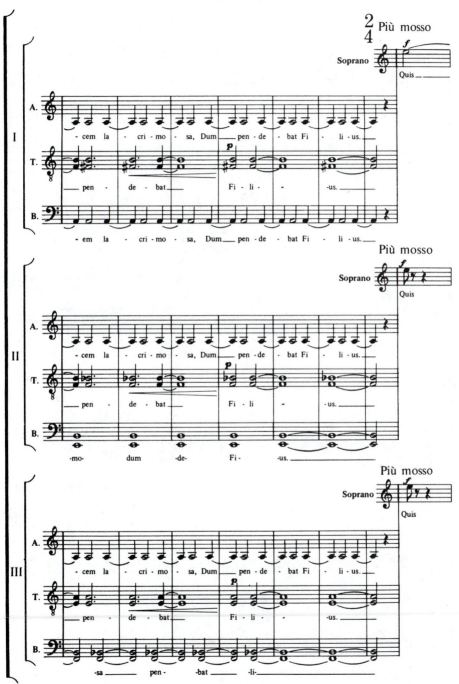

* = falsetto
** x = quasi recitando

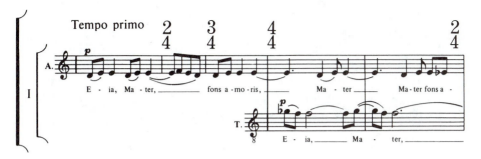

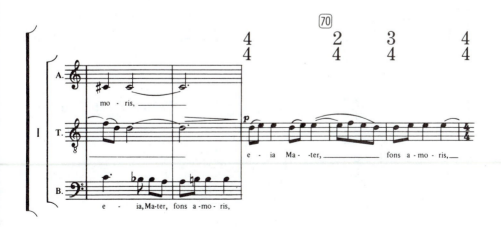

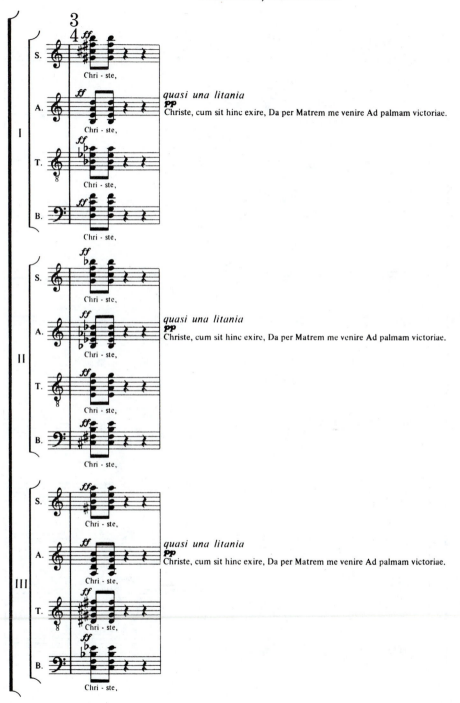

I

quasi una litania
pp
Christe, cum sit hinc exire, Da per Matrem me venire Ad palmam victoriae.

II

quasi una litania
pp
Christe, cum sit hinc exire, Da per Matrem me venire Ad palmam victoriae.

III

quasi una litania
pp
Christe, cum sit hinc exire, Da per Matrem me venire Ad palmam victoriae.

Penderecki, *Stabat Mater*

quasi una litania

I

S.	*p* Christe, cum sit hinc exire, Da per Matrem me venire Ad palmam victoriae.
A.	*p* Christe, cum sit hinc exire, Da per Matrem me venire Ad palmam victoriae.
T.	*p* Christe, cum sit hinc exire, Da per Matrem me venire Ad palmam victoriae.
B.	*p* Christe, cum sit hinc exire, Da per Matrem me venire Ad palmam victoriae.

quasi una litania

II

S.	*p* Christe, cum sit hinc exire, Da per
A.	*p* Christe, cum sit hinc exire, Da per
T.	*p* Christe, cum sit hinc exire, Da per
B.	*p* Christe, cum sit hinc exire, Da per

quasi

III

S.	*p* Christe,
A.	*p* Christe,
T.	*p* Christe,
B.	*p* Christe,

II

S.	Matrem me venire Ad palmam victoriae.
A.	Matrem me venire Ad palmam victoriae.
T.	Matrem me venire Ad palmam victoriae.
B.	Matrem me venire Ad palmam victoriae.

una litania

III

S.	cum sit hinc exire, Da per Matrem me venire Ad palmam victoriae.
A.	cum sit hinc exire, Da per Matrem me venire Ad palmam victoriae.
T.	cum sit hinc exire, Da per Matrem me venire Ad palmam victoriae.
B.	cum sit hinc exire, Da per Matrem me venire Ad palmam victoriae.

Penderecki, *Stabat Mater*

Stabat Mater dolorosa
juxta Crucem lacrimosa,
dum pendebat Filius.
Quis est homo, qui non fleret,
Matrem Christi si videret
in tanto supplicio?
Eia, Mater, fons amoris,
me sentire vim doloris
fac, ut tecum lugeam.
Fac, ut ardeat cor meum
in amando Christum Deum,
ut sibi complaceam.
Christe, cum sit hinc exire,
da per Matrem me venire
ad palmam victoriae.
Quando corpus morietur,
fac, ut animae donetur
paradisi gloria.

Grieving, the Mother stood
at the foot of that cross of sorrow
on which hung the Son.
Hard the man his tears refraining,
watching Mary, uncomplaining,
beat a sorrow like to none.
Lay that mother, fount of love,
inspire in me a cleansing sorrow
for the sacrifice of an innocent.
Make my heart increasingly ardent
in the love of Lord Jesus Christ,
and let me find comfort in him.
When in death my eyes are closing,
open them, Lord, to see reposing
victory's crown in Mary's hand.
When my frame by death is broken,
and my doom by Thee is spoken,
be it, Lord, the better land.

98. Luciano Berio,
Second Movement
from *Magnificat* (1949)

See page 3 for text.

99. Goffredo Petrassi,
Improperium from *Motetti per la Passione* (1965)

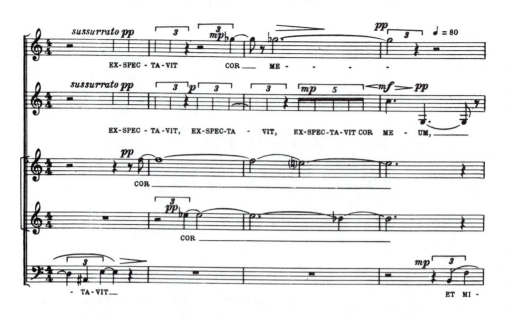

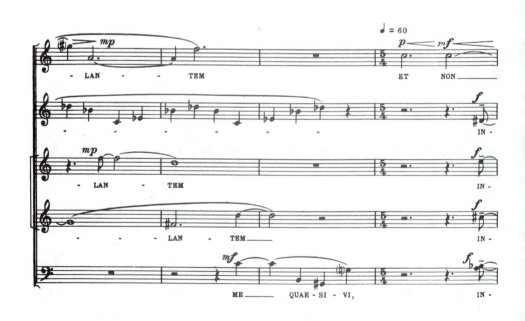

Improperium expectavit cor meum, et miseriam: et sustinui qui simul mecum contristaretur et non fuit; consolantem me quaesivi, et non inveni: et dederunt in escam meam fel, et in siti mea potaverunt me aceto.

My heart awaited reproach and misery: And I looked for one Who would grieve together with me But there was none; I sought for one who would comfort me And I found none: And they gave call for my food And in my thirst they gave me vinegar to drink.

Psalm 69:20–21

100. George Gershwin,
Sing of Spring (1936)

spring!   spring, and sing of spring!

spring!   spring, and sing of spring!

spring!   spring, and sing of spring!

spring!   spring, and sing of spring!

Text by Ira Gershwin

101. R. Nathaniel Dett, *Listen to the Lambs* (1914)

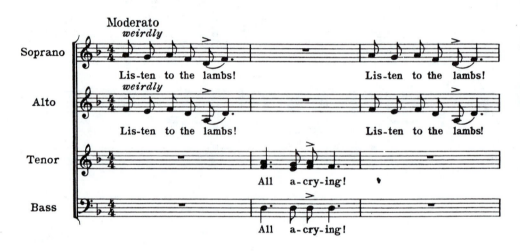

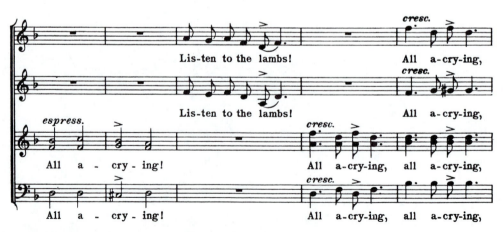

all__ a - cry - ing,___ all a - cry - ing!

all a - cry - ing,___ all a - cry - ing!

all__ a - cry - ing,___ all a - cry - ing!

all a - cry - ing,___ all a - cry - ing!

Meno mosso
SOLO SOPR.
molto espress.

He shall feed his flock like a shep-herd,__ and car-ry the young lambs in_his bo-som.

SOLO TENOR
con bocca chiusa (humming)

SOLO BASS I
con bocca chiusa (humming)

SOLO BASS II

TUTTI

He shall feed his flock like a shep - - herd, and carry the young lambs in his bo-som.

TUTTI

He shall feed his flock like a shepherd, like a shepherd, and carry the young lambs in his bo-som.

TUTTI

He shall feed his flock like a shepherd, like a shepherd, and carry the young lambs in his bo-som.

TUTTI

He shall feed his flock like a shepherd, and carry the young lambs in his bo-som.

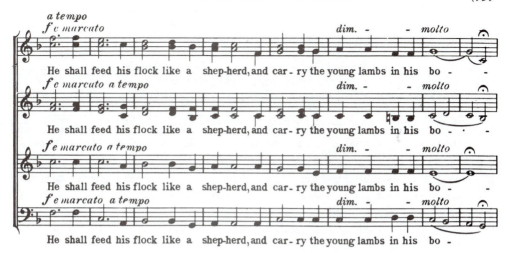

He shall feed his flock like a shep-herd, and car-ry the young lambs in his bo - -

He shall feed his flock like a shep-herd, and car-ry the young lambs in his bo - · -

He shall feed his flock like a shep-herd, and car-ry the young lambs in his bo - -

He shall feed his flock like a shep-herd, and car-ry the young lambs in his bo -

Soprano Solo

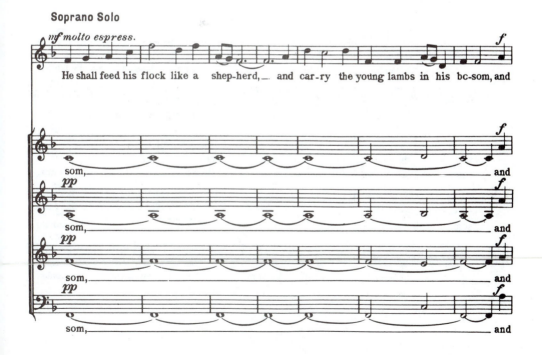

He shall feed his flock like a shep-herd, __ and car-ry the young lambs in his bc-som, and

som, _____ and

som, _____ and

som, _____ and

som, _____ and

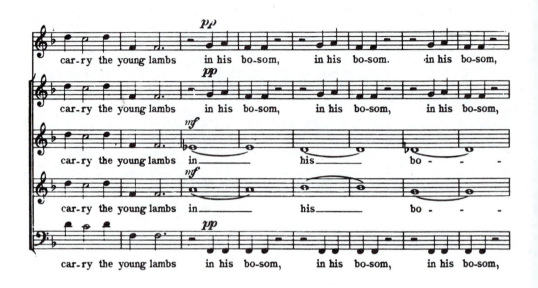

car-ry the young lambs in his bo-som, in his bo-som. in his bo-som,

car-ry the young lambs in his bo-som, in his bo-som, in his bo-som,

car-ry the young lambs in_____ his_____ bo - - -

car-ry the young lambs in_____ his_____ bo - - -

car-ry the young lambs in his bo-som, in his bo-som, in his bo-som,

in his bo-som, in his bo-som, in his bo-som the young lambs.

in his bo-som, in his bo-som, in his bo-som: lambs.

som,_____ the_____ young_____ lambs.

som,_____ the_____ young_____. lambs.

in his bo-som, in his bo-som, in his bo-som: lambs.

Dett, *Listen to the Lambs*

102. Charles Ives,
Psalm 67 (1898)

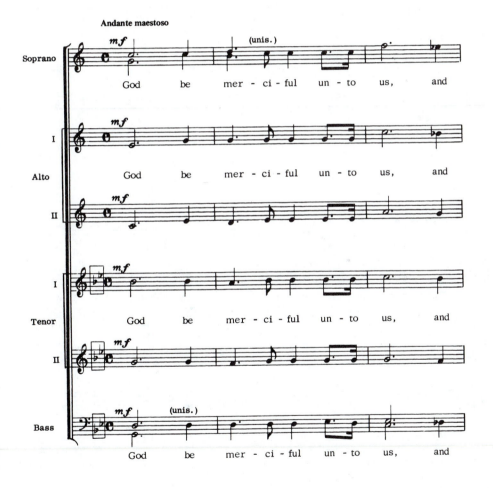

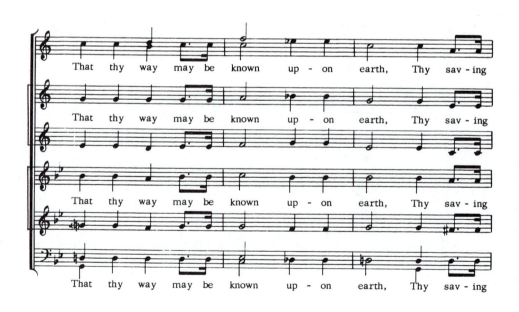

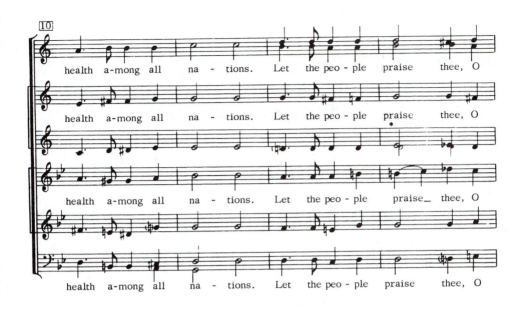

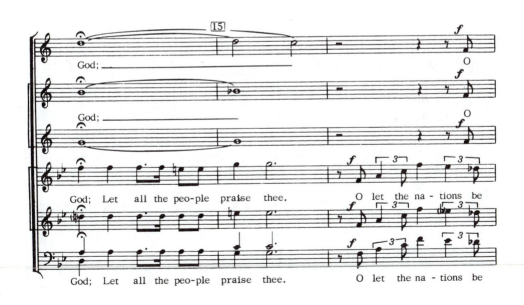

let the na - tions be glad and sing for joy:_____

let the na - tions be glad and sing for joy:

glad and sing for joy:

(unis.)
glad and sing for joy: For thou shalt judge the

glad and sing for joy: For thou shalt judge the

For thou shalt judge the peo - ple right-eous-ly,_____ And gov -

For thou shalt judge the peo - ple right - eous-ly,_____ And gov -

peo-ple, the___ peo - ple right-eous - ly, And___ gov - ern the

peo - ple___ right - eous - ly, _____ And gov - ern___

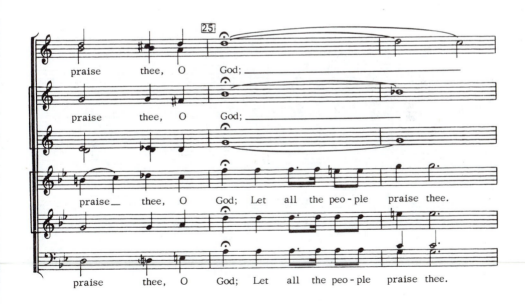

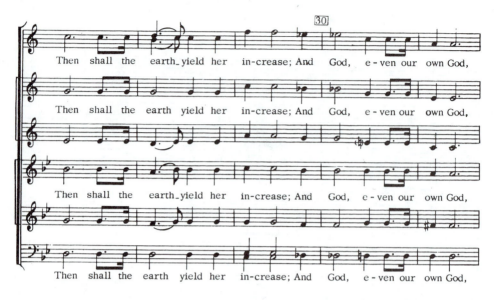

Then shall the earth_yield her in-crease; And God, e-ven our own God,

Then shall the earth yield her in-crease; And God, e-ven our own God,

Then shall the earth_yield her in-crease; And God, e-ven our own God,

Then shall the earth yield her in-crease; And God, e-ven our own God,

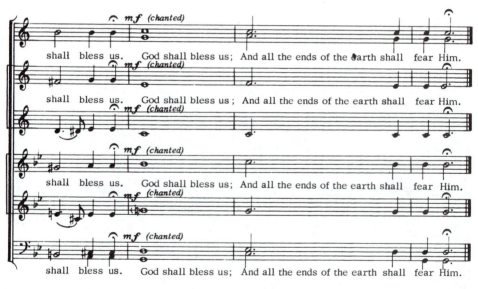

shall bless us. God shall bless us; And all the ends of the earth shall fear Him.

shall bless us. God shall bless us; And all the ends of the earth shall fear Him.

shall bless us. God shall bless us; And all the ends of the earth shall fear Him.

shall bless us. God shall bless us; And all the ends of the earth shall fear Him.

shall bless us. God shall bless us; And all the ends of the earth shall fear Him.

103. William L. Dawson,
There Is a Balm in Gilead (1939)

104. Louise Talma, *Let's Touch the Sky* (1952)

Text by e. e. cummings

105. Irving Fine, *Have You Seen the White Lily Grow* from *The Hour-Glass* (1949)

Text by Ben Jonson

106. Elliott Carter, *Musicians Wrestle Everywhere* (1945)

si - cians wres - tle ev - ery - where, ___ mu - si - cians ___ wres - tle ___

- ery - where, wres - tle ev - ery - where, _____

ery - where, ev - ery - where, ev - ery - where, mu - si -

cians wres - tle ev - ery - where, _____ ev -

___ ev - ery - where, mu - si - cians wres - tle ev

___ ev - ery - where: ___ All day, a - mong the crowd - ed air, I

___ ev - ery - where: ___ All day, a - mong the crowd - ed air,

- cians wres - tle ev - ery - where: All day, a - mong the crowd - ed air,

ery - where ___ All day, a - mong the crowd - ed air,

ery - where: ___ All day, a - mong the crowd - ed air,

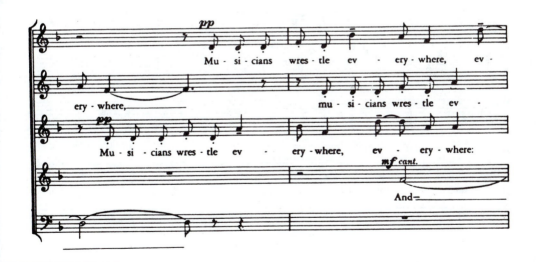

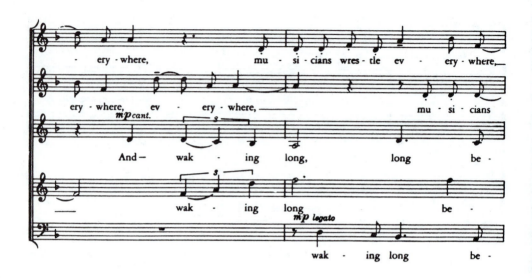

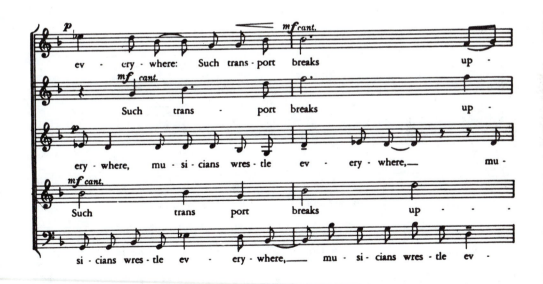

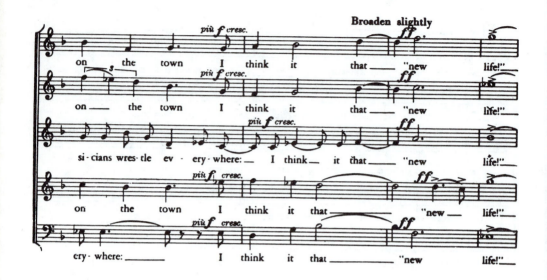

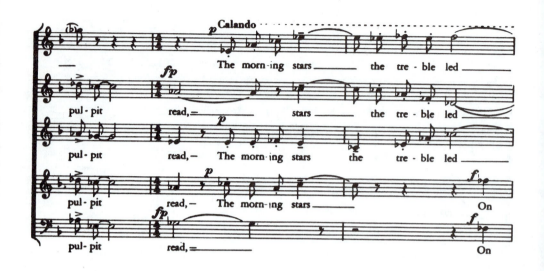

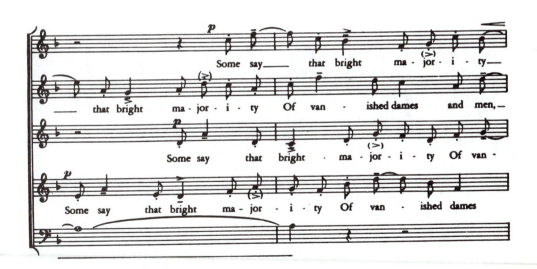

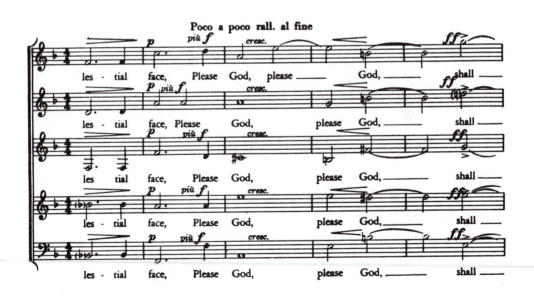

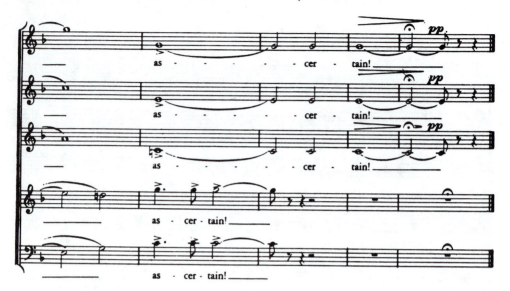

Text by Emily Dickinson

107. Samuel Barber, *The Coolin* from *Reincarnations* (1940)

Text by James Stephens

108. Vincent Persichetti, Kyrie from *Mass,* Op. 84 (1961)

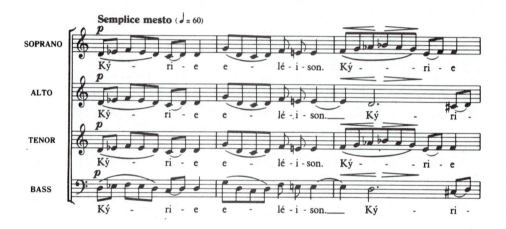

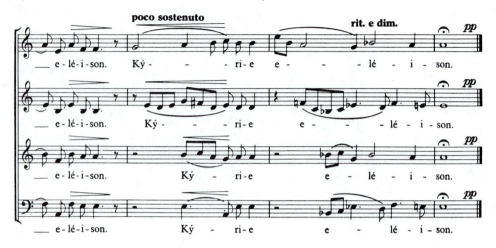

See page 15 for text.

109. Daniel Pinkham, First Movement from *Christmas Cantata* (1958)

* In this score, the trumpets are in C; however, the parts are written in B flat.

† Organ may be substituted for all of Brass Choir II. In the first movement, the tuba and baritone part may be doubled by the organ pedal.

Permission for use of this excerpt granted by the publisher, Robert King Music Co.

ia,
ia,
ia,
a2
a2
senza rallentare
al - le-lu - ia.
al - le-lu - ia.
al - le-lu - ia.
muted
muted

Quem vidistis pastores?

Dicite: Annuntiate nobis in terris
Quis apparuit.
Natum vidimus et choros angelorum

Collaudantes Dominum.
Alleluia.

Whom were you observing,
   shepherds?
Tell us: Describe the one who
appeared to us on earth.
We have seen him born and the
   chorus of angels
praising the Lord.
Alleluia.

110. Hale Smith, *Poème d'automne* from *In Memoriam–Beryl Rubinstein* (1952)

*P ⌐⌐⌐⌐⌐⌐ = Principal Voice, S ⌐⌐⌐⌐ = Secondary Voice.

court - e - sans   Wait-ing for their   lov - ers.

e - sans   Wait-ing for their   lov - ers.

e - sans   Wait-ing for their   lov - ers.

e - sans   Wait-ing for their   lov - ers.

⌣ As a weak beat

35 SOP. I
accel.   *a little faster*   *p sempre*

But soon___   The win - ter

SOP. II   *p sempre*

But soon___   The win - ter winds___

ALTO

TENOR   *p sempre*

But soon___

35
accel.   *a little faster*

mp   *f* *(tremolo optional)*   *(f)*

ff

Poem by Langston Hughes

111. Richard Felciano, *Hymn of the Universe* (1974)

"...you, my God, are the inmost depths, the stability of that eternal **milieu**, without duration or space, in which our cosmos emerges gradually into being and grows gradually to its final completeness, as it loses those boundaries which to our eyes seem so immense." **Teilhard de Chardin**

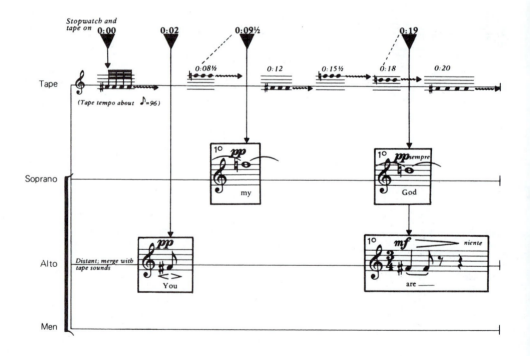

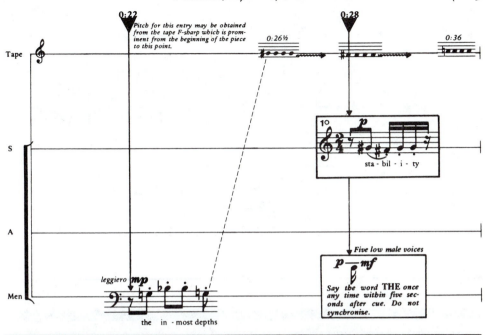

Alto: *rallentando molto, very fast to very slow so that last two notes are about two seconds apart. All notes should be very short. Figure should jump energetically out of the texture and then recede into it again. Conductor gives subsidiary cues for coordination.*

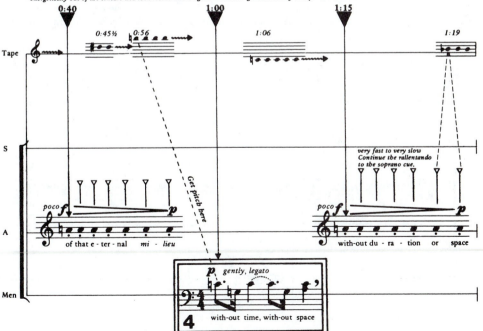

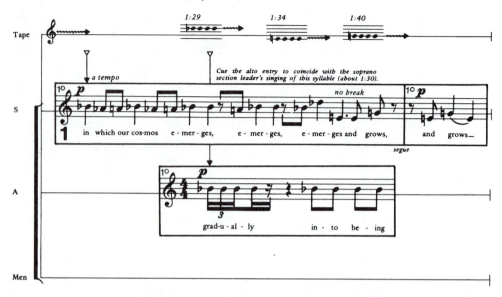

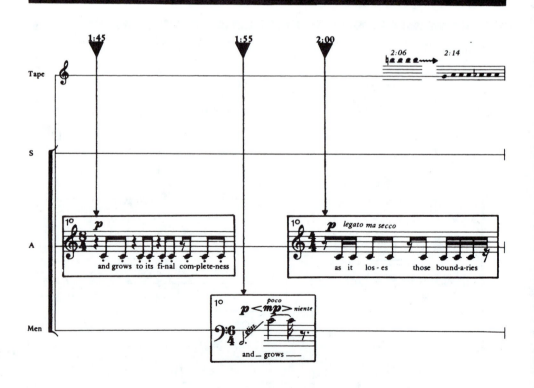

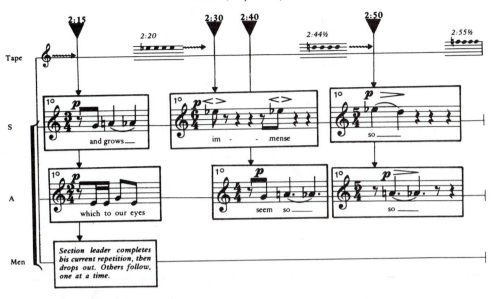

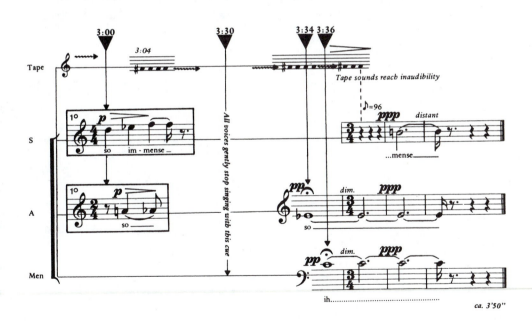

Text by Teilhard de Chardin

Glossary

a bocca chiusa (It.): with closed lips.

a cappella (It.): a term applied to choral music which is entirely without accompaniment (literally, "in the church style").

accelerando (It.): becoming faster.

adagio (It.): very slow.

affettuoso (It.): tender.

Alberti bass: a convetional figuration for the left hand in keyboard works, characterized by broken chords, associated with Domenico Alberti, an eighteenth-century composer.

allargando (It.): slowing down.

allegretto (It.): fairly fast, but not as fast as allegro.

allegro (It.): fast.

alternatim: a term used in reference to early liturgical compositions to indicate the alternation of polyphony and plainsong.

altus (Lat.): a term first appearing around 1450 and used in the later 15th and 16th centuries as an abbreviation for *contratenor altus,* the higher of the two contratenor parts then common (the other being *contratenor bassus*). In the Renaissance, such parts were usually sung by men using falsetto. In modern times, *alto* has generally been used to designate the lower of the two female (or boy) voice types.

andante (It.): moderately fast; literally, a "walking" tempo.

andantino (It.): somewhat faster than andante.

animato (It.): animated.

anthem: a paraliturgical choral composition in English. The anthem first appeared in England during the Reformation, where its function in religious services was similar to that of the motet in the Roman Catholic church, although its musical style was quite different. By the end of the 16th century, two types of anthem had evolved: the *full anthem* (using chorus only) and the *verse anthem* (using chorus and soloists). Anthem composition has continued in the 20th century in England, Canada, and the United States.

antiphon: a term for various types of Gregorian chant: 1) short texts, often from the Scriptures, set to melodies in syllabic style and sung as refrains to psalm verses; 2) texts from the New Testament set to moderately ornate melodies and used as processional pieces on certain feasts; 3) a special group of four texts in honor of the Virgin Mary (*Marian antiphons*) sung at the end of Compline (evening service in the Roman Catholic church), each one of which is proper to a particular season of the liturgical year. Types 2 and 3, though originally sung in conjunction with a psalm, were from an early time separated from their psalms and sung independently.

a tempo (It.): at the original tempo.

attacca (It.): an indication that the next movement of a work is to follow without pause.

ausdrucksvoll (Ger.): expressively.

balletto (It.): an Italian composition of around 1600, usually employing lively dance rhythms, homophonic writing (though often with imitation at the beginnings of phrases), and a refrain set to the syllables "fa-la." Imported to England by Thomas Morley, it was known there as the *ballett*.

basso continuo: *see* **continuo.**

basso ostinato (It.): a repeated bass line on which a set of continuous variations is built.

Bass stets unterordnen (Ger.): continually subordinate the bass part.

bassus (Lat.): a term which first appeared around 1450 and was used in the later 15th and 16th centuries as an abbreviation for *contratenor bassus*, the lower of the two contratenor parts then common (the other being the *contratenor altus*). In modern times, *bass* is generally used to designate the lower of the two male voice types.

belebt (Ger.): lively.

ben cantando (It.): singing well.

burden: 1) in the English carol of the 15th century, a musical refrain which was frequently sung by the chorus and on occasion may also have been danced; 2) any musical refrain.

calando (It.): slowing down and becoming softer.

canon: 1) in music of the 14th, 15th, and 16th centuries, any verbal directive intended to aid the understanding of the notation; 2) the strict imitation of a melody by one or more following parts, beginning on the same pitch as the original (canon at the unison) or at some other interval (canon at the major second, canon at the fifth, etc.), and at any time interval; 3) any composition employing canonic imitation.

cantata: 1) in 17th-century Italy, the most important type of secular vocal chamber music, which, by the end of the century, had become standardized as a work for soloist consisting of several da capo arias joined by recitatives; 2) in 17th- and 18th-century Germany, a type of concerted sacred music for chorus, orchestra, and soloists. Originally, such works were based on chorale texts and consequently often incorporated chorale melodies; but by the time of Bach, both of these characteristics became uncommon (except for the singing of a chorale at the end of a cantata); 3) generally, any multimovement choral work on a sacred subject.

canticle: a lyric passage from the Scriptures similar to a psalm but not occurring in the Book of Psalms. In the Roman Catholic church, the four greater canticles (*cantica majora*), taken from the New Testament (and including the *Magnificat* and *Nunc dimittis*), are used at Vespers, Lauds, and Compline. The fourteen lesser canticles (*cantica minora*), taken from the Old Testament, are used during the service of Lauds.

cantus (Lat.): In the Middle Ages, the Gregorian melody to which counterpoints were added in composing or improvising polyphony. In the 15th and 16th centuries, a general designation for the highest part in a polyphonic composition.

cantus firmus (Lat.): any preexistent melody incorporated into another composition.

carol: 1) a type of English vocal polyphony reaching its peak in the 15th century, usually of a devotional, ceremonial, or commemorative nature. Structurally, carols are characterized by the alternation of a refrain (sometimes two refrains), called the *burden* or *foote*, with a number of verses. 16th-century carols were freer in form and more restricted in subject matter, generally concerned with Christmas. 2) Any song for Christmas.

chaconne (It.: **ciaccona**): a variation procedure employing a continuously repeating harmonic pattern. The term is often confused with *passacaglia*, a similar procedure employing a ground bass. In actual practice during the 17th and 18th centuries, when the chaconne and passacaglia were most frequently used, the two terms were not applied with consistent meaning, and were often used interchangeably.

chanson (Fr.): song; in Renaissance music, a secular choral piece, often in less than four parts.

chorale (Ger.: **choral**): a hymn tune of the Lutheran church. Most chorales were written before the end of the Baroque period.

clavicembalo (It.): harpsichord.

concertante (It.): a term used to describe a work in which one or more solo instruments are prominent.

concertato style (It.: **stile concertato**): a term used to describe various kinds of contrasting sound groups used in much Baroque ensemble music.

conductus (Lat.): 1) by the 13th century, a designation for a composition in from one to four parts, setting a strophic metrical Latin text in syllabic style. All the voice parts proceed in a similar rhythmic movement and have the same text. Some conductus have introductory and concluding melismas called *caudae*, and are called *conductus cum caudis*. 2) The term *conductus style* has frequently been used to describe certain polyphonic compositions of the late Middle Ages and early Renaissance (particularly from England) which, although not strictly conductus, have one text and similar rhythm in all parts.

con grazia (It.): with grace.

con moto (It.): with movement.

con passione (It.): with passion.

con spirito (It.): with spirit.

continuo (It.): 1) a term used in the Baroque period for instruments (normally harpsichord and viola da gamba or cello) which play the basso continuo line; 2) a Baroque term used as an abbreviation for *basso continuo* (Eng.: *figured bass, thoroughbass*), a part designed to show the bass notes together with "figures" (numbers and symbols), which indicate the harmonies of the piece in a shorthand notation. The keyboard player supplied the harmonies along with the bass line, with the string player doubling the bass notes.

contratenor: in 14th-, 15-, and early 16th-century vocal music, a designation for a third voice part added to the two-voice complex of discantus and tenor.

cori spezzati (It.): divided choirs.

crescendo (It.): getting louder.

da capo (It.): repeat from the beginning.

declamato (It.): in a declamatory style.

diminuendo (It.): getting softer.

discantus (Lat.): a designation for the top voice in many compositions of the late Middle Ages and Renaissance.

dodecaphonic: a term referring to the twelve-tone method of composition.

dolce (It.): sweet.

duro (It.): harsh.

en dehors (Fr.): emphasized.

English discant: 1) a type of improvised polyphony thought to have been cultivated in England in the 14th and 15th centuries. Like fauxbourdon, English discant generally used Gregorian chants as cantus firmi and relied on parallel triads in the first inversion. Unlike fauxbourdon, the cantus firmus was generally in the lowest part. 2) The term *English discant style* is frequently used to designate certain English compositions of the 14th and 15th centuries making extensive use of parallel first-inversion triads.

espressivo (It.): expressive.

estremamente piano (It.): extremely soft.

falsetto (It.): a kind of harmonic produced vocally, used principally by male singers for notes above their normal range.

familiar style: vocal music in which the voices, usually four, move uniformly in regard to note values and text syllables.

fauxbourdon (Fr.): 1) a verbal canon used after the first quarter of the 15th century, indicating that a third part is to be added to a two-voice composition consisting of octaves and parallel sixths. This third part is to reproduce the upper part (the cantus firmus) a perfect fourth lower, creating a composition in three parts consisting of perfect sonorities at cadences alternating with parallel first-inversion triads in between. 2) The term *fauxbourdon style* is used to designate compositions of non-English origin making prominent use of parallel first-inversion triads.

figured bass: *see* **continuo.**

fliessend (Ger.): flowing.

folk song: a song of unknown authorship which has been transmitted orally and has become widely known in one locality or among one people.

frottola (It.): a designation for various types of Italian secular polyphony of the early 16th century. Frottole are normally chordal settings in three or four parts, with the melody in the upper voice.

fuging tune (fuguing tune): a type of hymn or psalm setting in homophonic style involving an imitative section at or near the end. Such settings were composed principally by late 18th- and early 19th-century Americans, although examples of fuging tunes may be found by 17th-century English composers.

fugue: a contrapuntal composition, often for the keyboard, generally consisting of an alternation of imitative sections (*expositions*) with freer sections (*episodes*). The expositions are usually characterized by successive appearances of the fugue subject with its answer (usually the subject repeated exactly or with slight modification a fifth higher) until all the parts have entered. The episodes, while usually remaining contrapuntal, are not strictly imitative and usually contain no obvious references to the subject; moreover, they are usually less stable tonally than the expositions.

ganz schlicht (Ger.): very simply.

Gebrauchsmusik (Ger.): utilitarian music, music intended primarily for social or educational purposes rather than as a form of self-expression.

getragen (Ger.): sustained.

giusto (It.): just, right, fitting.

grazioso (It.): gracious.

H̄: a symbol used by Arnold Schoenberg as an abbreviation for *Hauptstimme*, the main voice in a densely textured polyphonic composition.

haute-contre (Fr.): contertenor, male alto.

hexachord: a scale of six notes adopted by Guido d'Arezzo and incorporated into medieval theory.

hocket (Lat.: **hoquetus**): the breaking of a melody into single notes which are sung alternately by two or more voices, one having a rest while the other sounds.

hymn: a nonscriptural song of praise to God, usually with a relatively uncomplicated musical setting suitable for congregational rendition.

immer beschwingt (Ger.): continuously moving along.

isorhythm: a late-medieval compositional device in which a rhythmic pattern (*talea*) and melody (*color*) are repeated (sometimes with diminution) once or several times in the course of a composition.

Kapellmeister: *see* **maestro di cappella.**

Knabenchor (Ger.): boys' choir.

lai (Fr.): a type of medieval French song consisting of many sections of varying lengths, each of which is repeated before the next one is presented.

larghetto (It.): fairly slowly.

lebhaft (Ger.): lively.

legato (It.): smooth.

leggiero (It.): light.

lento (It.): quite slow, but not as slow as adagio.

lied (Ger.): song. Generally, any monophonic or polyphonic setting of a German secular text. Specifically, a 19- or 20th-century German song for solo
voice with a piano accompaniment which usually attempts to convey the
mood of the poem.

litania (It.): litany, chant.

luce (It.): light.

lunga (It.): long.

ma (It.): but.

madrigal: 1) a 14th-century Italian composition for two or three voices in AAB
or AABB form; 2) in 16th-century Italian music, a polyphonic vocal composition on a vernacular poem of some literary pretension. The madrigal
usually combined imitative and chordal writing and, especially at the end
of the century, used chromaticism and other musical devices to reflect
every emotional nuance of the text. Outside Italy, the 16th-century madrigal was most enthusiastically cultivated in England.

maestoso (It.): majestically.

maestro di cappella (It.) (Ger.: **Kapellmeister**): master of the chapel or director of music to a prince, bishop, or nobleman.

marcato (It.): stressed.

Mass: the central element of the Roman Catholic liturgy, signifying the mystical reenactment of the Last Supper and, through the doctrine of tran-
substantiation, of Christ's Crucifixion. The texts of the Mass may be
divided into two groups, those which change from service to service
(*Proper*) and those which remain unchanged (*Ordinary*). Musically, the
Proper is made up of the Introit, Gradual, Alleluia, Offertory, and Communion, and the Ordinary includes the Kyrie, Gloria, Credo, Sanctus,
Agnus Dei, and Ite missa est.

melismatic style: a style in which there are many notes to each syllable of text.

meno (It.): less.

mesto (It.): sad.

misterioso (It.): misterious.

moderato (It.): moderate.

molto (It.): much, very.

morendo (It.): dying away.

mosso (It.): lively.

motet: 1) from the 12th to the 15th century, a polyphonic composition for
two to four voices using two or more texts simultaneously and based on a
cantus firmus in the tenor; 2) in the 15th century, a free composition,

usually for three voices, with a Latin text generally in the top or top two voices (the lower voice or voices being instrumental); 3) generally, in the period after 1500, a sacred choral composition in four or more parts on a biblical or inspirational Latin text. The texture is usually imitative and contrapuntal, although sections of homophony are not uncommon.

musica ficta (musica falsa) (Lat.): in the Middle Ages and Renaissance, the extempore chromatic alteration of pitches in the written music, usually indicated in modern editions by cue-sized accidentals placed above the altered notes. The terms derive from the fact that such chromatic alterations necessitated using tones not part of the medieval tonal system.

neumatic style: a style of chant in which there are a few notes (two to six) for each syllable of text.

niente (It.): nothing.

noël (Fr.): a French Christmas carol.

non far sentire l'attacco (It.): do not let the attack be heard.

non troppo (It.): not too much.

obbligato (It.): a part, usually instrumental, which cannot be dispensed with in performance, as distinct from one which is optional or *ad libitum*.

ode: a choral composition similar to a cantata but not normally intended for a church service.

Office: the service of canonical hours in the Roman Catholic liturgy, the main purpose of which is the chanting of psalms. Musically, the most important Offices are Matins, Lauds, Vespers, and Compline.

oratorio: a semidramatic composition for soloists, chorus, and orchestra on a religious subject.

ossia (It.): or else; used to indicate an alternate version of a passage, usually one which is easier to perform.

paraphrase procedure: a free rendition or elaboration of a well-known melody. In early music, the term is used with specific reference to the elaboration of plainsong.

parlante (It.): approximating speech.

part-song: a homophonic choral composition in which the melody is usually in the top voice.

passacaglia: *see* **chaconne.**

Passion: a musical setting of the story of Christ's Passion, usually as told by one of the Evangelists.

perdendo (It.): dying away.

pesante (It.): heavily accented.

più (It.): more.

pleno (It.): indication for the full diapason chorus of the organ.

plus lent (Fr.): more slowly.

pochissimo (It.): very little.

poco (It.): little; **poco a poco:** little by little.

presto (It.): very fast.

primo tempo (I° **tempo**) (It.): return to the opening tempo.

psalm: one of the 150 lyrical poems contained in the Book of Psalms. In the Roman Catholic service, psalm singing is the main purpose of the canonical hours, where they are intoned to standard psalm tones. This type of recitation involves an introductory phrase (*intonatio*), followed by the delivery of the first half of the verse to the reciting tone (*tenor*), a medial cadence (*mediatio*), the recitation of the second half of the verse on the tenor, and a terminal formula (*terminatio*).

quasi (It.): almost, as if.

rallentando (It.): slowing down.

rechant (Fr.): refrain.

recitando (It.): reciting.

recitative: a vocal style which imitates the rhythms and inflections of natural speech, most often used in opera, where its function is to carry on the action to the next musical number. Two common types of recitative are *recitativo secco*, supported only by continuo, and *recitativo accompagnato*, supported by orchestra.

Requiem Mass: 1) the Mass for the Dead, so called from its Introit, *Requiem aeternam*. It differs from the usual Mass notably in omitting the Gloria and Credo, and substituting a Tract for the Alleluia, followed by the Sequence *Dies irae*. 2) The term is also applied to Protestant settings, as, for example, those by Schütz and Brahms, which use vernacular scriptural texts in place of those in the Roman Catholic version.

rinforzando (It.): a sudden accent.

ritardando (It.): slowing down.

ritornello (It.): 1) the last section of an Italian madrigal; 2) an instrumental piece in early opera; 3) the orchestral prelude, interludes, and postlude in a da capo aria; 4) a passage for full orchestra in a concerto.

rondeau (Fr.): 1) a form of medieval French poetry, written and set to music between the 13th and 15th centuries; 2) a form of French instrumental music in the Baroque period.

round: a canon in which each part continues to repeat *ad libitum*.

ruhig (Ger.): calm, quiet.

scherzando (It.): joking.

segue (It.): continue without pause.

semplice (It.): simple, plain.

sempre (It.): always, at all times.

senza (It.): without.

serenade: diversionary chamber music, either vocal or instrumental.

simile (It.): similarly.

sinfonia (It.): the 18th-century designation for opera overture; in choral works, a short instrumental introduction to the composition.

smorzando (It.): dying away.
sostenuto (It.): sustained.
sotto voce (It.): sing with a subdued vocal sound.
Sprechstimme (Ger.): a type of voice production midway between song and speech.
staccato (It.): detached, separated.
stets sehr zurückhaltend (Ger.): continually holding back considerably.
stringendo (It.): pressing forward.
strophic: a text setting in which the same music (sometimes with slight variants from verse to verse) is used for all of the verses.
subito (It.): suddenly.
submisse (It.): subordinated, suppressed.
superius (Lat.): the top voice in polyphonic compositions of the 15th, 16th, and 17th centuries.
sussurrato (It.): whispering.
syllabic style: a style in which there is one note for each syllable of text.

Tenebrae (Lat.): the Roman Catholic services of Matins and Lauds on Holy Thursday, Good Friday, and Holy Saturday.
tenor: in the Middle Ages and Renaissance, the voice part that carries the cantus firmus; in modern times, the higher of the two male voice types.
tenuto (It.): held.
testo solo (It.): narrator only.
tutti (It.): all, the entire ensemble.

una corda (It.): the soft pedal on the piano.

vif (Fr.): lively.
villanella (It.): a popular part-song in 17th-century Italy, the text of which often parodied the sentimental style of the madrigal.
virelai (Fr.): a medieval French song which begins with a refrain subsequently repeated after each verse.
vivace (It.): lively.

wie ein Wiegenlied (Ger.): like a lullaby.

zart (Ger.): graceful, tender.
Znamenny chant: the chant of the Russian church as used from the 12th through the 17th centuries. The term is derived from *znamia* (sign or neume).
zögern (Ger.): hesitate.

Appendix A: Biographical Sketches of Composers

JOHN ANTES (1740–1811) was born of a second-generation German American family at Frederick, Montgomery County, Pennsylvania. His father was a leader in the German Reformed church and a force behind the movement to unify the divergent religious denominations in his community. When his mission failed he joined the Moravian Brethren. John Antes received a classical education at the Moravian boy's school at Bethlehem, Pennsylvania, which he entered in 1752. He revealed an unusual talent for precision craftsmanship when, at the age of seven, he made a violin—perhaps the earliest violin built in America. While little is known about his musical training, we do know that he spent his adult years in Germany, Egypt, and England. From 1765 to 1769 he was apprentice watchmaker at the Moravian town of Neuwied on the Rhine. In 1769 he was ordained into the Moravian ministry and sent to Egypt as a missionary—the first American missionary to serve there. In 1781 he returned to Europe and became business manager of the Moravian Congregation at Fulneck, England, where he remained until his retirement in 1808. He died three years later in Bristol, England. His choral compositions include 25 sacred anthems and 12 chorales.

JACOB ARCADELT (c. 1504–c. 1568) was the youngest of the three most important composers of the early madrigal (the other two were Philippe Verdelot and Costanzo Festa). He may have been born in Liège, since he later held benefices at the churches of St. Barthélemy and St. Pierre in that city. He was in Florence in 1530 and was a singer in the papal chapel between 1541 and 1550. By 1555, he was in the employ of Charles of Lorraine, Prince of Guise, in whose service he apparently remained until the end of his life. He composed over 200 madrigals (some on sonnets of Michelangelo) and some 120 French chansons. He also wrote 3 books of Masses and about 20 motets.

JOHANN SEBASTIAN BACH (1685–1750) was born in Eisenach and educated there and in Ohrdrug and Lüneburg. He began his professional career in 1703 as a violinist in the chamber orchestra of Duke Johann Ernst in Weimar, but left the Duke's employ after several months to become organist in Arnstadt. Thereafter he was successively organist at the church of St. Blasius in Mühlhausen (1707), court organist and chamber musician to the Duke of Weimar (1708), and *Kapellmeister* to Prince Leopold of Anhalt-Cöthen (1717). In 1723, Bach took up the position he was to occupy for the remainder of his career, that of cantor of the St. Thomas School and *director musices* of the four city churches of Leipzig. He wrote 3 oratorios, 7 motets, 5 Masses (including the monumental *B-minor Mass*), 1 *Magnificat*, 300 sacred and 27 secular cantatas.

SAMUEL BARBER (b. 1910) enjoyed early success as a composer. A native of West Chester, a suburb of Philadelphia, he entered the Curtis Institute as a charter student in 1924 at the age of fourteen. In 1935 he won both the American *Prix de Rome* and the Pulitzer Prize, which he won again the following year. In 1938 he became the first American to have his works premiered by Arturo Toscanini and the NBC Symphony (*Essays for Orchestra No. 1* and *Adagio for Strings*). From 1939 to 1942 he served on the faculty of the Curtis Institute, teaching orchestration and conducting the chorus. He received the D.Mus. *honoris causa* from Curtis in 1945 (Harvard University awarded him the same degree in 1959). Barber's choral works are relatively few in number, but are performed with some regularity. They include 2 choruses, Op. 8; *A Stopwatch and an Ordinary Man*, Op. 15; the 3 choruses of *Reincarnation*, Op. 16; *Prayers of Kirkegaard*; *The Lovers*; and *Knoxville, Summer of 1915*. His two operas are *Vanessa* (1958) and *Anthony and Cleopatra* (1966).

BÉLA BARTÓK (1881–1945) was born in Nagyszentmiklós, a small village in what is now western Romania. His father was the director of an agricultural school and a gifted amateur musician. Béla received his first instruction in music from his mother, who gave him piano lessons when he was six. After graduation from the Gymnasium in Pozsony, Bartók was given the opportunity of studying in Vienna, but, on the advice of Ernö Dohnányi, chose to enter the Royal Academy of Music in Budapest where he worked with Istvan Thoman (piano) and Hans Koessler (composition). In 1905, Bartók made the first of his many field trips to study and record folk music, first Hungarian, then also Slovak, Romanian, and even North African. These studies had a decisive influence on his compositional style, freeing it from the "tyrannical rule of major and minor keys." In 1907 he joined the piano faculty of the Academy in Budapest (he never taught composition there). Because of the political situation in Europe, he left Hungary and came to the United States, where he remained until his death of leukemia in 1945. The influence of folk music is readily apparent in his compositional output in that all 62 of his choral works are either settings of actual Hungarian folk songs or melodically derived from them. All of them, however, are based on traditional Hungarian texts.

LUDWIG VAN BEETHOVEN (1770–1827) has long been recognized as the pivotal composer in the period of transition between Viennese Classicism and the full-blown Romantic movement in Germany. His seventeen choral works, although a very small part of his total compositional output, are nevertheless significant contributions to the literature, especially the Masses in C major and D major (*Missa Solemnis*). Though he was born in the Rhine town of Bonn, Beethoven spent most of his life in Vienna. His success as a composer and pianist was marred by a hearing disability, which by 1814 had become so acute that he was forced to abandon his concertizing career. In spite of this tremendous handicap he was able to compose during his last thirteen years a number of masterpieces, including the *Missa Solemnis, Ninth Symphony,* and the late quartets, works that in their intense subjectivity, vast dimensions, and formal innovations carry the unmistakable stamp of musical genius. Beethoven's choral compositions include the 2 Masses, 1 oratorio, *Christus am Ölberg (Christ on the Mount of Olives)*, and 8 cantata-like works.

LUCIANO BERIO (b. 1925) was born in Oniglia, a small Italian town near the French border. He was raised in a musical family and received his first instruction from his father, an organist and composer. In 1951 he graduated from the Conservatory in Milan, where he had studied composition with Giorgio Ghedini and Giulio Paribeni. Shortly thereafter, he went to Tanglewood to study serial technique with Luigi Dallapiccola. In 1955 he joined Bruno Madera in founding the electronic Studio di Fonologia at the Italian Radio in Milan, an association he maintained until 1961. For many years, Berio was active at Darmstadt, where many of his works were performed and where he gave lectures and seminars. He has lived in the United States since 1962 and now teaches composition at the Juilliard School of Music.

HECTOR BERLIOZ (1803–1869) wrote about thirty choral works, but he is, of course, best-known for his brilliant orchestral compositions. The son of a country doctor in a small town near Grenoble, he was sent to Paris at the age of eighteen to study medicine. Torn between his family's wishes and his own desire for a career in music, he eventually enrolled at the Paris Conservatory. Although he profited considerably from the instruction of Jean François Lesueur and Antonin Reicha (particularly the former), he seems to have developed many of his innovative orchestral ideas independently of any teacher (although certain works of Luigi Cherubini must be regarded as influences). Berlioz gave many concerts of his own music in Paris, but in his own lifetime he was better appreciated as a musical journalist and polemicist than as a composer. He was particularly successful in concerts he directed in St. Petersburg and Moscow, and memorable performances of his works were given by Franz Liszt in Weimar. His best-known choral works are those which combine large vocal and instrumental forces, such as the *Grande Messe des morts*, *Romeo et Juliette*, *La Damnation de Faust*, *L'Enfance du Christ*, and the *Te Deum*.

WILLIAM BILLINGS (1746–1800) was born in Boston where he first worked as a tanner, but later abandoned this trade to devote himself completely to music. He was largely self-taught, although he is said to have studied with John Barry, a local singer and choral conductor. His musical activities included the organizing and conducting of singing schools in various towns in the Boston area, the most famous of which was located in Stoughton, Massachusetts. He published six collections of vocal music, including 250 different hymn tunes and nearly 50 anthems (some of a patriotic nature), the most important of which were *The New-England Psalm Singer* (1770) and *The Continental Harmony* (1794). Billings is the most famous of a group of highly imaginative though (judged by European standards) unorthodox composers known as the Yankee Tunesmiths, a felicitous designation because it emphasizes the pragmatic nature of their musical creativity. Their favorite type of composition was the fuging tune, a hymn or psalm closing with a lively imitative section. As the vogue for "scientific" music increased at the close of the eighteenth century, the Yankee Tunesmiths lost favor with the public. Billings died in neglect and his widow and six children profited little from his many publications.

DIMITRI BORTNIANSKY (1751–1825) began his musical career as a choirboy in St. Petersburg, where he studied under Baldassare Galuppi. In 1769, he was awarded a stipend by Catherine II to study in Italy, where he began with his old teacher Galuppi in Venice, then went on to Rome and Naples. He returned to St. Petersburg in 1779 and devoted the next few years to the composition of French comic operas. In 1796, he became director of the Imperial Chapel, in which capacity he wrote a great deal of church music. Bortniansky is usually regarded as one of the important predecessors of the Russian nationalist movement, for he frequently incorporated Znamenny chants in his polyphonic church music.

JOHANNES BRAHMS (1833–1897) was born in Hamburg, of humble parentage. He received his first musical instruction from his father, who played the double bass in local theaters and bordellos. There were further musical studies with Otto F. Cossel (piano) and Eduard Marxsen (piano, theory), and by the time he was fourteen, he was making a living as a pianist. One of the few important nineteenth-century composers who was also a choral conductor, Brahms composed a considerable amount of music for choir. Between 1857 and 1859, he served as director of the court choir and as court pianist to the Prince of Detmold for part of each year, the remaining months being spent in Hamburg. In September of 1862, he moved to Vienna, where he was, for a short time (to 1864), the director of the Vienna Singverein. Although he returned to Hamburg for several years, his emotional attachment to Vienna was strong, and, in 1868, he settled there permanently. His works for chorus include the *Deutches Requiem* (German Requiem), *Schicksalslied* (Song of Destiny), *Nänie* (Elegy), *Rhapsodie* (Alto Rhapsody), the motets of Opp. 29, 74, and 110, and folk songs.

BENJAMIN BRITTEN (1913–1976) was born in the village of Lowestoft in Suffolk, where his father was a dentist and his mother an enthusiastic choir singer and secretary to the local choral society. He studied piano and viola as a child and, later, composition with Frank Bridge. At the age of sixteen he won a scholarship to the Royal College of Music, where he studied composition with John Ireland and piano with Arthur Benjamin. Upon graduation, he began writing music for documentary films and plays. His work in the theater brought him in contact with W. H. Auden, the poet and dramatist. They came to the United States together shortly before World War II, but Britten returned to England in 1942, settling in the coastal village of Aldeburgh. His choral works number approximately 35, including the *Spring Symphony, Te Deum, Rejoice in the Lamb, Hymn to St. Cecilia, A Ceremony of Carols,* the *War Requiem,* 10 part-songs, and 12 pieces for children's chorus.

ANTON BRUCKNER (1824–1896) was born of a devout Catholic family in Upper Austria. Orphaned at an early age, he attended the Volksschule in the village of St. Florian, where he became a chorister in the Abbey of the Augustine monks, studying piano, organ, and thoroughbass. In 1840 he enrolled in the Praperandie (Normal School) in Linz to prepare himself for a career as an elementary-school teacher. In 1845, he returned to St. Florian, where he was a teacher at the Volksschule and, during the years 1850–1855, provisional organist at the Abbey. At the end of 1855, Bruckner obtained the important post of cathedral organist in Linz. It was during this period that he first became acquainted with the operas of Wagner, and his reverance for the master's music knew no bounds after he heard *Tristan und Isolde* in 1865. He settled in Vienna in 1868, where he succeeded his teacher Simon Sechter as court organist and professor at the conservatory. In 1875 he received the appointment as lecturer in music at the University of Vienna. Tours of France (1869) and England (1871) made his name well known throughout Europe as an organ virtuoso. Bruckner's choral works include 6 Masses, a Requiem Mass, a *Te Deum,* a *Magnificat,* 5 psalms, and 36 smaller works.

DIETRICH BUXTEHUDE (1637–1707) was an important member of the North German school of organ composers, but his outstanding accomplishment lies in the field of choral music. He was probably born in Holstein, then under Danish rule, and, after studying with his father, he held successive appointments at Helsingborg (1657) and Helsingör (1660). In 1668 the church council of Lübeck offered him the prestigious position of organist at the Marienkirche, a post he retained for the rest of his life. Buxtehude's greatest reknown came from *Abendmusiken* (evening music) concerts established about 1673, held on the five Sundays preceding Christmas. About 120 of the cantatas written for these concerts during his tenure at Lübeck have been preserved. Their texts are derived from the Latin and German Bibles, from Lutheran chorales, from religious and even secular poetry. Buxtehude drew heavily on the chorale as the basis for his concerted choral works. Nearly half of the cantatas are based either wholly or partially on chorale melodies.

WILLIAM BYRD (1543–1623) was probably born in Lincolnshire and probably studied with Thomas Tallis. Nothing is known of his early life until 1563, when he was appointed organist at Lincoln Cathedral. Seven years later, he was designated a Gentleman of the Chapel Royal, but it was not until 1572 that he went to London to share with Tallis the position of organist of the Chapel. In 1575 these two men were granted a monopoly on the printing of music, and that same year they published a collection of motets under the title *Cantiones sacrae,* dedicated to Queen Elizabeth. Although Byrd composed madrigals, keyboard pieces, and instrumental music, his finest works are his sacred choral compositions scattered throughout various collections such as the *Psalmes, Sonets & Songs* (1588), two additional volumes of *Cantiones sacrae* (1589 and 1591), two books of *Gradualia* (1605 and 1607, apparently intended for the Catholic service), and the *Psalms, Songs & Sonnets* (1611). The surviving works include 3 Masses, (for three, four, and five voices, respectively), 60 anthems, and 12 sacred psalms.

GIACOMO CARISSIMI (1605–1674) is known primarily as a composer of chamber cantatas and oratorios. Born in the town of Marino (near Rome), he served the Cathedral of Tivoli, first as singer and then as organist, from 1624 to 1627. Following a short appointment as *maestro di cappella* at Assisi, he moved to a similar position in 1628 at the church of San' Apollinare in Rome, where he remained until his death in 1674. His oratorios were generally performed at San Marcello in Rome, and, like the cantatas, are characterized by careful text handling and an expressive melodic style. Examples of the larger works include the superb *Jepthe, Baltazar, Jonas,* and the *Judicium Salomonis.* Carissimi also produced a number of Masses and motets.

ELLIOTT CARTER (b. 1908) was born in New York City and studied at Harvard University with both Walter Piston and Gustav Holst. His early interest in music received encouragement from Charles Ives, but it was not until his last year as an undergraduate that he began serious, concentrated study in composition. Upon receiving an M.A. degree in 1932, he went to Paris and spent the next three years studying with Nadia Boulanger. In 1937 he became musical director of Ballet Caravan. About the same time he began to gain some prominence as a music critic, contributing articles to *The Saturday Review,* the *New York Herald Tribune,* and *Modern Music.* Carter received two Guggenheim fellowships in 1945 and 1950, won the American *Prix de Rome* in 1953, and in 1956 was elected a member of the American Academy of Arts and Letters. His academic career has included teaching stints at St. John's College in Annapolis, Yale University, M.I.T., Cornell, and the Juilliard School. But he is above all else a composer who devotes himself as much as possible to writing music. Carter has written some 15 choral works.

MARC-ANTOINE CHARPENTIER (1634–1704) was born in Paris, but went to Italy early in life, where he studied with Giacomo Carissimi in Rome. When he returned to France, he was invited to collaborate with Molière at the Théâtre Français, resulting in *Le Mariage forcé* (1672) and *Le Malade imaginaire* (1673). Following periods of employment by the Princess de Guise, the Jesuits, and the Duke of Orléans, he was named *maître de musique* at Sainte Chapelle, Paris, in 1698. Although Charpentier was a contemporary of Lully, he enjoyed neither the power nor the success which was lavished upon the latter. Charpentier was a gifted composer, who combined a lyricism reminiscent of his teacher, Carissimi, with the stateliness and ceremonial character of French music at the court of Louis XIV. His choral works include 12 Masses, 34 Latin oratorios, 30 psalm settings, motets for most of the feasts of the year, and settings of the *Te Deum* and *Magnificat.*

PAVEL GREGOR'EVICH CHESNOKOV (c. 1878–1944) devoted his creative life to producing harmonized transcriptions of the solemn chant traditions of Russia. He was born in the province of Vladimir, but very little else is known about his early life. Chesnokov wrote almost exclusively for the liturgical services of the Russian Church. His choral compositions number approximately 400, a large number of which are harmonized transcriptions of Slavonic chant. He also wrote an oratorio based on Lord Byron's poem *Heaven and Earth.* His earlier settings are characterized by a romantic style typical of most compositions written for the Russian Church of the late nineteenth century and the early years of the present century. The later works, however, reflect a more conservative style, while his harmonized transcriptions preserve intact the tradition of unison plainsong, as illustrated by the Znamenny chant included in this volume.

PETER MAXWELL DAVIES (b. 1934) is a British composer whose music reflects his interest in medieval and Renaissance techniques. He studied at the Royal College of Music in Manchester, with Goffredo Petrassi in Rome, and at Princeton University. His intensely personal style incorporates popular elements into an art-music context, emphasizes instrumental and vocal virtuosity, and reveals a high sense of the theatrical. Among Davies's vocal works are two cycles of carols with instrumental interludes, for choir soloists and orchestra; five motets for soloist with choir and orchestra; *The Shepherd's Calendar* for young singers and players; and the *Leopardi Fragments*.

WILLIAM DAWSON (b. 1898) was raised in Alabama and learned the trade of shoemaking as a youth. His ambition to attend Tuskegee Institute was realized in 1917. While there, he studied piano and harmony and learned to play most of the band and orchestral instruments. In 1926, after holding teaching positions in Topeka, Kansas, and Kansas City, Missouri, he won a scholarship to the American Conservatory of Music in Chicago, where he received the Master of Arts degree in music. He returned to Tuskegee in 1930 to organize and direct its School of Music. Under his leadership, the Tuskegee Institute Choir gained nationwide recognition. His first success as a composer came in 1934, when Leopold Stokowski and the Philadelphia Orchestra introduced his *Negro Folk Symphony*. He has written many choral works and arrangements of spirituals.

JOSQUIN DES PREZ (c. 1445–1521) was born in Picardie, perhaps in Condé. He was known in his lifetime as the "Prince of Musicians," and indeed he has come to represent for posterity the Renaissance ideal in music in much the same way as that other "Prince," Erasmus, represents this ideal in humanistic scholarship. He began his career as a choirboy in the collegiate church of St. Quintin, later becoming a canon and choirmaster here. He travelled to Italy early in his career, and records exist which identify him as a singer in Milan in 1459. At the same time, he probably served Duke Galeazzo Maria Sforza, though his presence in the Duke's service is not confirmed until 1474. From 1486 to 1494, he sang in the papal choir under Popes Innocent VIII and Alexander VI, and later was first chapel master in Ferrara (1499–1503), where he wrote his famous *Missa Hercules Dux Ferrariae*. He remained in the service of Louis XII, until the King's death in 1515. Toward the end of his life he was provost of Condé. Josquin developed an "international style" of polyphony in his Masses and motets, characterized by equality of voices (except where the tenor has a cantus firmus), pervading imitation, controlled dissonance, careful attention to text declamation, and an ingratiating, flowing melodic and rhythmic style.

R. NATHANIEL DETT (1882–1943) was born in Canada and came to the United States at an early age. He received a B.Mus. degree at Oberlin Conservatory in 1908, and continued his studies at the American Conservatory, Columbia University, Harvard University, the Eastman School of Music, and Howard University. His compositions include two impressive oratorios, three motets, choral settings of spirituals, and piano music. Under his leadership, the Hampton Institute Choir won international recognition with successful tours of Europe and the United States in 1930 and 1931.

HUGO DISTLER (1908–1942) was born in Nuremberg, Germany. Both his early training and his devotion to the church determined his compositional style. Following his studies at the Leipzig Conservatory, he became organist and cantor at the Jakobkirche in Lübeck. In 1933, he was appointed to the faculty of the Evangelische Kirchenmusikschule in Spandau (Berlin). Four years later, he began teaching at the Hochschule für Musik in Stuttgart, but returned to Berlin in 1940 as professor of church music at the Hochschule there. In 1942, he became conductor of the Berlin Cathedral Choir. Later that year, he took his own life in a supreme gesture of protest against the Nazi regime. As with Bach, most of Distler's choral works were intended to meet the practical needs of the church. They include 64 motets, 2 cantatas, a German Mass, a Passion, and the *Weihnachtsgeschichte* (Christmas Story). There are also 51 secular vocal compositions.

GUILLAUME DUFAY (c. 1400–1474) began his career as a choirboy at Cambrai Cathedral. By the time he was twenty he had journeyed to Italy where he served the Malatesta family of Rimini and Pesaro. Dufay held a number of positions in the next few years, including appointments in Rome, Florence, and Bologna. He returned to Cambrai around 1440, which became his permanent residence for the rest of his life. Like many other Netherlands composers, Dufay led a cosmopolitan life. He travelled extensively and was well educated in areas outside music, being a *Doctor utriusque iuris*—a doctor of both civil and canon law. In Dufay's music, particularly the secular works, the nonisorhythmic motets, and the later Masses, we can observe the transition, on the Continent, from the constructionist melodic style of the late Middle Ages (e.g., Machaut) to the free-flowing mellifluousness of the Renaissance—what his contemporary Martin Le Franc called *la contenance angloise*. Dufay's works comprise over 200 items, including approximately 8 Masses, 87 motets, and 67 French and Italian songs, together with Mass sections, hymns, and *Magnificats*.

JOHN DUNSTABLE (c. 1380–1453) was the most important English composer of the first half of the fifteenth century and the person commonly credited with being the first Renaissance composer. As a young man, he went to France in the service of John, Duke of Bedford, the brother of Henry V, possibly the "Roy Henry" of the Old Hall manuscript. To judge from the distribution of his works, most of his life was spent on the Continent, since few of his compositions are found in English sources. Dunstable is discussed by the theorist Tinctoris and the French writer Martin Le Franc as the founder of a new style of music, one which emphasized harmonic euphony and melodic grace. The motet *Quam pulcra es* is an example of this lyrical style, which was to be further developed by Dufay and Josquin. With the exception of three secular chansons (*Durez ne puis*, *Puisque m'amour*, and the questionably attributed *O Rosa bella*), the surviving vocal works of Dunstable all fall under the category of Latin church music.

JOHANNES ECCARD (1553–1611) was born in Mühlhausen, Thuringia. He studied in Weimar from 1567 to 1571, and during the next three years he was a pupil of Orlando di Lasso in Munich. He returned to Mühlhausen in 1574. The greater part of his life was spent in the distant outpost of Königsberg in East Prussia, where he was active in the court chapel after 1580, eventually becoming *Kapellmeister* in 1604. He moved to Berlin on July 4, 1608, to become *Kapellmeister* at the Electoral Chapel, and died there in 1611. Eccard's most important contribution to choral literature was his development of the chorale motet, which combined Franco-Flemish compositional sophistication with the Lutheran proclivity for chorale tunes. His 51 settings of well-known chorales in the important *Geistliche Lieder auf den Choral* (1597), compiled at the request of Georg Friedrich, Margrave of Brandenburg, and the two parts of his *Preussische Festlieder* (issued posthumously in 1642 and 1644) may be singled out among his numerous publications.

EDWARD ELGAR (1857–1934) was raised in a musical environment; his father was a violinist, organist, and successful music retailer in Worcester, England. The young Elgar played violin in the orchestra of the Three Choirs Festival and substituted for his father as organist at St. George's Roman Catholic Church. In the ensuing years he lived in Worcester, holding various minor musical posts and travelling to London and Leipzig. In 1891 he withdrew to Malvern, his estate in Worcester, where he spent the next thirteen years composing. In 1904 he moved to Hereford and a few years later, to London, where he remained until he returned permanently to Worcester in 1929. Elgar's music is closely tied to the Postromantic tradition, manifesting a clear interest in the English folk-song heritage as well. His 85 choral works include sacred and secular works both a cappella and with orchestra.

GABRIEL FAURÉ (1845–1924) was perhaps better known during his lifetime as a teacher than as a composer. Recognition of his importance as a creative figure had to wait until well after his death. Fauré was born in Pamiers, France, the son of a provincial inspector of schools. Observing the native musical ability of his son, the father took him to Paris at an early age, where he studied with Louis Niedermeyer and Camille Saint-Saëns. During his long life, he held numerous posts in Parisian churches; from 1877 to 1896 he served as organist at the Madeleine. A list of his students includes, among others, Maurice Ravel, Georges Enesco, Jean Roger-Ducasse, Raoul Laparra, Florent Schmidt, Louis Aubert, and Nadia Boulanger. In 1905, at the age of sixty, he was named to the prestigious post of director of the Paris Conservatory. Fauré's choral works number less than twenty, the most important of which are the *Cantique de Jean Racine* and the *Requiem*.

RICHARD FELCIANO (b. 1930), a native of California, holds degrees from Mills College, the Paris Conservatory, and the University of Iowa (Ph.D., 1959). His principal teachers of composition were Darius Milhaud and Luigi Dalla-piccola, with whom he worked during a year of residence in Florence. He has held grants from the French and Italian governments, a Fulbright grant, two Ford Foundation fellowships, and a Guggenheim fellowship. Since 1967 he has been a resident composer to the National Center for Experiments in Television in San Francisco. He is currently professor of music at the University of California at Berkeley and codirector of the University's electronic music studio.

IRVING FINE (1914–1962) was born in Boston and educated in the public schools of Boston and Winthrop, Massachusetts. He entered Harvard University in 1933, where he studied composition with Edward Burlingame Hill and Walter Piston, and choral conducting with Archibald T. Davison. His summers were spent at Tanglewood, where he associated with Serge Koussevitsky, Aaron Copland, and Igor Stravinsky. After a year of study in France with Nadia Boulanger, Fine returned to Harvard as director of the Glee Club (1939–1946) and Assistant Professor of Music (1946–1950). In 1950 he was appointed chairman of the School of Creative Arts at Brandeis University, a position he held until his death. Fine composed 27 choral works, the best known of which are the *Three Choruses from Alice in Wonderland* and *The Hour-Glass*, a cycle of 6 choral songs to poems by Ben Jonson.

JOSIAH FLAGG (c. 1738–c. 1794) was active in the musical life of Boston during the period of the American Revolution. An energetic bandmaster, he organized and trained the first regular militia band in New England. In his acquaintance with many European musicians and his introduction of their works to Boston audiences, he was influential in early American concert life. His *Collection of the Best Psalm Tunes*, engraved by Paul Revere and published in 1764, included some of the first English anthems published in New England. Flagg's other publication, issued in 1766, was the first sizable collection devoted primarily to anthems by New England composers.

STEVEN COLLINS FOSTER (1826–1864) wrote only one work for vocal ensemble, the four-part *Come Where My Love Lies Dreaming*. Although he had little formal training in music, his natural lyric gift led him to song composition at an early age. Because his family did not approve of a musical career, Foster was sent to Cincinnati to work as a bookkeeper for his brother. But his musical inclinations were not to be denied, and he soon abandoned the accounting profession. He remained in his native Pittsburgh until 1860, when he moved to New York. Though he wrote continuously throughout his life, many of his later songs were undistinguished. He died in the charity ward of Bellevue Hospital at the age of thirty-seven, penniless, alcoholic, and friendless.

GIOVANNI GABRIELI (1557–1612) was born in Venice, but was taken by Orlando di Lasso to Munich when he was eighteen. In 1585, when his uncle and teacher, Andrea, became first organist at St. Mark's, Giovanni was appointed second organist, a position he retained until his death. Through his composing (particularly the three collections of *Symphoniae sacrae*) and teaching, his influence upon the emerging concertato style of Baroque choral music was immense. His pupils included Hans Leo Hassler and Heinrich Schütz, both of whom carried this style to their native Germany, where it eventually had an important influence on Johann Sebastian Bach. Gabrieli was interested in the acoustical effects of massed ensembles alternating with soloists or other ensembles. His motets are almost all polychoral and dramatic in the Baroque musical sense.

GIOVANNI GASTOLDI (c. 1550–1622) is known primarily as a composer of balletti. We have no information concerning his early life, but he was probably assistant to Giaches de Wert at the court of Mantua. Gastoldi was *maestro di cappella* at the church of Santa Barbara in that city from 1582 until his death. His *Balletti a cinque voci* (Venice, 1591), with their lively rhythms and "fa-la-la" refrains, undoubtedly served as models for Thomas Morley's ballets. Gastoldi's compositions include 4 books of madrigals, a similar number of canzonetta collections, and assorted sacred works.

GEORGE GERSHWIN (1898–1937) has perhaps been most acclaimed for his successful merging of popular music, jazz, and art music. Born on New York's Lower East Side, he began to play the piano at the age of ten and went on to study harmony with Rubin Goldmark, counterpoint with Henry Cowell, and theory, composition, and orchestration with Joseph Schillinger. His first efforts in composition were in the popular-song style, and his hit song *Swanee*, made famous by Al Jolson, established him in Tin Pan Alley. His successes in musical comedy and song continued to grow, when his interest turned to jazz. *Rhapsody in Blue*, for piano and orchestra, was first performed in February, 1924, and marks Gershwin's first attempts to bridge the popular and classic styles, further exemplified by *An American in Paris* for orchestra, *Concerto in F* for piano, and the "folk opera" *Porgy and Bess*. Besides his concert music and hundreds of songs, Gershwin wrote 4 film scores and 16 musicals.

CARLO GESUALDO, Prince of Venosa (c. 1560–1613) is probably best remembered for one bizarre incident—his murder of his wife Maria and her lover, Fabrizio Carafa, on November 16, 1590. He seems to have had an exaggerated emotional temperament and this is often reflected in his music, particularly the later madrigals, which represent an almost unwholesome preoccupation with sharp emotional contrasts. Gesualdo's characteristic style is chromatic and full of word painting. His vocal works include 125 madrigals, printed in 6 books, 2 canzonettes, and 2 books of *Sacrae cantiones*.

ORLANDO GIBBONS (1583–1625) was born of a distinguished English family of musicians, and rose quickly to a place of prominence of his own. Recognized as one of the finest organists of the time, he was appointed in that capacity to the Chapel Royal in 1605, was virginalist to James I in 1619, and organist at Westminster Abbey in 1623. He received the degree of B.Mus. from Cambridge University in 1606. Gibbons's fame as a composer rests primarily on his church music, which includes 2 complete Anglican services, 40 anthems, 17 hymn tunes, 2 sets of psalms, and traditional polyphonic compositions. He made a special contribution in the establishment of the verse anthem form.

CLAUDE GOUDIMEL (c. 1510–1572) was born in Besançon and probably moved to Paris by 1549, for that date appears on a collection of his chansons published there by Du Chemin. He resettled in Metz, a Huguenot center, in 1557, and turned to Protestantism by 1560. The last music he composed for the Roman Church—a *Magnificat* and four Masses—appeared shortly before that year. Together with many other converts, he left Metz to seek safer quarters, returning first to his native town, then moving finally to Lyons. A prolific composer, his polyphonic settings are found in nearly all the psalmbooks published in various languages during the seventeenth and eighteenth centuries. Goudimel perished in the massacre following St. Bartholomew's Day in Lyons, in 1572.

GEORGE FRIDERIC HANDEL (1685–1759) is best known today as a composer of oratorios, but it was not until 1740, when he gave up opera altogether, that he turned his attentions to this genre. A gifted performer on the organ, harpsichord, violin, and oboe, Handel left his home town of Halle in 1703 for Hamburg, attracted by the theater there. Three years later he went to Italy, returning to Germany in 1610 to become *Kapellmeister* to the Elector Georg of Hanover. Before he could begin functioning in his new position, however, he journeyed to London, where he enjoyed enormous success writing and producing *opera seria* for the English musical stage. When, in 1715, the Elector became King George I of England, Handel moved permanently to London, becoming a British subject in 1727. Among his works for chorus are 2 Passions, 6 settings of *Te Deum*, 26 oratorios, and 11 anthems.

HANS LEO HASSLER (1564–1612) was the first important German composer of the Baroque to study in Italy. As a child he took lessons from his father, acquiring exceptional technical facility as an organist. In 1584, he went to Venice to work with Andrea Gabrieli, but returned to Germany after one year to assume the post of chamber musician in the court of Count Octavianus II Fugger in Augsburg. During his comparatively short life, Hassler served both the Protestant Elector of Saxony and the Catholic Prince Fugger. He composed Masses and Latin motets, although it appears that he was by persuasion a Protestant. His best-known composition is the secular song *Mein G'müth ist mir verwirret* (My Spirit Is Troubled), which was subsequently given a sacred text, *O Haupt voll Blut und Wunden* (O Sacred Head Now Wounded), and set five times by Johann Sebastian Bach. Hassler's vocal works include 8 Masses, 96 motets, 52 psalms, 70 chorale settings, 2 *Magnificats*, and a number of secular pieces.

FRANZ JOSEPH HAYDN (1732–1809) was born in the small Austrian village of Rohrau. As a young boy, he received instruction in voice, clavier, and violin from his uncle, J. M. Franck, of the neighboring village of Hainburg. His fine singing voice eventually earned him a place in the choir of St. Stephen's Cathedral in Vienna. After holding the post of music director at the court of Count Morzin at Pilsen (Bohemia) for one year, he entered the service of the Esterházy family (1760). Eventually, Haydn was given full direction of the musical forces of the Court of Prince Nicholas Joseph. On the death of the music-loving prince in 1790, Haydn accepted an invitation to appear at a series of concerts in London under the management of the violinist-impressario Johann Salomon. He returned to London in 1794 to complete the composition and performance of the last six of the twelve *London Symphonies*. After he returned to Vienna in 1795, he composed the last six Masses and the two oratorios *The Creation* (1798) and *The Seasons* (1801).

PAUL HINDEMITH (1895–1963) was born in Hanau and attended the Hochschule für Musik in Frankfurt. He was a gifted student of both violin and composition, and became, at the age of twenty, concertmaster of the Frankfurt Opera orchestra and violist in the Amar String Quartet. In 1927, Hindemith was appointed professor of composition at the Hochschule für Musik in Berlin. Branded a "cultural bolshevik" by the Nazi regime, he left Germany in 1938 and went to Ankara, Turkey, where he helped organize a state system of music education. In 1940, he became professor of theory and composition at Yale University. He returned to Europe and settled in Switzerland in 1953. Hindemith composed 25 works for chorus, 3 of which are with orchestra, 2 with piano, and 20 unaccompanied.

GUSTAV HOLST (1874–1934) maintained a life-long interest in sixteenth- and seventeenth-century English folk music as well as amateur music making and music education. His father wanted him to become a pianist, and in 1893 he enrolled in the Royal College of Music to pursue that career. Two years later, he won a scholarship to study composition with Sir Charles Stanford. In the meantime, a neuritic hand condition caused him to turn to the trombone as his major instrument. After leaving the Royal College of Music, he joined the Carl Ross Opera Company as first trombonist and *repetiteur*. In 1903, he began his career as a teacher, with appointments at St. Paul's Girls School (1905) and Morley College (1907), both of which he held to the end of his life. In 1919 he added the Royal College of Music to his teaching responsibilities. In the course of a trip to the United States in 1923, he lectured at Harvard University and the University of Michigan. Holst's choral compositions total about 115 works, 42 of which are with orchestra.

ARTHUR HONEGGER (1892–1955) was born in Le Havre, France, of German-Swiss parents, but lived most of his life in Paris. After two years at the Zurich Conservatory, he entered the Paris Conservatory (1912), where he studied harmony, counterpoint, and fugue under André Gédalge and Charles Widor, and conducting with Vincent d'Indy. Although Honegger was grouped together with five other composers (including Darius Milhaud and Francis Poulenc) designated as *Les Six*, he never had much in common with them. For the most part, he went his own way, pragmatically borrowing from the past or present as the situation demanded. The work that brought Honegger immediate recognition was the dramatic oratorio *King David* (1921). While he prized his operas above everything else (and believed *Antigone* to be his masterpiece), his choral works—*Le Roi David, Judith, Cantique des cantiques, Les Cris du monde, La Danse des morts, Jeanne d'Arc au bûcher* and *Chant de libération*—remain, to this day, his claim to immortality.

JEREMIAH INGALLS (1774–1828) was a singing master in Vermont and compiled the historically important tune book *The Christian Harmony* (1805). Although its influence at the time appears to have been slight, this unusually interesting collection is a significant source of early American folk hymnody. Little is known about Ingalls's life. He composed two outstandingly successful fuging tunes—*Northfield* and *New Jerusalem*—long before the publication of *The Christian Harmony*.

CHARLES IVES (1874–1954) was an original and independent musical personality, the first in a long line of anti-European experimental composers in America. As the son of a band director in Danbury, Connecticut, he was intimately associated with music from his earliest youth. After graduating from Danbury High School, he entered Yale University, where he studied composition with Horatio Parker and organ with Dudley Buck. After graduation, he went to New York, entered the insurance business, and began composing music in his free hours. By choice, he lived and worked generally apart from the music world of his time, although he was interested in furthering the cause of avant-garde music, supporting, for example, Henry Cowell's important periodical *New Music*. In 1947, his *Third Symphony* was awarded the Pulitzer prize, which Ives declined with characteristic New England saltiness, saying that "prizes were the badges of mediocrity." The list of Ives's published choral music includes nine psalm settings, the three *Harvest Home Chorales*, the cantata *The Celestial Country*, and smaller works. The important place that the principles of the New England Transcendalists occupied in Ives's work may be judged from the companion volume to the *Concord Sonata* entitled *Essays Before a Sonata*.

CLÉMENT JANEQUIN (c. 1475–c. 1560) was one of the creators of the sixteenth-century polyphonic chanson style. A student of Josquin, he may have been in the service of Louis Ronsard, father of the poet, at an early age. In about 1520, he was in Paris. Evidence also exists which places him in Bordeaux in 1529 in the service of the Cardinal of Lorraine. He was in Anjou after 1532, became a pastor of the village church of Unverre in 1548, and, in 1555, was named successively singer in the King's Chapel (Henry II) and *compositeur ordinaire*. However, he died in poverty at an advanced age in the Rue de la Sorbonne. There are some 286 chansons surviving from Janequin's works, many of them using the descriptive devices he loved so well in his later period, including *La Guerre, La Chasse, Les Cris de Paris,* and the *Chant des oiseaux.*

ORLANDO DI LASSO (c. 1532–1594), a prolific composer of over two thousand works representing every type of Renaissance vocal polyphony, died in Munich venerated by many of his contemporaries as the greatest of musicians. He had such a beautiful voice as a boy that he was abducted three times to sing in European courts. On the third occasion his parents allowed him to be taken to the Gonzaga court in Sicily. From there he went to Milan, where he completed his musical education in about 1550. He lived in Naples under the patronage of the Marchese della Terza, travelled to Florence, and then, in 1553, became choirmaster of the church of St. John Lateren in Rome. In 1555, he was in Antwerp, where his first musical publication appeared—a book of chansons, madrigals, and motets. The last thirty-eight years of his life, beginning in 1556, were spent in Munich, first in the service of Albrecht V, Duke of Bavaria, and later under his son, William V. His works include 53 Masses, 500 motets, 133 French chansons, 100 *Magnificats,* Italian madrigals, German lieder, and the celebrated *Penitential Psalms.*

LEONHARD LECHNER (c. 1553–1606), born in the South Tyrol (Etsch Valley), was trained as a chorister in the Bavarian court chapel under Lassus. From his birthplace comes the designation Athesinus which is usually appended to his name. Between 1575 and 1583, he served as an assistant schoolmaster at Nuremberg. While there, he began to compose motets and German songs in the madrigal style for various choral groups. His admiration for the music of Lassus is revealed in his 1568 edition of two books of Lassus's motets. Lechner was appointed *Kapellmeister* to Count Eitel Friedrich of Hohenzollern in 1584, but resigned one year later, possibly over religious differences caused by his conversion to Protestantism. After an unsuccessful application for a similar position at Dresden, he secured the post of *Kapellmeister* to the important court of Württemberg at Stuttgart, where he remained until his death. His vocal works include over 200 sacred and secular songs, 3 Masses, 8 *Magnificats,* 10 Introits, 7 penitential psalms, 1 Passion, 4 Italian madrigals, and a posthumous choral cycle, *Deutschen Sprüche von Leben und Tod* (German Sayings on Life and Death). Lechner's Passion motet based on the Gospel of St. John is considered the finest work of its kind by a sixteenth-century German composer.

CLAUDE LE JEUNE (c. 1528–1600) was prominent in Paris as a composer of chansons and metrical psalms. Few details of his life are known, except that he was born in Valenciennes and was in the service of King Henry IV of France after 1598. He was connected with the Académie de Poésie et Musique founded in 1570 by Antoine de Baïf to advance the cause of *vers mesurés à l'antique*—poetry "measured" (i.e., metered) according to the quantitative principles of classical prosody. In *Le Printemps*, Le Jeune published 39 settings of poems by Baïf, and in 33 of these, he caused the musical rhythm to correspond more or less exactly to the poetic one, so that the musical meter is a result of the irregular grouping of two values, long and short. The *musique mesurée* settings consist of *chants* (strophes) and *réchants* (refrains). In addition to such works, he wrote chansons, Italian madrigals, and Latin motets. Along with Claude Goudimel, he was one of the most important composers of psalm settings.

EDWARD ALEXANDER MACDOWELL (1861–1908) received what became the usual treatment for a young American aspiring to a career in music—he went to Europe for his education. After studying first in his native New York with Juan Buitrazo, Pablo Desvernine, and Teresa Carreño, he went to Paris (1876), where he studied at the Conservatory. Three years later, he went to Stuttgart and then to Wiesbaden, where he worked with Karl Heymann (piano) and Joachim Raff (composition). MacDowell remained in Europe for twelve years. When he returned to Boston in 1888, he was active as a composer, performer, and teacher. In 1896, he was appointed to the newly created Chair of Music at Columbia University, but he resigned in bitterness in 1904, proclaiming that the American university was not the place for serious musical study. MacDowell's vocal compositions, primarily part-songs, total 28.

GUILLAUME DE MACHAUT (c. 1300–1377) was born in Champagne, perhaps in the village of Machaut (today, the Ardennes). In 1323, he became secretary to King John of Bohemia, whom he accompanied on many trips and military campaigns. He was accorded various ecclesiastical benefices by Pope Benedict XII, the most important of which came in 1334 when he was named canon of Notre Dame in Rheims. He remained in this post until his death. The dominant composer of the fourteenth century, Machaut wrote the earliest known setting of the Ordinary of the Mass. He is unique among medieval composers in having supervised a complete edition of his own works, contained in six codices, most of which are in the Bibliothèque Nationale in Paris. His works include 19 *lais*, 23 motets, 1 *hoquetus*, 42 ballades, 21 rondeaus, and 33 virelais.

LUCA MARENZIO (1553–1599) was, together with Carlo Gesualdo, the leading composer of chromatic madrigals at the end of the Renaissance, and perhaps the most resourceful in expressiveness and technical facility. He was born in Coccaglio (near Brescia) and received his early musical training under Giovanni Contino, *maestro di cappella* at the Cathedral of Brescia. His musical career took him to Rome, Venice, Florence, and Cracow (Poland). Unusual for the time, Marenzio never held a church appointment, though he was associated with the papal court (not the Chapel) at the end of his life. In his lifetime, Marenzio published seventeen books of madrigals, totaling well over 200 items; five books of villanelle; three books of motets; a cycle of motets for the liturgical year; and a book of sacred concertos.

FELIX MENDELSSOHN (1809–1847), the son of a wealthy banker and the grandson of the celebrated philosopher Moses Mendelssohn, was raised in an environment of culture and refinement, receiving most of his education from private tutors. He made his public debut as a pianist when he was ten, and two years later began composition study with Carl Zelter, director of the Berlin Singakademie. In 1829, he played an important role in reawakening interest in the music of Bach by conducting (albeit in an abridged and edited version) the *St. Matthew Passion*, in all likelihood the first performance of the work since the death of the composer in 1750. Mendelssohn was a prolific composer of works in all genres. His choral compositions include 5 oratorios, 3 motets, 6 anthems, 8 psalms, a *Te Deum*, and 46 part-songs.

DARIUS MILHAUD (1892–1974) was born in Aix-en-Provence, the son of an almond merchant. He studied the violin as a youth and entered the Paris Conservatory in 1909, where his teachers were Charles Widor (fugue), Vincent d'Indy (composition), and Paul Dukas (orchestration). While still a student, he became associated with Erik Satie, Jean Cocteau, and Paul Claudel. When Claudel was appointed attaché at the French embassy in Brazil, Milhaud accompanied him as his secretary. Milhaud's name became known to an even larger public in 1920 as the result of a newspaper article in *Comoedia* associating him with *Les Six* (Georges Auric, Luis Durey, Arthur Honegger, Francis Poulenc, and Germaine Tailleferre). His life was disrupted in 1940, when he fled the Nazis and came to the United States as professor of composition at Mills College in California. In 1947, he returned to Paris and taught at the Conservatory. His later years were spent travelling between France and the United States, conducting, lecturing, and teaching. Milhaud was an extremely prolific composer who wrote hundreds of works, including 45 choral pieces.

CLAUDIO MONTEVERDI (1567–1643) embodies, within his music, the transition from the musical style of the Renaissance to that of the Baroque. Born in Cremona, the son of a prominent physician, he began his musical career there as a choirboy under Marc Antonio Ingegneri. At the age of twenty-three, he entered the service of Vincenzo Gonzaga, Duke of Mantua, as orchestral musician, singer, and composer, later serving as assistant conductor and *maestro di cappella* (1601). Unable to persuade his employers to increase his salary, Monteverdi resigned in 1613. One year later, he was appointed to the most coveted musical position in Italy, *maestro di cappella* at St. Mark's, Venice, where he remained for the rest of his life. His prodigious output includes operas, concerted sacred works, and 9 books of madrigals.

THOMAS MORLEY (c. 1557–1603) was a pupil of William Byrd and possibly also of Sebastian Westcote, organist of St. Paul's Cathedral. Between 1583 and 1587 he served as choirmaster of Norwich Cathedral. The following year he received the B.Mus. degree at Oxford, became organist at St. Paul's, and, in 1592, was appointed Gentleman of the Chapel Royal. Six years later, he was granted a monopoly on printing music. As a composer, Morley was especially gifted in writing madrigals, part-songs and balletts. His madrigal publications include *Canzonets to Three Voices* (1593), *Madrigals to Four Voices* (1594), *Balletts to Five Voices* (1595), and *Canzonets to Five and Six Voices* (1597). He is also remembered for his important book, A *Plaine and Easie Introduction to Practicall Musicke* (1597).

WOLFGANG AMADEUS MOZART (1756–1791) was born in Salzburg, Austria, the son of Leopold Mozart, violinist and court composer to the Archbishop of Salzburg. His early musical studies in clavier, violin, and composition were supervised by his father. In 1763, Leopold took the young Wolfgang and his gifted sister Marianne on a three-year performing tour of the principal cities of Europe. Five years later, they made another tour, this time to Italy. Between 1773 and 1781 Mozart lived in Salzburg, but spent much of the time composing and traveling, including an abortive trip to Paris in 1777. The final ten years of his life were spent in Vienna, where he composed, gave lessons, and appeared as soloist in concerts. Mozart composed a considerable amount of church music, including 4 litanies, 2 Vespers, 16 Masses, 1 Requiem Mass, 4 cantatas, canons, and a number of smaller pieces.

THEA MUSGRAVE (b. 1928), who was born in Scotland, studied at the University of Edinburgh before working with Nadia Boulanger for four years in Paris. She was the first British composer to win the Lili Boulanger prize. Her work is eclectic and reveals a fastidious musical mind. Her choral compositions include *The Phoenix and the Turtle* (1962); a dramatic work, *The Five Ages of Man* (1963); and *Rorate coeli* (1976).

JOHANNES OCKEGHEM (c. 1420–c. 1495) was a choir singer in the Cathedral of Antwerp in 1443 and joined the chapel of Duke Charles of Bourbon at Moulins from 1446 to 1448. In 1440 he studied under Dufay at Cambrai. Beginning in 1452, he served as first chapel singer and chapel master to three successive kings: Charles VII, Louis XII, and Charles VIII. He enjoyed the espect of his royal patrons, even becoming treasurer (between 1451 and 1459) of the great royal abbey of St. Martin at Tours. Josquin Des Prez and Pierre de La Rue were among his pupils. Ockeghem's compositions consist of 14 Masses, a Requiem Mass, 10 motets (including a *Deo gratis* for 36 voices), and 20 chansons.

GIOVANNI PIERLUIGI DA PALESTRINA (1525–1594) is considered the master of the Roman school of sacred polyphony. As a youth, he was a choirboy at the Basilica of Santa Maria Maggiore in Rome. In 1544, he became organist and choirmaster of the cathedral of his native town of Palestrina. When, in 1551, the Bishop of Palestrina became Pope Julius II, he invited the young composer to go to Rome as master of the Julian Chapel. Following Palestrina's dedication of his first book of Masses to Julius, the Pope recommended him for a position among the singers of the Sistine Chapel, even though Palestrina was not a priest and was also married with children (both of which were violations of the regulations). He was removed from the Sistine Chapel by Pope Paul IV on July 30, 1555. Shortly thereafter he became chapel master of St. John Lateran. Although offered positions in other cities of Italy and Europe, Palestrina spent the remainder of his life in Rome. Palestrina's works include 92 Masses, 600 motets, psalms, hymns, and a number of secular madrigals.

KRZYSZTOF PENDERECKI (b. 1933) has composed some of the most important choral music of the twentieth century. Born a Catholic in Poland, he was an adolescent during the Stalin and Gomulka periods. As a child, he took violin lessons in his home town of Debiça (near Cracow). He studied composition with Artur Malawski and Stanisław Wiechowicz at the Music Academy in Cracow, from which he received a diploma in 1958. One year later, he became an instructor at the Academy. He lectured on composition at the Volkwang Hochschule für Musik in Essen (1966–1968) and taught at the Yale School of Music in alternate years beginning in 1974. Penderecki's choral music is strong in social commentary. Of his 11 choral works, *The Psalms of David* (1958), *Stabat Mater* (1963), *St. Luke Passion* (1966), *Dies irae* (1966–67), *Utrenia* (1970), and *Magnificat* (1973–74) are the best known in this country.

VINCENT PERSICHETTI (b. 1915) is a native of Philadelphia, where he began his musical studies at an early age. At fifteen, he was appointed organist at St. Mark's Church. He continued his studies at the Combs Music College, was graduated in 1936, and later enrolled at the Curtis Institute for courses in conducting with Fritz Reiner. In 1939, he received a scholarship to the Philadelphia Conservatory, where he studied piano with Olga Samarof and composition with Paul Nordoff. That same year, he was named chairman of the composition department at Combs College, and later held the same position at the Philadelphia Conservatory. In 1947, he joined the faculty at the Juilliard School of Music. Among the numerous awards which he has received are the Koussevitzky Foundation Prize (1955), a Guggenheim Foundation scholarship (1958–1959), the Award of the Lincoln Center for the Performing Arts (1962), and the National Foundation for the Arts and Humanities Award (1966). Persichetti's choral works number over 30, including a Mass, *Magnificat*, *Stabat Mater*, three sets of choruses on poems by e. e. cummings, and other secular pieces.

GOFFREDO PETRASSI (b. 1904) began to study composition at the age of twenty-one. He received his early musical training as a chorister in Rome in the ancient school of San Salvatore in Lauro. While working as a clerk in a music store, he started taking lessons at the Santa Cecilia Conservatory. In 1939, he was appointed to the faculty of the Conservatory, where he is still active. Since 1947, he has served on various government commissions and in several private music organizations. He became known to American audiences in the course of a tour of this country in 1955–1956. His early influences were Alfredo Casella and Paul Hindemith; later he showed an interest in serial procedures. Petrassi has composed about 15 choral works, almost equally divided between sacred and secular.

DANIEL PINKHAM (b. 1923), a native of Lynn, Massachusetts, studied organ and harmony at the Phillips Academy and later attended Harvard University. His initial training in composition was with Walter Piston, followed by studies with Aaron Copland. His keyboard training included studies with E. Power Biggs (organ), Putnam Aldrich (harpsichord), and Wanda Landowska (harpsichord). He also worked at Tanglewood, where his teachers were Arthur Honegger, Samuel Barber, and Nadia Boulanger. He was awarded a Fulbright scholarship in 1950 and a Ford Foundation grant in 1962. He is presently a member of the faculty of the New England Conservatory of Music (since 1959), musical director of the King's Chapel in Boston (since 1958), a member of the Council of Arts and Humanities of Massachusetts, and of the United States Academy of Arts and Sciences. Pinkham's choral works include 3 cantatas, a Requiem, a *Stabat Mater*, a Passion, and about fifteen smaller works.

MICHAEL PRAETORIUS (1571–1621), the son of a Lutheran minister, attended the Latin school at Torgau, studied organ in Frankfurt, and then came into the service of the Duke of Braunschweig. He succeeded Thomas Mancinus as *Kapellmeister* in Wolfenbüttel in 1612 and remained there until his death nine years later. In spite of a prolific output, mostly written for the Lutheran service, he is best known for his theoretical writings. Besides the religious music in the nine volumes of the *Musae Sioniae* (1605–1610), which includes

⊥,244 vocal pieces by himself and others, there are numerous collections containing almost every type of sacred and secular music. His *Syntagma musicum* (3 volumes, 1615–1619) is an invaluable survey of performance practice up to and including his own time.

HENRY PURCELL (c. 1659–1695) began his musical education as a chorister in the Chapel Royal, where his teachers were Henry Cooke and Pelham Humfrey. In 1679, he succeeded his teacher, Henry Blow, as organist of Westminster Abbey. Three years later, he was appointed organist of the Chapel Royal and keeper of the instruments of Charles II. A prolific composer, Purcell wrote over 500 works, including over 70 anthems, 3 services, 9 hymns, 5 psalms, and 16 odes. One of the most original and gifted composers of his time, he was equally successful in operas, music for plays, cantatas, service music, chamber music, and keyboard works.

JEAN-PHILIPPE RAMEAU (1683–1764) was born in the city of Dijon, the son of a church organist. On the advice of his father, he went to study in Italy in 1701, but returned in one year to take a position as assistant organist and conductor at Avignon. After a short period there, he moved to the Cathedral of Clermont-Ferrand, where he composed church cantatas and completed his famous *Traité de l'harmonie* (1722). In 1723, he moved permanently to Paris, where he pursued his theoretical inquiries and was active as a composer of operas. His choral works include 4 motets and 8 cantatas.

MAX REGER (1873–1916) was born in Bavaria, the son of a teacher. Following conservatory studies in Wiesbaden with Hugo Riemann and a short term of military service, Reger went to Munich, where he held two minor posts: teacher at the Akademie der Tonkunst and conductor of the Porges Choral Society. In 1907, he was appointed musical director of the University of Leipzig and teacher of composition at the Leipzig Conservatory. He gave up the university post, but maintained the conservatory position until his death in 1916. During the Leipzig period, he wrote a number of choral works. In 1911, Reger was invited by the Duke of Meiningen to become director of his court orchestra. Upon the death of the Duke two years later, Reger retired to Jena to devote himself entirely to composition. Although known primarily for his organ and instrumental music, Reger wrote a considerable amount of choral music, including 3 motets, 4 cantatas, 24 choral arrangements, 8 sacred songs, and numerous folk-song settings.

GIOACCHINO ANTONIO ROSSINI (1792–1868) was born in Pesaro, the son of a government meat inspector who was also the town trumpeter. The young Rossini showed exceptional musical gifts by the time he was eight, and by fourteen had composed an opera. He entered the Liceo Musicale in Bologna in 1807, where he studied cello and piano and received instruction in composition. It was here that Rossini made an intensive study of the work of Haydn and Mozart, and developed an enthusiasm for the operas of Cimarosa. In 1810, his first opera was performed in Venice. Over the next thirteen years, he wrote more than thirty operas. His travels brought him to Milan, Naples, Rome, Lisbon, and Vienna. In 1824, he was appointed director of the Théâtre Italien in Paris. At the age of thirty-seven he gave up writing for the theater. He returned to Italy in 1836, livivng in Bologna and then Florence. In the 1850s he resettled in Paris, where he remained until his death in 1868. Rossini wrote some 42 choral works, among which the *Stabat Mater* and the *Petite Messe solennelle* are most famous.

ARNOLD SCHOENBERG (1874–1951) was born in Vienna, the son of a prosperous shopkeeper. When he was twenty, he took some counterpoint lessons from his future borther-in-law, the Polish conductor and composer Alexander von Zemlinsky, but he was virtually self-taught. In about 1900, Schoenberg was engaged to conduct various amateur choral groups in the Vienna suburbs, a circumstance which increased his interest in vocal music. The two-year period between 1901 and 1903 was spent in Berlin, where he composed and conducted cabaret music. With the support of Richard Strauss, he was awarded the Liszt Prize of the Allgemeiner Deutscher Musikverein. He returned to Vienna in 1903, where he worked for nine years as conductor and teacher. It was during this period that he became acquainted with Gustave Mahler and that Alban Berg and Anton Webern became his pupils. In 1925, he was appointed professor of composition at the Academy of Arts in Berlin. He left Germany when the Nazis came to power, first holding minor teaching posts in New York and Boston, and finally settling in Los Angeles as a professor at the University of California at Los Angeles. In addition to his approximately 25 choral works, Schoenberg wrote a number of books, including the *Hamonielehre* (1911), *Models for Beginners in Composition* (1942), *Twelve-Tone System of Composition* (1921), *Theory of Harmony* (1947), and *Style and Idea* (1950).

FRANZ SCHUBERT (1797–1828) was born in Liechtenthal, a suburb of Vienna. He had a fine soprano voice and was a choirboy at St. Stephen's Cathedral, the Imperial Court Chapel, and its seminary, Konvikt. He not only sang in the choir of the Court Chapel, but played violin and viola in the student orchestra as well. In 1813, after his voice changed, he left the Konvikt and entered the teacher-training institution of St. Anna. For three years, he taught in an elementary school, until his friend, Franz von Schober, made it possible for him to give up teaching and devote himself to composing. Schober shared his modest residence with Schubert and helped support him financially. Except for two summers during which he worked for the Esterházy family in Hungary, Schubert never had a regular position. He spent the remainder of his short life in Vienna, aided by his friends. A prolific composer, he wrote more than 1,200 works, including 6 Masses, a German Mass, an oratorio (*Lazarus*), 2 settings of *Tantum ergo*, 2 of *Stabat Mater*, several of *Salve Regina*, and a considerable number of shorter works for male chorus.

ROBERT SCHUMANN (1810–1856) was born in Zwickau, a town in Saxony about 40 miles from Leipzig. After law studies in Heidelberg, he returned to Leipzig in 1830 to study piano with Friedrich Wieck, who later became his father-in-law. Because of an injury to his right hand, he abandoned plans for a concert career and turned his creative energies to composing and literary pursuits. He became not only one of the primary composers of the Romantic movement but also its leading spokesman, by virtue of the many reviews and polemical articles he wrote for the *Neue Zeitschrift für Musik*. For a short time he served on the faculty of the Leipzig Conservatory, but he was unsuccessful as a teacher. After living in Dresden for the period 1844–1850, he accepted an invitation to become municipal music director of the Rhine town of Düsseldorf. But he was unsuited to this position, partly because his mental instability was becoming increasingly pronounced. In 1853, he was committed to a private mental asylum in Endenrich (close to Bonn), where he remained for the rest of his life. His choral compositions include 18 works with orchestra, a motet, 34 part-songs for mixed voices, 25 part-songs for men's voices, 12 part-songs for women's voices, and 31 vocal quartets with piano.

HEINRICH SCHÜTZ (1585–1672) was born in Köstritz near Gera in Thuringia, the son of a lawyer. He was, along with Hassler and Praetorius, a major figure in the transplanting of the Italian Baroque style (and particularly the Venetian polychoral style) to German soil. Schütz began his musical career as a choirboy in the court of Landgrave Moritz of Hessen. Under the Landgrave's patronage, he not only received his first musical training, but in 1609, he was sent to Venice to study with Giovanni Gabrieli. After Gabrieli's death, Schütz returned to Kassel, where he became court organist, a post which he relinquished four years later to become *Kapellmeister* at the Saxon court of Dresden. Beginning in 1629, he made repeated trips to Italy to buy instruments for the Dresden orchestra and to study the instrumental and dramatic music of Claudio Monteverdi. During the Thirty Years' War (1618–1648), Schütz was obliged to take employment elsewhere, working for a period in Hamburg, and, from the mid-1630s, serving at the Danish Royal Court in Copenhagen. When the war ended, he returned to his post at Dresden. His output includes motets in both the old imitative style (*Cantiones sacrae*, 1624) and the new polychoral

Venetian style (*Psalmen Davids*, 1619), madrigals (*Il primo libro de madrigali*, 1611), sacred works in the few- and multi-voice concertato style (*Symphoniae sacrae*, 1629, 1647, 1650; *Kleine geistliche Konzerte*, 1636, 1639), psalm settings (*Becker Psalter*, 1628) and oratorio-like works (*Historia der . . . Gebert Gottes*).

CLAUDIN DE SERMISY (c. 1490–1562) spent much of his professional life in the service of the kings of France. He was appointed *chantre-clerc* in the Royal Chapel of Louis XII in 1508, becoming chapel master under Francis I, a post he shared with Louis Hérault. When Francis I went to Italy in 1515, Sermisy accompanied him. He was also one of the musicians who entertained when Francis I and Henry VIII met at the Field of the Cloth of Gold in 1520. He composed some 200 chansons, 70 motets, 13 Masses, and 1 *Magnificat*, which were published in various collections in France, Italy, and the Netherlands. Many of his chansons were arranged for lute and keyboard and adapted to sacred texts, giving evidence of their immense popularity.

HALE SMITH (b. 1925) is a native of Cleveland, Ohio, where he received his early musical training. After military service he enrolled in the Cleveland Institute of Music and completed the B.Mus. (1950) and M.Mus. (1952) degrees there with a major in composition. A composer for all media, he has had works performed by the New Haven Symphony, Dallas Symphony, New York Philharmonic, Symphony of the New World, Springfield Symphony, Atlanta Symphony, and Richmond Symphony. He is presently a member of the music faculty of the University of Connecticut. His choral works include a cantata *Comes Tomorrow, In Memoriam—Beryl Rubinstein, I'm Coming Home* (with piano or jazz section), *Two Kids*, and *Tucson l'ouvert*.

IGOR STRAVINSKY (1882–1971) was born into a privileged family in prerevolutionary Russia. His father was a famous bass singer at the Imperial Opera and his mother, an excellent pianist. As a young man, Stravinsky studied law, but Nicolas Rimsky-Korsakov influenced him to turn to music. Stravinsky's association with the impressario Sergei Diaghilev brought him to Paris in 1909. Between 1910 and 1914, he lived in Switzerland and, during this time, composed for Diaghilev those ballets which first brought him fame (*The Firebird, Petrushka*, and *The Rite of Spring*). In Switzerland, Stravinsky became acquainted with the conductor Ernest Ansermet, who took a great interest in the young composer's work. Stravinsky never returned to Russia, living first in Paris between 1920 and 1940 and subsequently in the United States, where he first settled in California, later moving to New York. He was for most of his life the best representative of the movement known as Neoclassicism, though after 1950 he came increasingly under the influence of serial music, particularly that of Anton Webern. Stravinsky composed 15 works for chorus, of which *Symphony of Psalms, Mass, The Dove Descending Breaks the Air, Cantata, Canticum sacrum,* and *Les Noces* are best known.

JAN PIETERSZOON SWEELINCK (1562–1621), the last great Flemish composer, spent virtually all of his life in Amsterdam, where his father was organist at the Oude Kerk. Young Sweelinck inherited his father's post in 1573 and remained in it for 48 years; his own son succeeded him in 1621. Sweelinck, a prolific composer, was highly respected as a performer and teacher. His works include 153 *Psalms of David* set to the French translation of Clément Marot and Théodore de Bèze, 37 *Cantiones sacrae* with figured-bass accompaniment, 3 *Epithalamia* (wedding pieces) to Latin texts, 22 French chansons, 4 Italian madrigals, and 7 canons to Latin words.

THOMAS TALLIS (c. 1505–1585) began his career at Waltham Abbey in Essex and was organist there at the time of the dissolution of the monasteries in 1540. From 1540 to 1542 he was organist at Canterbury and, in 1542, was appointed Gentleman of the Chapel Royal, a post he held until his death. He shared the position of organist at the Chapel Royal with William Byrd from 1572 on. In 1575, he and Byrd were granted a twenty-year monopoly on printing music. In the same year, Byrd and Tallis published jointly the *Cantiones sacrae,* a collection of 34 Latin motets (each wrote 17). Among his surviving works are 2 Masses, 2 settings of the *Magnificat,* 2 of *Lamentations,* 52 motets, 18 English anthems, and 3 sets of psalms.

LOUISE TALMA (b. 1906) is one of the fortunate group of Americans who studied with Nadia Boulanger. Although born in France, she received her early musical training in New York at the Institute of Musical Art (now the Juilliard School of Music), then earned degrees at New York University (B.Mus., 1931) and Columbia University (M.A., 1933). In 1926, she went to study in France at the Fontainebleau School of Music and worked with Isidore Philipp (piano) and Nadia Boulanger (harmony, counterpoint, fugue, composition, organ). Miss Talma was the first woman composer elected to the American Academy and Institute of Arts and Letters and the first woman to be awarded the Sibelius Medal in London. Her choral works include *Let's Touch the Sky* (1955), *La Corona* (1955), and *A Time to Remember* (1966).

GEORG PHILIPP TELEMANN (1681–1767), a most prolific composer, was born in Magdelburg and, like his contemporary and close friend Handel, first intended to pursue a career in law. While a student at the University of Leipzig, he founded an amateur student musical group (the Collegium Musicum) and played the organ at the Neue Kirche, so that gradually his attention turned entirely to music. He had no formal training in this subject, but by diligence and practice he developed his native abilities. His early appointments in-cluded that of *Kapellmeister* to the Polish Prince Promnitz at Sorau (1704), to Duke Johann Wilhelm of Sachsen-Eisenach (1708), and to the Prince of Bayreuth (1712–1721). In 1721, he took over the important post of director of music at the Johanneum in Hamburg, with the responsibility for the music of the five main churches in the city. Here he remained until his death. One of his duties in Hamburg was to compose a Passion every year during Holy Week. His works include 44 Passions, 40 operas, 12 complete sets of services for the church year, 32 Services of Installation for Hamburg clergy, 20 ordina-tion and anniversary services, 12 funeral and 14 wedding services.

MICHAEL TIPPETT (b. 1905) was educated at Stanford Grammar School in Lincolnshire and at the Royal College of Music, where he studied composition with Charles Wood and R. O. Morris, and conducting under Sir Adrian Boult and Sir Malcolm Sargent. Tippett is sensitive to social issues, and this is re-flected in his music. In World War II, he was a conscientious objector and was imprisoned for his refusal to serve. A *Child of Our Time* (1941), which in-corporates Negro spiritual as chorales, was an outgrowth of this experience. Tippett's other choral compositions include A *Song of Liberty*, *The Weeping Babe*, *Plebs Angelica*, *Vision of St. Augustine*, and 2 part-songs.

RALPH VAUGHAN WILLIAMS (1872–1958) studied piano, violin, and harmony as a child but was never a professional performer. After completing his public-school education at Charterhouse, he entered the Royal College of Music and studied composition with Sir Hubert Parry. He then took the B.Mus. and B.A. degrees from Trinity College, Cambridge, and later (1901) the D.Mus. de-gree from that same institution. In 1896, he went to Berlin to study with Max Bruch. Upon returning to England, Vaughan Williams joined the English Folk-Song Society. Shortly after World War I, he was appointed professor of composition at the Royal College of Music, and except for a few months of study with Maurice Ravel in Paris and three trips to the United States (1923, 1932, 1956), he remained in England for the remainder of his life. Vaughan Williams was a prolific composer of choral music. His works for this medium include a Mass, 3 motets, 3 services, a *Te Deum*, 32 compositions with orchestra, 41 part-songs, and a large group of smaller sacred pieces.

GIUSEPPE VERDI (1813–1901) was born at Le Roncole, a small village near Bus-seto in the Duchy of Parma. His musical education was guided by the local church organist, who instructed him in music theory and taught him to play the organ. At the age of eleven Verdi became organist at Le Roncole and Busseto. He demonstrated sufficient ability to convince a local merchant, An-tonio Barezzi, to support him for one year at the Milan Conservatory. However, this plan was frustrated when the Conservatory refused to accept him. Undaunted, Verdi took private lessons under Vincenzo Lavigna. Working tirelessly during these three years in Milan, he prepared himself in the basics of musical composition. Verdi made his debut as an opera composer at La Scala in 1839 with *Oberto* and was immediately a success. Further successes brought him European recognition and commissions from Venice, Rome, London, Paris, and St. Petersburg. Most of his energies were devoted to opera composition. Consequently, Verdi wrote few works in other forms. After the death of a friend, the great Romantic writer Alessandro Manzoni, Verdi composed his *Requiem* (1874). Hs last compositions were the *Four Sacred Pieces* (1898).

TOMÁS LUIS DE VICTORIA (1548–1611), along with Cristóbal de Morales, is considered the leading composer of the Spanish Renaissance. There are no details available concerning his early life in Avila, but he was probably a choirboy at the cathedral. In 1565, he went to Rome and entered the Collegium Germanicum to prepare for the priesthood. Since he also studied at the Roman Seminary where Palestrina was *maestro di cappella*, it is likely that he studied with that composer. Four years later, he became chapel master and organist at the church of Santa Maria di Montserrato and, in 1571, replaced Palestrina at the Roman Seminary. After a period of 20 years in Rome, Victoria returned to Spain and settled in Madrid in the service of the widowed Empress Marie, daughter of Charles V. Among his surviving works, which are all sacred, there are 20 Masses, 45 motets, 18 *Magnificats*, an Office for the Dean, an Office for the Sunday before Easter, and a number of hymns, litanies, psalms, and other liturgical works.

ANTONIO VIVALDI (c. 1675–1741) was a celebrated violinist and composer. Born in Venice, the son of a violinist at St. Mark's Cathedral, he received his early musical training from his father and completed his musical studies with Giovanni Legrenzi. He studied for the priesthood and received Holy Orders in 1703, a year before he was appointed to the faculty of the Conservatorio dell' Ospedale della Pietà. He was promoted to *maestro de' concerti* in 1716, a position he held until 1740. In later life, Vivaldi travelled extensively, visiting Germany, the Netherlands, and possibly France. He died, destitute, in Vienna. While known primarily for his instrumental compositions, he composed a variety of choral works, including 2 oratorios, a Gloria, a *Magnificat*, 24 secular cantatas, 14 Vespers, 2 motets, a Kyrie for 8 voices, 2 settings of *Salve Regina*, and other sacred works.

JOHANN WALTHER (1496–1570) was a friend of Martin Luther and one of the first musicians to compose for the Lutheran Church. In 1517, he entered the service of the Elector Friedrich the Wise of Saxony as a bass singer. On the death of the Elector (1525), he was appointed cantor of the Latin School in Torgau and director of the Stadtkantorei. In 1548, the new Elector of Saxony brought him to Dresden as *Kapellmeister* of the court chapel, where he remained until 1554, when he retired to Torgau on a pension. Walther issued his *Geystliche gesangk Buchleyn* (Little Book of Sacred Songs) in 1524, a publication which contained 38 polyphonic sacred songs to German texts (including *Ein' feste Burg ist unser Gott*) and 5 Latin motets. His *Passion on the Gospel of St. Matthew* (c. 1525) is the earliest example of a work of this type in German.

ANTON WEBERN (1883–1945) was one of the most important of the early serialists. He was born in Vienna and studied musicology at the university there under Guido Adler, writing a doctoral dissertation on the music of Henricus Isaac. He studied with Arnold Schoenberg from 1904 to 1908. Thereafter, he was active as an opera conductor in Vienna, Teplitz, Danzig, Stettin, and after 1922, Prague. After 1922, he participated in Schoenberg's Verein für musikalische Privataufführungen (Society for Private Music Performances), an organization dedicated to the fostering of modern music, from whose performances the critics were barred. Webern adopted Schoenberg's dodecaphonic method, and all of his later works are serial. He was accidentally shot by an American soldier during a curfew after World War II. His choral works include *Entflieht aus leichten Kähnen*, 2 cantatas, and 2 songs from Goethe's *Chinesisch-deutsche Jahres- und Tageszeiten*.

THOMAS WEELKES (c. 1575–1623), a friend of Thomas Morley, was the most daring of the English madrigal composers. His chromatic harmonies as well as his emotional style were well in advance of anything being written in England at the end of the sixteenth century. His first book of madrigals, published in 1597 when he was organist of Winchester College and still in his early twenties, reveals remarkable maturity of style. In 1602, he took the B.Mus. degree at Oxford and, shortly thereafter, was appointed organist at Chichester Cathedral, for which he wrote a considerable amount of church music. His vocal works include 10 services, 45 anthems, 69 madrigals and balletts, and 26 *Ayres or Phantasticke Spirites* (Tavern Songs).

SAMUEL SEBASTIAN WESLEY (1810–1876), the son of Samuel and nephew of Charles, both important composers, was a choirboy in the Chapel Royal. At the age of sixteen, he began his career as an organist in London churches. Appointments followed at Hereford Cathedral (1832), Exeter Cathedral (1835), Leeds Parish Church (1842), Winchester Cathedral (1849), and Gloucester (1865). In 1839, he received the degrees of B.Mus. and D.Mus. at Oxford. Wesley's fame as a composer rests primarily on the volume of twelve anthems, published in 1853. Among his works are 26 anthems, 5 services, psalms, glees, and related other short compositions.

JOHN WILBYE (1574–1638) was perhaps the finest of the English madrigal composers. He was born in Norfolk and, as a young man, entered the service of the Kytson family at Hengrave Hall. Following the receipt of a land grant in 1613, he seems to have concentrated more on his property than on composing music. Among the English madrigal composers, Wilbye came closest to an understanding of the Italian techniques. He employed texts that were of an obviously higher literary quality than those set by his predecessors. His first book of 30 madrigals appeared in 1598, the second of 34 in 1609. One of his madrigals, *The Lady Oriana*, appeared in Thomas Morley's *The Triumphs of Oriana*; two motets were published in William Leighton's *Teares and Lamentacions* (1614).

Appendix B: Commentary on
the Individual Works

1. Anonymous, *Magnificat anima mea*

The *Magnificat* (or Canticle of the Blessed Virgin) was sung in the Latin liturgy of the Roman Catholic Church at the Office of Vespers. It consists of twelve verses (including the Doxology, verses 11 and 12) sung to a standard *tonus* or recitation formula. The *Magnificat* tones are similar to the psalm tones in that the larger portion of the text is sung on one note, the *tenor,* which is embellished with inflections at the beginning (called the *initium*), the middle (the *mediatio*), and the end (the *terminatio*). There is a *Magnificat* formula for each of the eight modes and each tone is provided with a number of different terminations (called *differentiae*) to effect a smooth transition between the tone and the beginning of the antiphon with which it is sung. The present example is in the first tone with termination on F.

2. Anonymous, *Hodie Christus natus est*

The most common type of antiphon is that used in connection with the singing of a psalm or canticle. Such antiphons are usually in neumatic style, with those for the *Magnificat* often somewhat more elaborate than those for the psalms. This antiphon for Second Vespers at the Feast of the Nativity of Our Lord is an excellent example of the neumatic style—each syllable of text is set either to one note or to one *neume* (a single notational symbol representing a composite of from two to five pitches).

3. Anonymous, *Haec dies, quam fecit Dominus*

The second item of the Proper of the Mass, the Gradual, is sung immediately after the first Lesson. It is, therefore, one of the few musical parts of the Mass which does not accompany an action. Perhaps for this reason it early became (together with the Alleluia) a musical showpiece, characterized by a highly ornate, melismatic style. Graduals (like Responsories, which they resemble) are in two parts: the choral respond (begun by the soloist) and the solo verse (concluded by the choir). Unlike the verses of the Responsories (which are normally sung to standard tones), the verses of the Graduals have independent melodies, which are closely related one to the other within a given mode by employing certain standard phrases. This Gradual for Easter Sunday is an example of the highly melismatic quality of this type of chant, with some syllables of the text decorated with more than thirty notes. *Haec dies* is also noteworthy in that it belongs to an ancient group of closely related pieces usually called the Gradual-type *Justus ut palma*, all of which are assigned to the second mode on D but end on the alternate final A.

4. Guillaume de Machaut, Kyrie from *La Messe de Nostre Dame*
The Machaut Mass is famous as the first complete setting of the items of the Ordinary (including the *Ite missa est*) known to be by one composer. (There are other fourteenth-century Ordinary settings which are anonymous.) Two styles are evident in this work, a more melismatic one superficially resembling the motet (used in the Kyrie, Sanctus, Agnus Dei, and *Ite missa est*), and a syllabic one reminiscent of the thirteenth-century conductus. The former type sets a cantus firmus, the latter does not. Unlike the Masses of the fifteenth century and after, which are usually based on cantus firmi not part of the Mass liturgy, the Machaut Mass uses the appropriate Gregorian melodies for the Kyrie, Sanctus, Agnus, and *Ite missa est*. These sections are also isorhythmic, consistently so in the tenor voice, but in the other voices as well. In the Kyrie, the isorhythmic structure of the tenor (which is based on the Kyrie *Cunctipotens Genitor*) is as follows: Kyrie I (4 measures × 7), Christe (7 measures × 3), Kyrie II (8 measures × 2), Kyrie III (7 measures × 4). This edition is based on the manuscript Paris, Bibl. Nat., fr. 1584, with several missing notes supplied from other sources.

5. Guillaume Dufay, Gloria from *Missa Se la face ay pale*
This movement illustrates several techniques which became important later in the Renaissance. First, it is part of a cantus firmus Mass, in which a pre-existent melody not part of the Ordinary appears, usually in the tenor voice, in each movement of the work (as opposed to the earlier practice in which cantus firmi were drawn from the appropriate parts of the Ordinary; see no. 4). Second, the cantus firmus is non-Gregorian; the use of secular melodies became quite common in the late fifteenth and in the sixteenth century. (It has been suggested that this Mass was written for the wedding of Carlotta of Savoy to the future Louis XI of France, which took place on March 9, 1451. If this be true, then this Mass represents a continuation of the practice, formerly observed by Dufay in his isorhythmic motets, of composing works for a particular occasion based on a symbolic cantus firmus.) Third, the cantus firmus is

set out in each movement in different proportional relationships, these relationships specified by a Latin canon at the beginning of each movement. In the Gloria, the tenor melody is repeated three times, first in tripled values, then in doubled ones, lastly in the original ones. Finally, the fact that in this work Dufay borrows the cantus firmus from another polyphonic composition (the tenor of his own ballade *Se la face ay pale*) is an anticipation of the many Masses to be constructed on *res factae* in the later Renaissance.

6. Johannes Ockeghem, Credo from *Missa Mi-Mi*

This work typifies Ockeghem's contrapuntal style by its low range (here transposed), long-breathed melodic lines, and nonrepetitive structure. Unlike Josquin and others in the next generation (see no. 7), Ockeghem does not make extensive use of imitation, relying instead on a rich texture of four or more independent melodic lines. However, this work is atypical, since it uses neither a cantus firmus nor a specific technical procedure as a means of unification. The title of this Mass derives from the motive heard at the beginning of each section in the bass part (E–A), which, in the untransposed version, would be *mi* in the natural hexachord on C and the soft hexachord on F.

7. Josquin Des Prez, *Missa Pange lingua*

This work exemplifies the so-called paraphrase procedure, in which an underlying cantus firmus permeates the entire structure, rather than being confined to the tenor, as in earlier compositions. Josquin's procedure here, using the Gregorian hymn *Pange lingua gloriosa*, is to break the chant melody into thematic fragments, vary them in a subtle manner, and then elaborate them in imitative fashion equally in all four parts. This style is noteworthy for its use of various combinations of two and three parts to alternate with the four-part tutti.

8. Giovanni Pierluigi da Palestrina, Sanctus and Benedictus from *Missa Papae Marcelli*

The *Missa Papae Marcelli* was apparently written in 1562 to commemorate the passing of Palestrina's patron Cardinal Marcello Cervini, who reigned as Pope Marcellus for three weeks in 1555 (succeeding Julius II). This work illustrates several important aspects of Palestrina's style, which, especially in the 104 Masses, represents the final stage in the development of Renaissance counterpoint begun by Ockeghem and Obrecht. These aspects include: 1) an expansion in the number of parts, so that works written in five and six voices become common around the middle of the sixteenth century; 2) a careful control of dissonance, with all nonharmonic tones prepared as suspensions, anticipations, passing tones, etc.; 3) a preponderantly diatonic, triadic tonal style calling for a minimum of *musica ficta*; and 4) the use of pervading imitation, in which a melodic motive is associated with a phrase of text and appears successively in most or all of the voices. Such passages often alternate with clearly chordal sections. Although the story disseminated by Palestrina's nineteenth-century biographer Giuseppe Baini that Palestrina's *Missa Papae Marcelli* saved elaborate church music from eradication by the Council of Trent has long been discredited, the work does reflect, in its restraint and careful text declamation, the Counter-Reformation attitude toward sacred music.

9. William Byrd, Agnus Dei from *Mass for Four Voices*
Byrd, a Catholic working in Protestant England, composed three Masses and other liturgical music for the Roman Catholic Church. The first of the Masses is for three voices, the second for four, and the third for five. They are all conservative in style and all use the head-motive device. The Mass for three voices includes considerable homophonic writing, but the other two are skillfully contrapuntal. The Agnus Dei from the four-voice Mass begins with a duet section, expands to a trio, and concludes with a tutti, thereby building dramatic tension. The composer makes greater use of chromaticism than does Palestrina. Moreover, his works exhibit the asymmetrical rhythms typical of the English tradition of choral music (see, for example, mm. 15–16 in the bass part).

10. John Dunstable, *Quam pulcra es*
The early Renaissance style, which emphasized harmonic euphony, gracefully proportioned melody, and careful text declamation, first appeared in England in the early fifteenth century in the works of a group of composers of whom the theorist Tinctoris said, "Dunstable stood forth as chief." *Quam pulcra es*, a motet based on the processional antiphon for the Blessed Virgin, is typical of the many functional liturgical pieces (antiphons, hymns, sequences) which exhibit this new style: the upper voice carries the melody, all voices sing the same text in a simple conductus style, and there is considerable use of parallel first-inversion triads (English-discant style).

11. Guillaume Dufay, *Ave Regina coelorum* (*a 3*)
This motet (not to be confused with Dufay's better known setting of the same text in four parts) is, like the previous example, a piece of functional liturgical music (even though there is no plainsong cantus firmus) in which text comprehensibility, melodiousness, and harmonic euphony are emphasized. It exhibits the so-called fauxbourdon style, which is characterized by perfect intervals at the beginnings and ends of phrases and first-inversion triads, for the most part, in between.

12. Josquin Des Prez, *Ave Maria, gratia plena*
This motet represents a compositional technique practiced by Josquin in which a Gregorian melody, figure, or motive is announced in one voice and then

imitated by the other voices in succession. In this so-called point-of-imitation style, the intervals, contour, and rhythmic shape of the original melody may be duplicated exactly or with slight modification in any number of different ways. At times a phrase may occur in one part in longer notes, but in most cases no single voice prevails over another. The original material is usually treated with rhythmic freedom. Each phrase of the text is treated separately, in imitation, in a homophonic style, or in a mixture of the two. Sometimes, as is common in Josquin's music, variety is achieved through reduced texture and paired voices in imitation (see the opening measures). Particularly significant words of the text are set in chordal style (often called *familiar style*), and this serves to add further variety. The motet represents the classical phase of the Renaissance motet in its pliant lyricism, flexible imitative technique, and careful attention to details of form and text declamation.

13. Orlando di Lasso, *In hora ultima*

The motets of Lasso are among the finest examples of sixteenth-century works in this genre. Whereas the strict and invariable text of the Mass seemed not to inspire him, the motet, with its virtually unlimited range of texts on many subjects, led him to his finest efforts. *In hora ultima* was perhaps intended as a satire on the style of the serious motet through the use of many exaggerated madrigalesque devices. The texture does not consist of a free-flowing unfolding of imitative sections, but rather a series of words, each set to its own distinctive (primarily rhythmic) motive. The most extreme examples of descriptiveness occur on such words as *tuba* ("trumpet") and *saltus* ("jump"). This motet illustrates the cosmopolitan attitude and variety of compositional technique more characteristic of Lasso's music than of Palestrina's.

14. Giovanni Pierluigi da Palestrina, *Ave Maria, gratia plena*

As with the Masses, Palestrina's motet style is characterized by the systematic use of imitation, careful text declamation, and restrained harmonic style. In contrast to the rich effect typical of Lasso's works, Palestrina's motets take on a mystical character. In place of thematic unity, each portion of the text evokes a symbolic or pictorial musical idea. The cantus firmus, which is the melody of the Vespers antiphon *Ave Maria* for the Feast of the Annunciation, is heard mainly in the tenor voice.

15. Tomás Luis de Victoria, *O quam gloriosum*

This motet is an example drawn from the large corpus of church music produced in seventeenth-century Spain. In addition to Victoria, several composers attained international stature, such as Cristóbal de Morales and Francisco Guerrero. Victoria's style shares much with Palestrina, in that the use of pervading imitation and the careful control of dissonance characterize his motets.

However, Victoria's are often more interesting because of his frequent, but judicious, use of text painting. An example may be found in the present work, where he sets the word gaudent ("rejoice") to increasing rhythmic activity and rising scale patterns in the lower voices. This work is an excellent example of the composer's restrained style.

16. Giovanni Gabrieli, O magnum mysterium

O magnum mysterium, published by Gabrieli in his *Concerti* of 1587, utilizes, for the first time, the technique of *cori spezzati* (divided choirs). It differs from the motets written by the composers of the so-called Roman school in at least two important ways: it is essentially homophonic and nonimitative, and dramatic contrast plays an important part in its style. (In the emerging Baroque period, this was designated as *stile concertato*.) The two choirs differ in range, the first one being higher. The work falls into four large sections; the final one begins (characteristically for Gabrieli) in triple meter. The influence of the architecture of St. Mark's Cathedral in Venice on the development of polychoral music has been exaggerated, for there were many other cities in which such music could be heard. But because of Gabrieli's particularly opulent style, the polychoral manner has been most closely identified with him and the church in which he worked. In Germany, such music was written by Michael Praetorius, Hans Leo Hassler, and Heinrich Schütz, among others.

17. Thomas Tallis, O nata lux de lumine

Unlike the majority of Tallis's Office hymns, *O nata lux* is not based on a cantus firmus. Its texture is homophonic throughout, similar in style to the many functional liturgical pieces composed in this manner by English musicians since the time of Dunstable (see no. 10). The setting treats only the first two verses of the hymn text (with a repetition of two lines at the end), differing from the composer's other settings, which are mostly *alternatim*. The rhythmic style is extremely repetitive, characteristic of English instrumental music of the period.

18. William Byrd, Ave verum corpus

This motet comes from the first volume of Byrd's *Gradualia*, a publication unquestionably intended for the Catholic community in Protestant England. It contains settings of the Proper of the Mass for important festivals throughout the year, as well as music not specifically liturgical (i.e., motets) but suited to performance during the service. Although the text is that of the Sequence for the Feast of Corpus Christi, it probably was not intended as a liturgical item (since most sequences were abolished by the Council of Trent) but as a motet. However, unlike other motets in the *Gradualia*, which are often elaborately contrapuntal, this one is primarily homophonic.

19. Johann Walther, *Ein feste Burg ist unser Gott*

Soon after the Reformation movement commenced, composers began writing vocal settings of Lutheran chorale tunes. Although these chorale-based compositions varied considerably in style, one of the more popular techniques was to place the plain chorale tune in the tenor and surround it with three or more parts in free-flowing polyphony. Johann Walther's setting of the Martin Luther text *Ein feste Burg* is representative of this style, which was not intended for the congregation, but for the choir or for devotional purposes at home.

20. Johannes Eccard, *Christ lag in Todesbanden*

While most of the chorale motets of the period have the chorale cantus firmus in the tenor, this familiar tune was placed in the top voice by Eccard. In this work the influence of the Netherlands composers is evident as the voices move melodically and rhythmically in an independent manner.

21. Hans Leo Hassler, *Komm, Heiliger Geist*

This simple, chordal setting of the familiar Lutheran chorale is an example of the type of chorale harmonization intended for congregational use in the worship service. In earlier times, these chorales were performed by the congregation as a single-line melody. In this example the melody retains the rhythmic structure of the original chorale tune. It is in the top voice, and is supported by four fully harmonized parts. The personal style of the composer is revealed in the rich harmonization and the high degree of craftsmanship.

22. Leonhard Lechner, *Historia der Passion und Leidens unsers einigen Erlösers und Seligmachers Jesu Christi*

Many polyphonic settings of the Passion appeared in Germany during the sixteenth century; Friedrich Blume has called Lechner's "the outstanding work in the history of the through-composed Passion." This work (the title means "History of the Passion and suffering of our only Redeemer and blessed Jesus Christ") is a work for four unaccompanied voices. The German text from the gospel of St. John is composed in the manner of a motet in five scenes, including the Seven Last Words. All possible combinations of voices are used to create a texture that ranges from simple choral harmonization to sixteenth-century polyphony. Since there are no soloists in the through-composed Passion, the individual choir parts serve in the role of the Evangelist, and the bass part sings the role of Jesus. Only the first section, "Arrest and trial before the Sanhedrin," is included in this anthology.

23. Claude Goudimel, *Ainsi qu'on oit le cerf bruire*

Psalms were used by the leaders of the French Reformation as the basis for their congregational singing, and Psalters including collections of these songs began to appear around the middle of the sixteenth century. The most famous of these, the Genevan Psalter, was published in 1542. This collection, prepared under the direction of John Calvin, included rhymed metrical versions of all 150 psalms, with tunes selected and arranged by Louis Bourgeois. This composition is based on Théodore de Bèze's translation of the 42nd psalm, which first appeared in the 1562 edition of the Genevan Psalter, set to a tune attributed to Louis Bourgeois. Goudimel's setting of this metrical text places the tune in the soprano part. The texture is basically chordal, with some embellishing passages of an imitative character in the three lower parts.

24. Jan Pieterszoon Sweelinck, *Chantez à Dieu chanson nouvelle*
This setting of the Marot–de Bèze translation of Psalm 96 is an example of one of the more elaborate and forward-looking psalm compositions of the seventeenth century. Here Sweelinck places the Genevan Psalter tune in the top voice, while the other three parts support the melody in a free and highly imitative manner. Word painting occurs throughout that is similar to effects found in the French chanson.

25. William Byrd, *Sing Joyfully*
This six-voice full anthem is believed to be the earlier of two settings Byrd composed of this nonliturgical text from Psalm 81. The texture of the music closely follows the mood of the text, opening with polyphonic and imitative writing. Of special interest in this through-composed composition is the outline of a major triad in the manner of a trumpet call on the text "Blow the trumpet." The chordal style at that moment presents a vivid contrast to the linear texture which predominates at all other times. In spite of the fact that this work derives its technique from the continental tradition, it is completely free of the expected compositional influences of the Netherlands school and is thoroughly English in spirit.

26. Orlando Gibbons, *This Is the Record of John*
In contrast to the full anthem, the verse anthem employs one or more solo voices alternating with full choir. This one is a narrative in three parts, and each solo statement is accompanied by strings. The accompaniment is independent of the voice parts in the verse sections, but doubles the choral lines in the full sections. Each of the three solo statements is followed by the chorus, which repeats some of the words already sung by the soloist. At its first entrance the choir takes up the concluding phrase of the soloist in strict chordal texture, but the melodic material is then varied throughout its imitative statement. The second choral section is a repeat of the text sung by the soloist, but in the final part only the soloist's concluding phrase is repeated.

27. Claudin de Sermisy, *J'ay fait pour vous cent mille pas*
Claudin specialized in a type of chanson characterized by delicate lyricism,

and his texts often dealt with love. This work illustrates the similarity of style between the Parisian chanson of c. 1530 and the early Italian madrigal (see no. 30). It is basically homophonic, diatonic, and syllabic, with clear phrase lengths. There is some incidental use of descriptive writing, as, for example, the brief step-progression on the words "cent mille pas." Characteristic of the genre are the many repeated notes in the melody and the structural repetition of material at the beginning and end of the piece (producing the pattern ababcdEE for the seven-line stanza, in which the last line is repeated).

28. Clément Janequin, *Le Chant des oyseaux*

Janequin is the most famous composer of the program chanson, a composition in which descriptive devices are used in profusion. One of these, *La Guerre*, depicts the confusion of battle, and another, *Les Cris de Paris*, the cacaphony produced by the hawking of the street vendors. *Le Chant des oyseaux* imitates the sounds produced by different birds. Attributes of Janequin's style illustrated by this work include the use of many rapid repeated notes to effect an excited declamatory style (often occurring in conjunction with static harmony), phrases which begin imitatively but continue homophonically, and clear sectionalization. In this work, each section but the first begins with the same melodic motive (the first section is related to the others rhythmically), and is then developed differently with respect to the realistic effects employed.

29. Claude Le Jeune, *Revecy venir du printans*

Le Jeune was one of the leading composers of *musique mesurée*, the basic principle of which was to set to music agogically texts written in imitation of the quantitative meters of ancient Greek and Latin poetry. Since the number of short syllables preceding a long syllable will vary in such poetry, *musique mesurée* settings are characterized by what in modern times is called mixed meter. Because the setting was syllabic and agogic in all parts, the resulting texture was always homophonic. The texts of chansons of this type often exhibit a rondo-like form consisting of an alternation of strophes (called *chants*) with a refrain (called *réchant*). In this work, the music of all the strophes is related in that many of the same melodic phrases reappear in each strophe in reordered sequence. Each new strophe adds a voice part, the first being for two parts, the last for five.

30. Jacob Arcadelt, *Il bianco e dolce cigno*

The early Italian madrigal was simple and diatonic, influenced by the style of the contemporary French chanson as well as that of the indigenous frottola. The present work illustrates this statement by its melodic emphasis in the upper part, homophonic texture, clear phrase lengths, and unambiguous harmonies. Noteworthy is the repetition of the last line of text in the manner of a French chanson (see no. 27), this same passage being the only imitative section in the work. *Il bianco e dolce cigno* was extremely popular in the sixteenth century, and was copied and rearranged innumerable times.

31. Giovanni Gastoldi, *Il bell' umore*

This balletto, published in a collection entitled *Balletti a Cinque Voci* (1591), represents a lighter form of the madrigal. Dancelike in rhythm and sprightly in tempo, *Il bell' umore* is a five-voice work with a refrain of "fa-la-la" syllables at the end of the first and last lines of the text. The compositional style is characterized by a simple chordal texture with fast declamatory and rhythmic accents throughout. There is a close relationship between the balletto and the instrumental dance music of the period.

32. Claudio Monteverdi, *Ecco mormorar l'onde*

Monteverdi's 9 books of madrigals document the transition from the Renaissance style to that of the Baroque. This work, from his second book, of 1590, is still rather conservative in style compared to those contained in books five on. Characteristic of Monteverdi is the pairing of voices (sometimes in dialogue with another pair, as in mm. 72 ff.), the variety of texture building to a tutti climax at the end, the free oscillation between imitative and homophonic writing, the descriptive rendition of certain words of the text (as on "ecco mormorar" and on "tremolar le fronde"), and the frequent use of two melodic motives simultaneously. The harmonic boldness and third relationships so typical of Monteverdi's later work are here little in evidence (but see m. 19 *et passim*).

33. Luca Marenzio, *Crudele acerba*

The works of Luca Marenzio and Carlo Gesualdo represent the final stage in the development of the Renaissance madrigal. In this period, the affective representation of the text becomes an almost narcissistic preoccupation. If the early madrigal may be said to be Mozartean in its nimbleness and lyrical qualities, the later one must certainly be Wagnerian in its turgidity and delight in chromatic harmonies juxtaposed in ambiguous tonal relationships. This ambiguity is accomplished through the frequent use of third relationships, modal inflections (changing from major to minor, and vice versa), and nonharmonic tones, particularly suspensions. Notice that the text, with its expression of sharply contrasting emotional states in close proximity one to the other, lends itself to this kind of musical treatment.

34. Carlo Gesualdo, *Moro lasso*

The vogue of the Italian madrigal plumeted to earth at the beginning of the seventeenth century like ripe fruit, succulent and sugary, falling from the tree, its connection with the lifegiving plant severed by the weight of its own development. This is nowhere better observable than in the last works of Carlo Gesualdo, a composer who, along with Marenzio, is associated with the final stage in the long development of the Renaissance madrigal. Stylistically, many of the features observed in Marenzio's work apply equally well to Gesualdo's *Moro lasso*. One encounters the same abundant use of nonharmonic tones, the same proclivity for chromatic third relations and chromatic harmony in general, the mixing of chordal and imitative writing, and the preoccupation with text painting. The difference between the two composers lies, perhaps, in the matter of degree, for Gesualdo, even more than Marenzio, seemingly delighted in keeping the listener in an almost continual state of emotional ambivalence and tonal disorientation.

35. Thomas Morley, *Fire, Fire*

This ballett was strongly influenced by the Italian balletti of Giovanni Gastoldi, which it resembles in its sprightly rhythm and "fa-la-la" refrain. *Fire, Fire,* one of the most popular of Morley's works in this genre, is full of the innovations with which he transformed this Italianate form: the inclusion of contrapuntal sections, the lengthening of the structure, and the change from duple to triple meter in short sections.

36. Thomas Weelkes, *When David Heard*

This five-voice setting of II Samuel 18:33 is an excellent example of the classic madrigal style applied to a sacred text. The constant use of minor seconds, the repeated words and phrases, and the resourceful employment of imitative techniques all serve to highlight the poignancy of the grief of the king upon learning of the death of his son Absolom.

37. John Wilbye, *Adieu Sweet Amarillis*

In spite of the aggressive nationalism of Elizabethan England, the musicians and writers of the time were very much under the influence of the Italians and were eager to emulate their accomplishments in the arts. The popularity of the madrigal in England during the last twenty years of Queen Elizabeth's reign can be explained by two factors: the strong native tradition of part-song writing and the influence of the Italians. *Adieu Sweet Amarillis* is a representative work of the English madrigal school, which is generally lighter and gayer in mood than its Italian counterpart, and is created almost entirely for the amateur singer. In this short piece the finest features of the English style are exemplified: contrapuntal writing, delicate harmonies, sensitivity to the text, contrast in texture from polyphony in the first section to homophony in the last, and a change in tonality from the minor mode in the beginning to the major at the end.

38. Claudio Monteverdi, *Laetatus sum*

Of all the new elements in the compositional technique of the Baroque, the *concertante* principle was the most spectacular. Growing out of the Venetian experiments in *cori spezzati* (divided choirs), a style developed in which short phrases are heard alternately in various sections of the total ensemble, literally competing with each other in the arena of sound. This motet, based on Psalm 122 and composed for St. Mark's Cathedral, is a perfect example of this technique. Using brilliant and rivaling vocal and instrumental forces, Monteverdi unified the work with a basso ostinato (G–G–C–D), which is used throughout the five sections, except for a small deviation in one passage. While this passacaglia is occuring in the bass, an exciting variety of vocal and instrumental activity takes place in the upper parts.

39. Giacomo Carissimi, *Plorate filii Israel* from *Jepthe*

In his oratorio *Jepthe*, Carissimi drew together all the resources of contemporary instrumental and operatic music in one composition. This work is representative of a new seventeenth-century form which dramatically links together significant episodes in the life of a biblical figure, yet is distinguished from opera by its sacred subject matter, its narrator, its choral passages for dramatic, narrative, and meditative purposes, and its concert, rather than staged, presentation. The chorus assumes a major role in the oratorio, with simply harmonized phrases that contribute to the dramatic action, the key element that transforms the oratorio into a choral drama. *Plorate filii Israel*, with its powerful dissonance and its expressive declamation of the Old Testament text, closely resembles the style of Monteverdi's late motets and Wilbye's sacred madrigals.

40. Antonio Vivaldi, *Magnificat, Et exsultavit,* and *Et misericordia* from *Magnificat*

Throughout the eighteenth century, the *Magnificat* remained the most popular scriptural text outside the psalms to be set to music. Vivaldi's setting of the canticle of Mary highlights the distinctive instrumental writing that is characteristic of the choral music of the Italian Baroque. There are symphonic episodes, instrumental ritornelli reminiscent of concerti, and figurative instrumental passages (Alberti bass, walking bass, running violin obbligati, etc.) that identify this music unquestionably as Italian in style.

41. Marc-Antoine Charpentier, Kyrie from *Messe de minuit pour Noël*

The historical significance of this Mass lies in that it appears to be the first work in this form to use popular French tunes (*noëls*) as melodic material. Charpentier, who effectively scored the work for solo voices, four-part chorus, flutes, strings, and organ, incorporates ten such French carols into its musical texture. By the simplest means he is able to adapt the original tunes to their liturgical setting without destroying their popular and naïve quality. The thematic material for the Kyrie is taken from the French tunes *Joseph est bien marié*, *Or nous dites Marie*, and *Une jeune pucelle*.

42. Jean-Philippe Rameau, *Laboravi clamans*

This motet is a highly contrapuntal one-movement work for five voices with a figured bass in the organ continuo part. Rameau reprinted this work in Book IV of the *Traité de l'harmonie* (Treatise on Harmony, 1722) to illustrate the chapter on fugue. *Laboravi* contains four fugues, or subjects, each one illustrating a clause in the text from the third verse of Psalm 69. In this context the term *fugue* is used to describe both the subjects and the movement as a whole, but the basic contrapuntal texture is less clearly defined than in the late Baroque fugue.

43. Henry Purcell, *Come, Ye Sons of Art* from *Come, Ye Sons of Art*

The seventeenth century English ode is a genre similar to the anthem, in several movements and usually composed in free form. Some of the best choral writing of the period is found in odes and anthems, most of which are unknown today because their texts are unsuitable for any purpose other than the specific one for which they were composed. *Come, Ye Sons of Art*, which Purcell wrote to celebrate the birthday of Queen Mary, the wife of William III, is scored for two oboes, two trumpets, timpani, strings, and continuo. It clearly shows the influence of the Italian music of the period, especially in the opening overture, intervening instrumental ritornelli, clear-cut rhythmic patterns, and brilliant melodic writing.

44. George Frideric Handel, *And There Came All Manner of Flies* from *Israel in Egypt*

Israel in Egypt is unique among Handel's oratorios in that the chorus carries the narrative throughout the work. This is due, in part, to the nature of the text, which deals with the destiny of a group of people rather than with an individual (i.e., *Messiah*, *Samson*, *Saul*, etc.). This might well be considered a "parody" oratorio, in that Handel borrows from the music of other composers for sixteen out of the twenty-five arias, duets, and choruses in the work. For example, this double chorus, taken from the *Seranata* by Alessandro Stradella, is typical of the composer's ability to transform a conventional piece of music into a unique example of descriptive choral writing.

45. Michael Praetorius, *Psallite*

The chorale motets of Praetorius occupy a special place in the history of choral literature, for they are among the earliest examples of a genre that culminated in the motets of J. S. Bach. This four-voice setting, composed in three-part

(ABA) form, is representative of the concertato principle, in which the upper and lower voices "compete" with each other within a texture that is primarily chordal. The text is macaronic: Latin words are intermixed with the venacular German.

46. Heinrich Schütz, Opening Section from *Musikalische Exequien*

The *Musikalische Exequien*, one of the most important funeral compositions of the entire seventeenth century, was written in 1636 in memory of the composer's friend, patron, and musical collaborator Prince Heinrich of Reuss. Like many other polychoral pieces of the period it exhibits a free use of chorale melodies in its musical setting. Called "A Concert in the Form of a German Funeral Mass" by the composer, the work is built in three sections: an opening section for six soloists and six-voice chorus, based on scriptural texts; the second section, consisting of an antiphonal motet for double chorus; and the final section, a concertante *Nunc dimittis* for a large five-voice chorus and a small group of three soloists (two sopranos and baritone). The text includes sayings that the Prince chose to have carved on his casket. The opening, a German paraphrase of the Kyrie—"Herr Gott Vater im Himmel, erbarm dich über uns" (God, Father in heaven, have mercy on us), "Jesu Christe, Gottes Sohn, erbarm dich über uns" (Jesus Christ, Son of God, have mercy on us), "Herr Gott Heiliger Geist, erbarm dich über uns" (God the Holy Spirit, have mercy on us)—incorporates marked textural contrasts.

47. Dietrich Buxtehude, *In dulci jubilo*

The most striking characteristic of this cantata for the Christmas season is the manner in which the composer embellishes the chorale tune to elaborate the macaronic text. This may be considered a typical chorale cantata, with the chorale melody and text constituting the primary musical material for the entire work. Writing for three voices (soprano, alto, bass), two violins, and organ, the composer keeps the hymn tune in the soprano as he sets each of the five verses with progressively richer embellishment on each successive phrase. Even in this early form of the chorale cantata there are many typical Baroque features, such as the sculptured shape of the vocal lines and the idiomatic and thematically derived instrumental writing of the two violin obbligato parts. There is also a marked contrast between the declamatory homophony of the choral sections and the more imitative writing in the intervening passages for solo voices and instruments.

48. Johann Sebastian Bach, *Jesu, meine Freude*

The six motets occupy a special place among Bach's sacred works for chorus. Four of the six were composed in Leipzig on commission for funeral services. *Jesu, meine Freude* (Jesus, My Joy), an elaborate work in eleven movements, is the composer's longest motet and his only chorale motet. Five of the eleven movements are set for five voices, including the middle movement (section six), a fugue, which provides a contrast in texture to the four movements based on the Johann Cruger chorale melody. In choosing a text, Bach combined the popular chorale by Johann Franck with passages from chapter eight from St. Paul's Epistle to the Romans (Romans 8:1–2, 9–11). The motet's tonality centers around E minor, with eight of its eleven movements in this key.

49. Johann Sebastian Bach, *Nach dir, Herr, verlanget mich*

This cantata dates from Bach's Weimar period, having been composed between 1706 and 1710. It is basically of the old concertato type, incorporating short sections of contrasting texture, and requiring a soloist. (In this case, the soprano soloist sings an aria which can be performed by the entire section, if desired.) The instrumental forces consist of two violins, bassoon, and continuo. The text is based on verses 1, 2, 5, and 15 of Psalm 25, with three original free verses in between, which Bach's biographer Charles Sanford Terry attributes to the composer. The work opens with a short Sinfonia, leading to a chorus, adagio and then allegro. Following the third movement—the soprano aria mentioned above—there is a second chorus, in which the composer amplifies the text "Lead me in your truth" with a diatonic scale passage that begins in the bass, moves measure by measure through the four vocal parts, and then culminates in the two violins. A simple, songlike trio (for alto, tenor, and bass) follows, preceding a third chorus which is related in structure to the second and fourth movements. The final chorus is in the form of a chaconne, the theme of which later appeared in Cantata 12 (1714), *Weinen, klagen, sorgen, zagen*.

50. Johann Sebastian Bach, *O Haupt voll Blut und Wunden* from St. Matthew Passion

Chorale harmonizations were considered functional music by eighteenth-century Lutheran composers, who had no higher artistic goal than to involve the congregation meaningfully in the worship service. This was Bach's purpose in the chorales he harmonized for his Passions, of which this piece is a typical example.

51. Georg Philip Telemann, *Laudate Jehovam, omnes gentes*

The new instrumental style and the clear-cut homophonic texture of the pre-Classical period is an evident influence in the later works of Telemann. This motet reveals a compositional simplicity, wherein the choral writing tends to be chordal, the contrapuntal writing largely confined to short passages of fugato, and the thematic material imitated at regular intervals. The harmony consists primarily of reiterated tonic and dominant chords, which serve to establish a definite tonal center and point directly to the Viennese Classical style.

52. William Billings, *I Am Come into My Garden*

This anthem is one of two compositions in *Continental Harmony* that take their texts from the biblical *Song of Solomon*. (The other is *I Am the Rose of Sharon*.) In contrast to many of Billings's more primitive works, *I Am Come into My Garden* reveals considerable compositional craftsmanship. In this through-composed work for mixed chorus and three solo voices (soprano, tenor, bass), the tonality of A minor is strongly established early on by the use of the melodic interval of the fifth (A–E) and a consistently raised leading tone (G sharp). This piece is clearly one of the gems of the American colonial period.

53. Josiah Flagg, *Hallelujah*

Colonial American composers were fond of setting the psalms. *Hallelujah*, a short work for five-voice chorus taken from Flagg's *A Collection of the Best Psalm Tunes* (Boston, 1764), is an interesting example of the use of imitation. Here the trumpetlike theme appears in stretto and augmentation.

54. Jeremiah Ingalls, *Northfield*

Although the Colonial fuging tune superficially resembled the polyphonic motets of Elizabethan England, there was actually no musical cross-influence between the two. *Northfield*, by the Vermont singing master and composer Jeremiah Ingalls, is representative of the fuging tunes of the period. It begins with a short homophonic section ending on a dominant cadence. The section which follows consists of separate entrances of the voices (the "fuge" in free imitation). The third part is a recapitulation of the fuging technique. In some settings this ABB form was varied, but this piece is rather typical of the formal practice of the time. The harmonic devices, including open fifths, parallel fifths and octaves, modal inflections, and some mild dissonances, give the work its somewhat primitive flavor.

55. John Antes, *Christ the Lord, the Lord Most Glorious*

Based on a text by Johann Müller (1756–90), a German Moravian minister who served in England, this hymn is one of twelve chorales by John Antes that were harmonized and freely edited from the figured-bass notation by Thor Johnson and Donald M. McCorkle. The tunes, bound together with the composer's twenty-five anthems in an autograph manuscript book, were discovered in 1955 in the Moravian Church Archives in Winston-Salem, North Carolina. This chordal setting contains very little of the chromaticism associated with the Bach chorales. The present edition is transposed from D major.

56. Wolfgang Amadeus Mozart, *Dixit* from *Vesperae solennes de confessore*, K. 339

Vespers, the evening service of the Roman Catholic church, includes the singing of five psalms and the *Magnificat*. Because the various movements are distributed throughout the service, there is no unifying influence within the work. This through-composed setting of Psalm 110 is written for four-voice choir, four soloists, and orchestra consisting of two trumpets, three trombones, timpani, two violins, and basso continuo. The trombones double the three lower voice parts and offer a significant contrast to the short, punctuated trumpet and timpani scoring, and the rich, figurative writing in the violins.

57. Wolfgang Amadeus Mozart, *Ave verum Corpus*, K. 618

This motet, written in the composer's last year (1791), is a miniature masterpiece. Like most other sacred works of the Viennese Classical period, it includes an instrumental accompaniment, in this case two violins, viola, and continuo. Composed in a chordal setting, the string instruments maintain a steady, quarter-note rhythm throughout, with a two-measure introduction, a three-measure interlude beginning at measure 19, and a three-measure cadential pattern at the end. The simplicity of the rhythmic movement, expressive melodic lines, and economy of musical forces combine to produce a simple, yet moving, setting of this liturgical text.

58. Wolfgang Amadeus Mozart, Introit and Kyrie from *Requiem*, K. 626

The choral style which developed in Vienna during the second half of the eighteenth century was primarily instrumental. The influence of the symphony and opera created a conflict, since liturgical leaders frowned upon the use of instruments and disapproved the rhythmic techniques of Italian opera which were so much a part of the symphonic-choral style of the period. Mozart's solution to this dilemma was to return to the ornate contrapuntal texture of the late Baroque. The opening movement of the *Requiem*, with its extended fugal phrases in both the slow Introit and the quick Kyrie, must be considered an obeisance to the past.

59. Franz Joseph Haydn, Gloria from *Missa brevis St. Joannis de Deo* (*Kleine Orgelmesse*)

The reforms which Joseph II instituted in order to diminish the powers of the Catholic church within his empire became law in April, 1783. And, while these measures were for the most part short-lived, they did produce some changes in the ritual of the church that are felt in Austria to this day. The *Missa brevis* (short Mass) was one way of creating economy and simplicity in an abbreviated service; the text of the Mass was radically shortened by having two or more parts sing different words simultaneously, a process that was usually reserved for the Gloria and Credo. By having all four parts singing different sections of the text at the same time, Haydn was able to reduce the Gloria of the *Kleine Orgelmesse* (Short Organ Mass) to thirty-one measures. The instrumentation of two violins and continuo, often called the Vienna church trio, is typical of Haydn's short masses.

60. Franz Joseph Haydn, Agnus Dei from *Mass in C* (*Paukenmesse*)
Haydn's last six Masses are significantly influenced by the instrumental style of the Classical period. H. C. Robbins Landon has suggested that "it was the deeply religious Haydn's ultimate aim to extend and perfect the purely orchestral apparatus of the symphony by means of the High Mass, embodying as it does the central mysteries of the Christian religion." After a hiatus of fourteen years (1782–96), Haydn returned to the large-scale orchestral Mass. His late works in this form are in reality symphonies for voice and orchestra utilizing a liturgical text. The *Mass in C* of 1796 (known also as the *Paukenmesse*, or Kettledrum Mass, and as *Missa in tempore belli*, or Mass in Time of War) is scored for a large orchestra, which includes flutes, oboes, clarinets, bassoons, horns, trumpets, timpani, strings, and organ. The solo quartet is used alone or together with the choir according to the text or form of the movement; often one half of a sentence is sung by one or more soloists, and the other half is completed by the choir.

61. Franz Joseph Haydn, *Vollendet ist das grosse Werk* from *Die Schöpfung*
Haydn's successful handling of the oratorio may be attributed to his familiarity with Handel's works as well as his personal experiences in England. Incorporating into the Baroque genre a touch of Handelian breadth along with his own mature symphonic style, he was able to carry on in the tradition of *Israel in Egypt* and *Messiah* with three works of his own: *Die Schöpfung* (The Creation), *Die Jahreszeiten* (The Seasons), and a choral arrangement of his instrumental work *The Seven Last Words*. This chorus, which ends the second part of *The Creation*, is set in the grand Baroque style. The movement includes fugato writing, imitation, and melodic sequences. Except for the figurative patterns written for the strings, the large orchestra doubles the chorus most of the time.

62. Ludwig van Beethoven, Gloria from *Mass in C*, Op. 86
Beethoven employed the same technique of form expansion in the symphonic Masses that he used in his symphonies. For this reason these works are generally unsuitable for the liturgical service and more successful in the concert hall. The Gloria of the *Mass in C* is 379 measures long and consists of four extended sections: the first, for chorus and orchestra (72 measures); the second,

for tenor solo, chorus, and orchestra (65 measures); the third (*Qui tollis*), for alto solo, vocal quartet, chorus, and orchestra (75 measures); and the fourth (65 measures). It is through this autonomous formal structure, the independent interpretation of the Mass text, the free and imaginative treatment of choruses and vocal solos that Beethoven established the model for the symphonic Mass in the nineteenth century.

63. Franz Schubert, *Der Tanz*

This part-song represents Schubert's lighter style of composition for mixed voices. The setting is simple, primarily chordal, with the melodic interest in top voice. Part-songs were designed for *Liedertafeln* (popular singing clubs); they could also be performed in the home, as the vocal quartet was staple entertainment in the cultured, nineteenth-century Austrian home. Notice that the piano accompaniment immediately establishes the mood of the text.

64. Franz Schubert, *Des Tages Weihe*

Whereas the songs Schubert composed for the *Liedertafeln* were in simple, folk-song style, there were a group of secular part-songs written for the *Musikvereine* (singing organizations) which were more serious in their musical intent. Concerned on a higher artistic plane, they were probably composed for choirs rather than the singing clubs or the informal vocal quartet. In contrast to the battle song or drinking song, the literary quality of the texts of these secular part-songs were comparable to those of the lied.

65. Anton Bruckner, *Christus factus est*

The influence of the Cecilian movement, a nineteenth-century attempt to revive the a cappella style of the sixteenth century and restore Gregorian chant to its original form, is apparent in this motet for unaccompanied four-voice chorus. Here is a clear mixture of styles: the opening chantlike phrase, the a cappella ideal, the dynamic contrast, the chromaticism, and the high-Romantic sensibility, all pointing to an eclectic work. Yet this mixture is so personal, naïve, and original that it appears timeless to the listener and performer, much like the mystery of the Christian ritual itself. This is music that is circumscribed by a deep devotion to the militant faith of the Roman Catholic Counter-Reformation and fertilized by the long tradition of choral music that dates from the Renaissance.

66. Hector Berlioz, *Le Ballet des ombres*

The individuality of Hector Berlioz is at once apparent in this choral work, based on a text by Albert Duboys. The piano part is singularly free of the conventions that we generally associate with that instrument. Here, instead, we find the unpredictable: harmonic progressions selected for their color, non-functional chord changes, vocal writing that is conceived instrumentally, and a piano part that is not idiomatic to the keyboard. Although conceived in the imagination of a composer who is an unabashed romantic, this composition receives its formal shape by means of a fastidious and restrained structural plan. Its three sections (AA¹A² Coda) are linked by the eight-measure minor-third figure in the piano bass line and the C-minor tonality. Another item of interest in this scherzolike work may be found in the distribution of voices: the soprano and tenor I parts are identical.

67. Gabriel Fauré, *Cantique de Jean Racine*
The lyricism that is associated with Fauré's songs is also found in this work, one of the gems of nineteenth-century sacred French choral music. In this setting for four-voice chorus with keyboard accompaniment, Fauré has created a Romantic work that exhibits definite Classical tendencies: warm and flowing melodic lines, a placid triplet accompaniment, smooth interpretation of the French language, clear-cut ABA form, and a harmonically rich chordal texture. Even the chromaticism and the free succession of seventh chords exist within a clearly recognized tonal center. Here we find a genuine affirmation of religious faith expressed in the most direct musical terms.

68. Felix Mendelssohn, *Heilig*
This is one of three sacred pieces by Mendelssohn without opus number, and probably dates from a late period in his compositional output. The influence of the English cathedral style is at once apparent with the synthesized double-chorus texture (in contrast to *coro spezzato*), the Anglican text, and the harmonic construction on thirds. This motet is through-composed and homophonic.

69. Felix Mendelssohn, *He That Shall Endure to the End* from *Elijah*
Whereas in his first oratorio, *St. Paul*, Mendelssohn revealed the influence of Bach (with particular reference to the chorale and the *St. Matthew Passion*), in *Elijah* he was much closer to the English oratorios of Handel. This work, which served as the model for English composers in the nineteenth century, is classical in concept, but admits to gentle suggestions of the chorale. In contrast to the Bach chorale settings in the Passions, this excerpt incorporates elements of dynamic contrast, imitation in all voice parts, and a rich orchestration consisting of flutes, oboes, clarinets, bassoons, strings, and organ. The text for this chorale is taken from the New Testament (Matthew 24:13), even though the oratorio centers around the life of an Old Testament hero.

70. Johannes Brahms, *Schaffe in mir, Gott, ein reines Herz*, Op. 29, No. 2
The influence of Bach and the chorale motet of the Baroque period is nowhere more apparent than in the two Op. 29 motets of Johannes Brahms. This six-voice motet is an excellent example of the composer's craftsmanship: its

four sections contain two fugues, each preceded by a canon, and a fugato in the final movement. Based on a text from the Psalm 51 (verses 10, 11, and 12), this masterpiece is written for unaccompanied chorus.

71. Johannes Brahms, *Im Herbst*, Op. 104, No. 5

Two styles are apparent in the secular choral works of Brahms's later period: a lilting folk-song style and the dark, introspective, and pastoral style that is represented by *Im Herbst* (In the Autumn). The spirit of resignation that is characteristic of all five songs in this opus is heightened in this final piece. Based on a poem by Klaus Groth, the three verses in strophic form are set in a sombre harmonic and tonal structure. Originally written in A minor, it was transposed up a minor third when the singers at the first rehearsal had difficulty with the unusually low tessitura.

72. Robert Schumann, *Zigeunerleben*, Op. 29, No. 3

This part-song, written during the composer's "song" year (1840), is one of three lied settings with piano accompaniment on a text by Emanuel Geibel. Entitled *Drei Gedichte* (Three Poems), the first is set for two sopranos, the second for three sopranos, and the *Zigeunerleben* (Gypsy Life) for soprano, alto, tenor, and bass. These lieder are, in reality, a duet, trio, and quartet for voice with piano accompaniment. This third setting reveals the restlessness of the Romantic spirit. The melodic line is angular and explosive, while the harmonic colors are vivid. Notice how the piano part supports the text, highlighting the moments of climax.

73. Edward Elgar, *Go, Song of Mine*, Op. 57

This is the composer's most ambitious part-song. Composed to D. G. Rossetti's translation of the thirteenth-century Guido Calvacanti text, the work is written for six-voice mixed chorus consisting of one soprano part, two alto, two tenor, and one bass. The tone colors tend to be on the darker side, in deference to the solemn poem. In form the piece falls into three sections, each ending softly at a double bar. And, while the melodic interest is focused on the top part, the tenors are given the thematic material before the end of the first and last sections on the text "Go, song of mine."

74. Samuel Sebastian Wesley, *Wash Me Throughly from My Wickedness*

Wesley brought new life into the English anthem, a form which had by the 1800s become very mechanical and conventional. This piece is one of the best examples of his compositional style, which is characterized by sonorous and beautifully constructed harmonies, diatonic suspensions, and accented passing tones. There is very little counterpoint in this music. It is cathedral music and needs the resonance of the lofty arched Gothic architecture for a full realization of its style in performance.

75. Gioacchino Rossini, Kyrie from *Petite Messe solennelle*

This extended Mass, written when the composer was past seventy, was conceived as a dignified and reverent setting of the Mass text. Set for the unusual combination of four soloists, four-voice chorus, two pianos, and harmonium (a portable reed organ), it is clearly influenced by the composer's operatic style. The solo writing is of a virtuoso character, the choral writing, massive, and the accompaniment, brilliant (it was later revised to include a full orchestral accompaniment). The Kyrie contains some lovely contrapuntal writing, especially in the Christe section, where the choral parts enter one measure apart in a style suggestive of earlier periods.

76. Giuseppi Verdi, *Ave Maria* from *Quattro pezzi sacri*

Toward the end of his life, Verdi composed four choral works which his publisher Ricordi brought out together as *Quattro pezzi sacri* (Four Sacred Pieces). The *Ave Maria*, designed as an exercise in tonality, was written for four-voice unaccompanied chorus. Verdi based the work on what he called an enigmatic scale: one which followed its own pattern of half steps and whole steps. The ascending octave (C–D♭–E–F♯–G♯–A♯–B–C) differed from the descending pattern (C–B–A♯–G♯–F–E–D♭–C). The composer explained this exercise in tonality as a "study in the style of the experiments of Willaert and Rore."

77. Pavel Chesnokov, *Praise the Name of the Lord*, Op. 11, No. 5

The doctrines and traditions of Byzantine Orthodoxy profoundly influenced art forms in early Russia and in the Graeco-Slavonic Church, the state church of Russia. Similarly, the early Slavonic chants were greatly influenced by their Byzantine counterparts. The principal monophonic chant of the Church, called Znamenny after its manner of notation, preserved many characteristics of its Gregorian precursor, and conformed to a comparable system of eight tones or *octoechoi*. Unlike the scalar modes of the West, however, the eight tones of the Eastern church consisted of a system of eight different musical domains, each one recognizable by its own distinctive melodic pattern. The fact that no man-made instrument was permitted in the church service probably encouraged Russian composers of the time to exploit to the fullest the sonorities of the "choral instrument."

78. Dimitri Bortnianski, *Cherubic Hymn*

The Cherubic Hymn holds the same relative place in the liturgy of the Graeco-Slavonic Church as the Agnus Dei serves in the Roman Catholic Mass: it is sung during the blessing of the elements in the Communion service. The slow opening section is repeated three times, once each time the priest elevates the chalice containing the water and the wine. At the conclusion of the third statement, the choir sings the Amen while the priest partakes of the elements.

The concluding section is a hymn of praise which is usually sung at a rapid tempo. Bortnianski's setting is basically chordal and remains in D major throughout.

79. Stephen Foster, *Come Where My Love Lies Dreaming*

This is the only work Foster wrote for mixed voices; he composed no other choral pieces, and this composition is classified technically as a vocal quartet. Its texture is homophonic, with the melodic interest in the soprano part, accompanied by a tenor-dominated trio. The form is strophic with a short coda at the end.

80. Edward MacDowell, *The Brook*, Op. 43, No. 1

The text is the most important element in the vocal works of MacDowell. This part-song is characteristic of his emphasis on the declamatory aspect of the poetic idea. He wrote that a composer "should declaim the poems in sounds: the attention of the hearer should be fixed upon the central point of declamation." In this example the melodic interest is in the soprano part, with the lower three parts serving merely as a background for the statement of the text. The texture is chordal, and the words are sung on the pulse beats of the 6/8 measure.

81. Arnold Schoenberg, *De profundis*, Op. 50b

This through-composed work in seven sections dates from Schoenberg's last compositional period, when he synthesized all his previous styles. It was composed to the original Hebrew words of Psalm 130. Although Schoenberg rejected the use of the traditional chants in this setting, he did study them in order to absorb the melodic inflections of the language. The rhythmic and formal structure of the work reflects that study.

82. Anton Webern, First Movement from *Cantata No. 1*, Op. 29

The term "pointilistic," used to describe the style of Anton Webern's first cantata, is borrowed from the visual arts; it describes a technique of utilizing sounds as isolated points or dots rather than as parts of a melody or phrase. The first entry of the chorus reveals the elements of this style as the four serial forms unfold in a chordal texture, giving the entire first movement a homophonic character. As in the song cycles of Opp. 23 and 25, the vocal medium prompts Webern to apply this fragmentary style of writing with less consistency and rigidity than is apparent in his instrumental works; he treats the voices in a more sustained manner and strives for a warmer, more lyrical mode of expression. *Cantata No. 1*, set for soprano, mixed chorus, and orchestra to a text by Hildegard Jone, is representative of the composer's mature style: an extremely sparse texture, a pointilistic technique, the use of silence as a principle of musical construction, a predilection for canonic writing, a prevalence of low dynamics, and a tendency to extreme formal compression.

83. Max Reger, *O Tod, wie bitter bist du*, Op. 110, No. 3

This motet, composed two days before the composer's death, is a dark and somber expression of the text, which comes from the apocryphal book of wisdom by Jesus, Son of Sirach, *Ecclesiasticus* (not to be confused with the Old Testament book of Ecclesiastes). Set for five-voice mixed chorus, including two independent soprano parts and divided lower voices, the thick and highly chromatic texture proceeds slowly in a declamatory style. The tempo, lingering chromaticisms, and various alternations between solo passages and choral sections all contribute to the work's sober mood.

84. Paul Hindemith, *En Hiver* from *Six Chansons*

Hindemith conceived of his chansons and madrigals as chamber music: "Only the string quartet in its purest form as created by Haydn, Mozart, and Beethoven even approaches the earlier ideal, but in my opinion the quartet never quite attained the uttermost balance of compositional virtuosity, ideal treatment of materials, and complete answering of the needs and abilities of the users" (preface to the madrigals). This chanson is the shortest of the six in French style. It is illustrative of the mild dissonance characteristic of all his choral works. Major seconds and minor sevenths are present in almost every cross-section of the texture. In form this chanson is through-composed.

85. Hugo Distler, *Es ist ein Ros entsprungen* from *Weihnachtsgeschichte*, Op. 10

Distler here revives the chorale motet preserving the original flowing meter of the Lutheran chorale tune in the soprano part. A striking characteristic of this piece from the *Weihnachtsgeschichte* (Christmas Story) is the use of different meters in all four voices, thereby allowing for a kind of independence that is reminiscent of Renaissance polyphony. In general, the rhythmic structure tends to follow the meter of the text, a device that makes the polymetric technique quite convincing. Other stylistic traits that appear in this motet are melismatic passages which intensify key words, melodic sequence, and imitation.

86. Arthur Honegger, *Je t'amerai, Seigneur* from *Le Roi David*

The dramatic oratorio *Le Roi David* (King David) was originally composed as incidental music to a play by René Morax, but was later rewritten for concert performance as a symphonic psalm in three parts. To unify the solos, choruses, and instrumental interludes, the composer employs a narrator to describe the state action. Many of the choruses are psalm settings, such as *Je t'aimerai, Seigneur* (I will extol thee, O Lord). Based on the Clément Marot translation of Psalm 18, this movement is constructed in three-part ABA form. In the first and third sections, the melodic material is presented in the soprano part and is supported by a rich harmonic accompaniment built primarily on open fourths and fifths. After an introductory theme by the basses, the middle section employs full choir in chordal texture accompanied by instrumental obbligato. In this work the composer uses an unusual orchestra consisting of woodwinds, brasses, double bass, piano, and harmonium. This instrumentation, combined with an eclectic use of Handelian counterpoint, folk-song melodies, exotic, oriental-sounding textures, and polytonality, helps create a spirit and atmosphere appropriate to the Old Testament text.

87. Darius Milhaud, *Babylone* from *Les Deux Cités*

The first of three impressionistic choral movements, this through-composed setting is striking in quality and bold in color. The rich texture is spiced with triplet figures in the melodic parts and supported by an essentially harmonic structure built on intervals of fourths and fifths. The interspersed solos for soprano bring a haunting quality to the lament of the fallen city Babylon. The text is by Paul Claudel, under whom Milhaud worked as cultural attaché in the French Embassy.

88. Gustav Holst, *I Love My Love*, Op. 36, No. 5

Holst, like Ralph Vaughan Williams, was an enthusiastic collector of English folk songs. It is thus not surprising that the six choral settings of Op. 36 are based on folk materials. *I Love My Love*, the fifth of the set, is an original Cornish folk song in six verses, each of which is elaborated to highlight the text. One other point should be made about the work: the folk style itself establishes the basis for a new kind of free composition.

89. Ralph Vaughan Williams, *O vos omnes*

This motet represents a serious side of Vaughan Williams's compositional style. In contrast to his choral pieces in folk-song style, *O vos omnes* looks back to an earlier era of English church music. Here is a work that exhibits all the elements of the English cathedral tradition: modality, English discant, parallel sixth chords, free rhythm, chantlike passages, meters which lend themselves to the polyphonic texture, and Latin text. The grand tradition of English nationalism is here preserved in a new and fresh setting.

90. Benjamin Britten, *Jubilate Deo*

The individual character of Britten's personal idiom is often characterized by the use of melodic and rhythmic musical patterns, expanded motives interspersed within the texture of the composition. This work, completed in 1961 at the request of the Duke of Edinburgh for St. George's Chapel in Windsor, is representative of the composer's use of linear patterns in a stratified manner.

The highly configured organ accompaniment proceeds throughout the piece without regard for or relation to the more legato character of the voice arts.

91. Peter Maxwell Davies, *Alleluia, pro Virgine Maria* from *O magnum mysterium*

This contemporary English carol points to an earlier, medieval vocal style. The composer organizes the meter freely so that the rhythm of the words determines the metrical structure. The form, based on the fourteenth-century burden (refrain), also guides the order of performance: Burden–Verse 1–Burden–Verse 2–Burden–Verse 3–Burden. The mildly dissonant harmonic texture contributes to the austere setting of the text.

92. Michael Tippett, *Nunc dimittis*

Tippett's *Magnificat* and *Nunc dimittis* were composed for the 450th anniversary of the founding of St. John's College, Cambridge. The *Nunc dimittis*, the Song of Simeon (Luke 2:29–32), is representative of Tippett's severely dissonant style; it is a work that is mystical in concept and sparse in texture. In the program notes of the first performance (March 13, 1962), the composer wrote: "in contrast to the display of the *Magnificat* the organ part of the Nunc dimittis is reduced to primitive onomatopoesis of the thunderings of God." The choral setting is written for solo treble voice over quiet sustained dischords from the three lower voices.

93. Thea Musgrave, *Rorate coeli*

This boldly linked setting of two poems by William Dunbar (c. 1460–c. 1513), one relating to Christmas and the other to Easter, is set for four-voice mixed chorus unaccompanied and five soloists. It is a brilliantly composed work that includes improvisatory and chance elements which are described in precise detail for singer and conductor. The opening statement of the macaronic text is especially stunning, with its controlled dynamic range and the spacing of the dominant-seventh chord echoed back and forth between soloists and choir. A chorale setting appears in the middle of the work, over which the *Dies irae* is sung in free rhythm.

94. Béla Bartók, *Wedding Song from Poniky* from *Four Slovak Folk Songs*

Bartók's folk-music style is well-represented in these Slovak songs that date from 1917. They are composed in a simply harmonized note-against-note and unison setting. Written for four-voice mixed chorus with piano accompaniment, these songs have a relatively uncomplicated structure: large sections are sung in unison or fall into chordal form. This first song, with a strong Lydian and tritonal flavor, is a dialogue in 3/4 meter between a mother and the daughter she gave to a wicked man in a foreign country. The accompaniment is unusual in that the pianist is instructed to perform the opening arpeggiated chords from the top note downward, rather than in the usual manner.

95. Igor Stravinsky, Sanctus from *Mass*

This concise setting of the Ordinary is written for a choir of men and boys and a double wind quintet consisting of two oboes, two English horns, two bassoons, two trumpets, and three trombones. Stravinsky clearly intended the work for a liturgical rather than a concert setting: "My Mass was not composed for concert performance, but for use in the church." There are certain passages that suggest the homorhythmic style of an earlier period, but the austere and impersonal nature of the texture removes all traces of Romantic sentimentality and places it securely in a Neoclassical framework. When considered from the standpoint of its overall form, the Mass is constructed like an arch: the Kyrie and Agnus Dei are related, the Gloria and Sanctus both have solo sections, and the Credo, the longest movement, stands by itself in the center. Of special interest in the Sanctus is the clearly classical fugal section, beginning at measure 13 on the text "Pleni sunt coeli."

96. Igor Stravinsky, *Anthem*

Stravinsky turned to serial technique relatively late in his career, around 1954. His personal style, however, emerges so strong that the result is not so much an extension of Schoenberg's style as a transformation of the twleve-tone method to suit his own purposes. The *Anthem* is based on a tone row that is used in all four transformations: original, inversion, retrograde, and retrograde inversion. But it is not employed in a strict sense; at times the row is moved from one voice to another, and some notes are repeated within each statement to reflect the repetitions of the text.

97. Krzysztof Penderecki, *Stabat Mater*

The *Stabat Mater*, which the composer later incorporated into the *Passion according to St. Luke*, combines both traditional and contemporary elements, thus establishing itself as a striking example of a work that utilizes voices in a delicate, sympathetic, and remarkably effective manner. Scored for three a cappella choirs, it begins with a plainchant, which recurs throughout the composition, moves to a Bach-like repeated-note theme that is developed imitatively, and eventually introduces the clusters which build up into tense bands of twelve-tone complexity. The vocal effects, range, and register create variations in verbal intensity, ranging from whispers and hisses to ecstatic cries. As the work unfolds there is little or no reference to tonality, so that the sudden appearance of a familiar major triad on the final Gloria seems surprising but perfectly in keeping with the essence of the composition.

98. Luciano Berio, Second Movement from *Magnificat*

The *Magnificat* is one of Berio's early works, dating from his student period. Written in 1949, this eclectic work reflects the influences of Schoenberg, Milhaud, Hindemith, Bartók, and Webern, composers whose works were forbidden in Italy during the years of the fascist regime. The traditional text of Mary's canticle is composed in a highly coloristic setting that reveals elements of polytonality, whole-tone melodic figures, dissonance, and a strong rhythmic texture. Yet the melodic writing is lyrical in a style typical of Italian church music. The work is scored for 2 sopranos, 4-part mixed chorus, 2 pianos, and an instrumental ensemble consisting of flute, oboe, 2 clarinets, 2 horns, 2 trumpets, 2 trombones, double bass, and percussion (timpani, vibraphone, snare drum, cymbal, 3 tam-tams).

99. Goffredo Petrassi, *Improperium* from *Motetti per la Passione*

The influence of serial and *Sprechstimme* techniques are clearly evident in Petrassi's *Motetti per la Passione* (Motets for the Passion). *Improperium* (Reproach), the second of this collection of four motets, is a highly dissonant setting of Psalm 69:20–21. Each phrase of the text introduces a tone row (or fragment of one) that builds to a climax consisting of a chord of all the tones in that fragment. Between each phrase the reiterated text "Expectavit cor meum" (My heart awaited) is spoken by one of the five voice parts on an indefinite pitch but in a prescribed rhythm. The final spoken statement is chanted by a solo baritone, and the movement ends softly on a choral statement of the tone row that commences in the soprano and works its way down in a dissonant chordal texture to the bass part.

100. George Gershwin, *Sing of Spring*

The musical language which became the basis of the Gershwin style was based in ragtime, blues, and jazz. As a serious composer who believed that material derived from the American popular idiom could be used for a broader audience, Gershwin wrote a number of works for the concert stage. *Sing of Spring*, a charming piece for mixed chorus and piano in ABA form, was composed for the filmed musical *Damsel in Distress*, in which a madrigal group sings two ballads as background music. As the film is set in England, Gershwin aimed for an English flavor. What resulted was somewhere between a madrigal and a Gilbert and Sullivan chorus, but with the unique Gershwin touch.

101. R. Nathaniel Dett, *Listen to the Lambs*

Dett was a thoroughly trained composer whose aim was to bring black art into the mainstream of American musical culture. He sought to accomplish this by incorporating the characteristics of indigenous black American music within Romantic forms and techniques. In contrast to the spiritual arrangements by Dett's contemporaries, *Listen to the Lambs* is an original composition for eight-voice mixed chorus and soprano solo. Called "A religious characteristic in the form of an anthem," it employs alternation between full and chamber choir, between thick and sparse chordal textures, and between chromatic and diatonic scale elements. Considered an eclectic work, it fuses African and European compositional elements to produce an anthem that is popular in appeal, yet stylistically representative of the nineteenth-century European Romantic tradition.

102. Charles Ives, *Psalm 67*

The most striking characteristic of *Psalm 67* is its harmonic structure. At a time when extreme and consecutive dissonances were unknown in choral writing, Charles Ives used them without hesitation whenever they constituted the most powerful harmonic force for his purpose. In his literary writings he expressed a frank distaste for hymn harmonizations which displayed "well-worn and easy" chords, thereby placing unnecessary limitations on a religious expression that should be "expanding and universal in scope." An intensely devout man himself, he experimented continuously to add a mysterious grandeur to his sacred works. To this end, Ives divides the chorus into two independent choirs and writes three-part triads for each group. The choirs never sing the same triad together, however, and the result is a constant bitonality.

103. William Dawson, *There Is a Balm in Gilead*

Whereas *Listen to the Lambs* is an original composition in the style of a Negro spiritual, Dawson's *There Is a Balm in Gilead* is a spiritual arrangement for mixed voices and soprano solo. Loosely based on a biblical text from Jeremiah 8:22, the setting is primarily chordal throughout, with the tenor part imitating the soprano statement of the main refrain theme. The form is similar to the medieval English burden, alternating the choral refrain with the soloist who sings the two verses to the accompaniment of the full choir.

104. Louise Talma, *Let's Touch the Sky*

The rhythmic vitality of this thoroughly American choral setting derives directly from the e. e. cummings poem. This is music with a strong rhythmic impulse. The accents are placed with artful asymmetry, resulting in syncopations that possess the element of surprise. Like many other American composers who developed under the influence of Nadia Boulanger, Talma expresses a deep interest in finding a meaningful connection between music and the life about her, in searching for a musical venacular to become an accessible language to her listeners. Written for flute, oboe, bassoon, and four-voice chorus, this work exhibits an economy of means, a transparency of texture, and a preciseness of tonal vocabulary that places it clearly within a Neoclassical framework.

105. Irving Fine, *Have You Seen the White Lily Grow* from
     The Hour-Glass

This setting of the popular Ben Jonson poem achieves the nineteenth-century ideal of melodic breadth combined with harmonic opulence. Soaring melodic lines in the women's voices accompanied by rich, widely spaced four-voice chords in the men's registers produce vivid tonal colors which effectively highlight the pastoral text. Fine's careful use of mild dissonance goes hand in hand with fastidious taste, clarity of intention, and logical three-part design. This is a musical language that is readily accessible to the listener.

106. Elliott Carter, *Musicians Wrestle Everywhere*

This madrigal, one of the composer's most prominent works from the 1940s, is set for five-voice chorus a cappella or with strings to a poem by Emily Dickinson. In style it resembles his *Piano Sonata,* especially the rare vitality of the melodic material and the shifted accents, which combine with a free polyphonic setting to produce a highly successful cross-accented counterpoint. The madrigal represents a new high point in Carter's treatment of rhythm, one example of the craftsmanship that has become the hallmark of his work.

107. Samuel Barber, *The Coolin* from *Reincarnations*

The lyricism that is associated with Barber's songs and instrumental music is readily apparent in this choral setting of a poem by James Stephens. The smooth and expressive interpretation of the text reveals a carefully constructed multimetric texture, a siciliano-like rhythm, and a mastery of vocal colors. Neoromantic in style and traditional in form, this four-voice unaccompanied work flows evenly in a mildly dissonant tonal setting and gives the impression of the warmth and refinement that mark the composer's early compositions for chorus.

108. Vincent Persichetti, Kyrie from *Mass,* Op. 84

Based on a chantlike theme, this three-part Kyrie maintains its Gregorian flavor in spite of the mildly dissonant contemporary idiom. The opening section is thoroughly linear with the soprano–tenor and alto–bass sections singing the diatonic line in octaves. In contrast, the Christe introduces a less linear style with the four voices singing in a quasi-chordal texture. In the final Kyrie, the alto and soprano share the thematic material. The effect is a neo-Renaissance choral style composed in a tightly knit and compact formal structure.

109. Daniel Pinkham, First Movement from *Christmas Cantata*

This movement, written for mixed chorus and two brass choirs, is brilliant in sound and musical effect. Through rhythmic and harmonic freedom, and by a clear understanding of instrumental and vocal sonorities, the composer has demonstrated in this work an ability to devise musical effects which are both unusual and inviting. Here is a texture that is predominately linear, but spiced with striking rhythmic emphases. Pinkham has a fondness for varying the metric signature, in this case to follow the accentuation of the Latin text. When considered in its entirety, this cantata hints back to the spirit and style of medieval vocal polyphony.

110. Hale Smith, *Poème d'automne* from *In Memoriam—Beryl Rubinstein*

The three-movement choral suite *In Memoriam—Beryl Rubinstein* was first composed for voices and piano, and was orchestrated by the composer six years later, in 1959. The second movement, *Poème d'automne*, a somber setting for a Langston Hughes poem, incorporates many twentieth-century tendencies. Originally composed in memory of two acquaintances of the composer (his uncle and the director of the Cleveland Institute), this atonal choral piece reveals an economy of means and clear musical craftsmanship. Of special interest are the rhythmic vitality of the piano introduction and the sudden shifts in meter, the primarily chordal sections for unaccompanied chorus, the clear references to serial techniques, and quite dramatic tempo changes.

111. Richard Felciano, *Hymn of the Universe*

The electronic medium is especially appropriate for a text by Teilhard de Chardin. The synthesis of voices and tape allows the creation of a new kind of spatial polyphony, symbolizing the immensity of the universe and the omnipresence of the Creator. By blending the three-voice chorus (soprano, alto, and men) with a succession of sound events which assume a linear counterpoint to the voices, the composer establishes zones or planes of foreground and background in a seemingly infinite montage of sound. The gentle, floating, and sustained choral parts merge graciously with electronic sound masses and are quickly surrounded by their new environment.

Appendix C: Source List

1. *Magnificat anima mea*, ed. Dennis Shrock. Hinshaw Music, Inc.
2. *Hodie Christus natus est*, ed. Dennis Shrock. Hinshaw Music, Inc.
3. *Haec dies, quam fecit Dominus*, ed. Dennis Shrock. Hinshaw Music, Inc.
4. Machaut, *La Messe de Nostre Dame*, ed. William Dalglish. Hinshaw Music, Inc.
5. Dufay, *Missa se la face ay pale*, ed. Heinrich Besseler. Bärenreiter-Verlag 1912.
6. Ockeghem, *Missa Mi-Mi*. Edwin F. Kalmus (Belwin-Mills Publishing Corp.) 6357.
7. Josquin, *Missa Pange lingua*. Edwin F. Kalmus (Belwin-Mills Publishing Corp.) 6148.
8. Palestrina, *Missa Papae Marcelli*, ed. Rudolf Ewerhart. Associated Music Publishers, Inc. (Breitkopf & Härtel) A-530.
9. Byrd, *Mass for Four Voices*, ed. Frederick Hudson. Optional chamber organ acc. Edition Eulenberg, Ltd. 997 (miniature score).
10. Dunstable, *Quam pulcra es*, ed. Dennis Shrock. Hinshaw Music, Inc. HMC-246.
11. Dufay, *Ave Regina coelorum a 3*, ed. Manfred F. Bukofzer. Includes a 4-part setting, rehearsal acc. T. Presser Co. (Mercury Music Corp.) 352-00116.
12. Josquin, *Ave Maria, gratia plena*, ed. Paul Boepple. T. Presser Co. (Mercury Music Corp.) 352-00044.
13. Lasso, *In hora ultima*, ed. Alan Harler. Rehearsal acc. Roger Dean Publishing Co. CA-104.
14. Palestrina, *Ave Maria, gratia plena*, ed. Ray Robinson. Hinshaw Music, Inc.
15. Victoria, *O quam gloriosum*, ed. Ray Robinson. Hinshaw Music, Inc.
16. Gabrieli, *O magnum mysterium*, ed. Richard Hynson. Hinshaw Music, Inc. HMC-248.
17. Tallis, *O nata lux de lumine*, ed. Edmund H. Fellowes, rev. ed. Anthony Greening. Rehearsal acc. Oxford University Press TCM 82 (rev.).
18. Byrd, *Ave verum Corpus*, ed. R. R. Terry, rev. ed. John Morehen. Latin and English, optional acc. Oxford University Press TCM 3 (rev.).
19. Walther, *Ein feste Burg ist unser Gott*, ed. Dennis Shrock. Hinshaw Music, Inc.
20. Eccard, *Christ lag in Todesbanden*, ed. Dennis Shrock. Hinshaw Music, Inc. HMC-249.
21. Hassler, *Komm, Heiliger Geist*, ed. Dennis Shrock. Hinshaw Music, Inc.
22. Lechner, *Historia der Passion und Leidens unsers einigen Erlösers und Seligmachers Jesu Christi*, ed. Konrad Ameln. Bärenreiter-Verlag 2968.
23. Goudimel, *As a Hart Longs for the Brooklet (Ainsi qu'on oit le cerf bruire)*, ed. A. B. Couper. French and English, rehearsal acc. T. Presser Co. (Mercury Music Corp.) 352-00436.

24. Sweelinck, *Psalm 96 (A Huguenot Psalm)*, ed. Paul Boepple. French and English. T. Presser Co. (Mercury Music Corp.) 352-00004.
25. Byrd, *Sing Joyfully*. Rehearsal acc. Stainer & Bell, Ltd. CCL 559.
26. Gibbons, *This Is the Record of John*, ed. William Palmer. Novello & Co., Ltd. Anth. 1330.
27. Sermisy, *J'ay fait pour vous cent mille pas*, ed. Ray Robinson. Hinshaw Music, Inc.
28. Janequin, *Le Chant des oyseaux: Reveillez-vous*, ed. Ray Robinson. Hinshaw Music, Inc. HMC-250.
29. Le Jeune, *Revecy venir du printans*, ed. Dennis Shrock. Hinshaw Music, Inc.
30. Arcadelt, *Il bianco e dolce cigno*, ed. Dennis Shrock. Hinshaw Music, Inc.
31. Gastoldi, *Il bell' umore (I will have a gay life)*, ed. Maynard Klein. Italian and English, rehearsal acc. G. Schirmer, Inc. 11450.
32. Monteverdi, *Ecco mormorar l'onde (Hark! low murmurs the water)*, ed. H. F. Redlich. Italian and English, rehearsal acc. Edition Schott (London) 10972.
33. Marenzio, *Crudele acerba*, ed. Dennis Shrock. Hinshaw Music, Inc.
34. *A Treasury of Early Music*, ed. Carl Parrish. 50 selections. W. W. Norton & Co., Inc.
35. *European Madrigals for Mixed Voices*, ed. Egon Kraus. 23 selections. G. Schirmer, Inc. ED 2601.
36. Weelkes, *When David Heard*, ed. Walter Collins. Rehearsal acc. Associated Music Publishers, Inc. (G. Schirmer, Inc.) NYPM 11.
37. *Invitation to Madrigals*, Book 2, ed. Thurston Dart. 20 selections. Galaxy Music Corp. (Stainer & Bell, Ltd.).
38. Monteverdi, *Laetatus sum*, ed. James McKelvy. Latin and English, keyboard realization. Mark Foster Music Co. MF 109 score (performance material available).
39. Carissimi, *Historia de Jepthe*, ed. Gottfried Wolters. Keyboard realization by Mathias Siedel. Möseler Verlag Wolfenbüttel, score (choral score available).
40. Vivaldi, *Magnificat Ossencensis*, ed. H. C. Robbins Landon. Universal Edition UE 13191 score.
41. Charpentier, *Messe de Minuit pour Noël*, ed. H. Wiley Hitchcock. Concordia Publishing House 97-5196 score (performance material available).
42. Rameau, *Laboravi clamans*. Latin and English, keyboard realization. Associated Music Publishers, Inc. (G. Schirmer, Inc.) A-410.
43. Purcell, *Come Ye Sons of Art*, ed. Michael Tippett and Walter Bergmann. Keyboard realization. Schott & Co., Ltd. (London) 11080.
44. Handel, *Israel in Egypt*, ed. Friedrich Chrysander. Edwin F. Kalmus (reprint of original Breitkopf & Härtel) 1311.
45. Praetorius, *Psallite*, ed. Kurt Stone. Latin and German, English, rehearsal acc. Joseph Boonin, Inc. B.111.
46. Schütz, *A German Requiem (Musikalische Exequien)*, ed. Arthur Mendel. German and English. G. Schirmer, Inc. ED 2270.
47. Buxtehude, *In dulci jubilo*, ed. Bruno Grusnick. German and Latin. Bärenreiter-Verlag 620 score (performance material available).
48. Bach, *Jesu, meine Freude*, BWV 227, ed. Konrad Ameln. Bärenreiter-Verlag BA 5132.
49. Bach, *Nach dir, Herr, verlanget mich*, BWV 150. Breitkopf & Härtel 4650 score.
50. Bach, *Matthäus-Passion*, BWV 244, ed. Alfred Dürr. Bärenreiter-Verlag 196 study score (performance material available).
51. Telemann, *Laudate Jehovam, omnes gentes*, ed. Paul Thomas. Latin and English, keyboard realization by Fritz Oberdoeffer. Concordia Publishing House 97-4838

score (performance material available).

52. *The Bicentennial Collection of American Choral Music (1790–1900),* ed. Mason Martens. 26 selections. McAfee Music Corp. (Lorenz Industries).
53. Flagg, *Hallelujah,* ed. Ray Robinson. Hinshaw Music, Inc.
54. Ingalls, *Northfield,* ed. Irving Lowens. Rehearsal acc. E. B. Marks Music Corp. (Belwin-Mills Publishing Corp.) JS 70.
55. Antes, *Twelve Moravian Chorales,* ed. Donald M. McCorkle. Boosey and Hawkes, Inc. 5201.
56. Mozart, *Vesperae solennes de confessore,* K. 339. Breitkopf & Härtel (performance material available).
57. Mozart, *Mozart Anthem Book,* Vol. 2, ed. James Boeringer. 4 selections. Concordia Publishing House 97-5275.
58. Mozart, *Requiem,* K. 626. Edwin F. Kalmus (Belwin-Mills Publishing Corp.) 179 miniature score (performance material available).
59. Haydn, *Missa brevis St. Joannis de Deo (Kleine Orgelmesse),* ed. H. C. Robbins Landon in collaboration with Karl Heinz Füssl and Christa Landon. Bärenreiter-Verlag TP 95 miniature score (performance material available).
60. Haydn, *Paukenmesse,* ed. H. C. Robbins Landon. Bärenreiter-Verlag TP 94 miniature score.
61. Haydn, *Die Schöpfung (The Creation).* Edition Eulenburg, Ltd. (C. F. Peters Corp.) 995 miniature score (performance material available).
62. Beethoven, *Mass in C major,* Op. 86. Edwin F. Kalmus (Belwin-Mills Publishing Corp.) 436 miniature score (performance material available).
63. Schubert, *Der Tanz,* ed. Ray Robinson. Hinshaw Music, Inc. HMC 247.
64. Schubert, *Des Tages Weihe,* ed. Dennis Shrock. Hinshaw Music, Inc.
65. Bruckner, *Christus factus est.* Arista Music Co. AE 157.
66. Berlioz, *Songs with Piano Accompaniment,* Vol. 1. French, English, and German, 8 selections. Edwin F. Kalmus (Belwin-Mills Publishing Corp.) 1231 miniature score.
67. Fauré, *Religious Music.* 8 selections. Edwin F. Kalmus (Belwin-Mills Publishing Corp.) 6177.
68. Mendelssohn, *Twelve Sacred Choral Works.* Edwin F. Kalmus (Belwin-Mills Publishing Corp.) 1209 miniature score.
69. Mendelssohn, *Elias (Elijah),* Op. 70. German and English. Universal Edition, Philharmonia 29 miniature score.
70. Brahms, *Two Motets for 5-Part Mixed Chorus,* Op. 29. Rehearsal acc. Edwin F. Kalmus (Belwin-Mills Publishing Corp.) 6105.
71. Brahms, *Im Herbst,* ed. Ray Robinson. Hinshaw Music, Inc. HMC-251.
72. Schumann, *Ausgewähte Gesänge für gemischten Chor.* 10 selections. C. F. Peters Corp. 4694.
73. Elgar, *Go, Song of Mine,* Op. 57. Rehearsal acc. Novello & Co., Ltd. part-song book 1164.
74. Wesley, *Wash Me Throughly from My Wickedness.* Rehearsal acc. G. Schirmer, Inc. 10403.
75. Rossini, *Messe solennelle.* Ricordi & Co., Ltd. (Belwin-Mills Publishing Corp.).
76. Verdi, *Ave Maria.* Rehearsal acc. E. B. Marks Corp. (Belwin-Mills Publishing Corp.). MC 7.
77. Chesnokov, *Praise the Name of the Lord,* ed. Charles Hirt. Hinshaw Music, Inc.
78. Bortnianski, *Cherubic Hymn,* ed. Ray Robinson. Hinshaw Music, Inc.
79. *The Bicentennial Collection of American Choral Music (1790–1900),* ed. Mason Martens. 26 selections. McAfee Music Corp. (Lorenz Industries).

80. *Ibid.*
81. Schoenberg, *De profundis (Psalm 130)*. Hebrew and English, rehearsal acc. by P. Gradenwitz. MCA Music (Belwin-Mills Publishing Corp.) 1193-062.
82. Webern, *Cantata No. 1*, Op. 29. German and English. Universal Edition, Philharmonia 447 miniature score.
83. Reger, *O Tod, wie bitter bist du*, Op. 110, No. 3. Bote & Bock (Associated Music Publishers, Inc.).
84. Hindemith, *En Hiver*. French and English, rehearsal acc. Belwin-Mills Publishing Corp. (Schotts Soehne, Mainz) AP 39.
85. Distler, *Es ist ein Ros entsprungen*, ed. Bruno Grusnick. Bärenreiter-Verlag BA 681.
86. Honegger, *Le Roi David*. Edition Foetisch (Lausanne, Switzerland).
87. Milhaud, *Babylone*. French and English. G. Schirmer, Inc. 8921.
88. Holst, *I Love My Love*. Rehearsal acc. G. Schirmer, Inc. (J. Curwen & Sons) 8117.
89. Vaughan Williams, *O vos Omnes*. Rehearsal acc. J. Curwen & Sons 80594.
90. Britten, *Jubilate Deo*. Oxford University Press S 551.
91. Davies, *Alleluia, pro Virgine Maria*. Rehearsal acc. Schott & Co., Ltd. (London).
92. Tippett, *Magnificat* and *Nunc dimittis*. Schott & Co., Ltd. (London) Edition 10873.
93. Musgrave, *Rorate coeli*. Novello & Co., Ltd.
94. Bartók, *Four Slovak Folk Songs*. English, German, Hungarian, and Czechoslovakian. Boosey & Hawkes, Inc.
95. Stravinsky, *Mass*, for mixed chorus and double wind quintet. Boosey & Hawkes, Inc. Hawkes Pocket Scores 655.
96. Stravinsky, *Anthem (The Dove Descending Breaks the Air)*. Boosey & Hawkes, Inc. 5438.
97. Penderecki, *Stabat Mater*. Belwin-Mills Publishing Corp. S.B. 892.
98. Berio, *Magnificat*. Belwin-Mills Publishing Corp. EL 2290.
99. Petrassi, *Motetti per la Passione*. Edizioni Suvini Zerboni 6533.
100. Gershwin, *Sing of Spring*, ed. Gregg Smith. Lawson Gould Music Publishers, Inc. (G. Schirmer, Inc.) LG 51964.
101. Dett, *Listen to the Lambs*. Rehearsal acc. G. Schirmer, Inc. 5956.
102. Ives, *Sixty-seventh Psalm*. Rehearsal acc. Associated Music Publishers, Inc. (G. Schirmer, Inc.) A-274.
103. Dawson, *There Is a Balm in Gilead*. Rehearsal acc. Neil A. Kjos (Music Press) T105.
104. Talma, *Let's Touch the Sky*. Hinshaw Music, Inc.
105. Fine, *Have You Seen the White Lily Grow*. Rehearsal acc. G. Schirmer, Inc. 9969.
106. Carter, *Musicians Wrestle Everywhere*. Rehearsal acc., optional strings. T. Presser Co. (Mercury Music Corp.) 352-00119.
107. Barber, *The Coolin*. G. Schirmer, Inc. 8910.
108. Persichetti, *Mass*, Op. 84. Rehearsal acc. T. Presser Co. (Elkan-Vogel, Inc.).
109. Pinkham, *Christmas Cantata (Sinfonia sacra)*. Latin and English. Robert King Music Co. Music for Brass 602.
110. Smith, *In memoriam—Beryl Rubinstein*. Rehearsal acc., optional chamber orchestra. Galaxy Music Corp. (Highgate Press) HP 56.
111. Felciano, *Hymn of the Universe*. E. C. Schirmer Music Co. 2944.

Index of Composers

Index of Titles

Index of Genres